Lecture Notes in Artificial Intelligence 9318

Subseries of Lecture Notes in Computer Science

More information about this series at http://www.springer.com/series/1244

Matteo Baldoni · Luciano Baresi
Mehdi Dastani (Eds.)

Engineering Multi-Agent Systems

Third International Workshop, EMAS 2015
Istanbul, Turkey, May 5, 2015
Revised, Selected, and Invited Papers

 Springer

Editors
Matteo Baldoni
Dipartimento di Informatica
Università degli Studi di Torino
Torino
Italy

Luciano Baresi
DEIB - Politecnico di Milano
Milano
Italy

Mehdi Dastani
Department of Information and Computing
  Sciences
Utrecht University
Utrecht
The Netherlands

ISSN 0302-9743   ISSN 1611-3349   (electronic)
Lecture Notes in Artificial Intelligence
ISBN 978-3-319-26183-6   ISBN 978-3-319-26184-3   (eBook)
DOI 10.1007/978-3-319-26184-3

Library of Congress Control Number: 2015954626

LNCS Sublibrary: SL7 – Artificial Intelligence

Printed on acid-free paper

Springer International Publishing AG Switzerland is part of Springer Science+Business Media
(www.springer.com)

Preface

The engineering of multi-agent systems (MAS) is a multi-faceted, complex task. These systems consist of multiple, autonomous, and heterogeneous agents, and their global behavior emerges from the cooperation and interactions among the agents. MAS have been widely studied and implemented in academia, but their full adoption in industry is still hampered by the unavailability of comprehensive solutions for conceiving, engineering, and implementing these systems.

Being at the border between software engineering and artificial intelligence, they can benefit from both disciplines, but at the same time they lack proper mainstream solutions. For example, even if the artificial intelligence side has been proposing conceptual models for years, there is still a lack of proper abstractions unanimously recognized as effective design solutions for the conceptions of agents and of their interactions. Similarly, there is still a significant gap between the availability of "standard" software engineering implementation and validation solutions and their adoption in the conception of MAS. More recently, the emergence of self-adaptive software systems, and in general the idea of software systems that can change their behavior at runtime, has imposed MAS as one conceptual solution for their realization, but it has also emphasized the need for proper and sound engineering solutions. Conversely, design artifacts (e.g., agent or MAS models) can be also used to support and assist the testing and debugging of conventional software, while the use of agent-oriented programming languages results in programs that are more readily verifiable. Their many pieces belong to the same puzzle, but significant work is still needed to put them together.

As said, many solutions have already been proposed. They address the use of common software engineering solutions for the conception of MAS, the use of MAS for ameliorating common software engineering tasks, and also the proper blending of the two disciplines to conceive MAS-centric development processes. Academia has been working on ideas and solutions; industry should have exploited them to improve the state of the art. The cross-fertilization is needed to make the two sides of the same coin cooperate, and a single, common venue can help to exchange ideas, compare solutions, and learn from one another.

The International Workshop on Engineering Multi-Agent Systems (EMAS) aims to be this comprehensive venue, where software engineering and artificial intelligence researchers can meet together and discuss the different viewpoints and findings, and where they can also try to present them to industry. EMAS was created in 2013 as a merger of three separate workshops (with overlapping communities) that focused on the software engineering aspects (AOSE), the programming aspects (ProMAS), and the application of declarative techniques to design, program, and verify (DALT) MAS. The workshop is traditionally co-located with AAMAS (International Conference on Autonomous Agents and Multi-agent Systems) and thus this year it was held in Istanbul (Turkey).

This year the workshop was a single-day event. We received 19 submissions, and after a double review process, 10 papers were selected for inclusion in this volume. All the contributions were revised by taking into account the comments and discussions at the workshop. Moreover, the volume includes two papers by the invited speakers, Brian Logan, from the University of Nottingham, and Mirko Viroli, from Università di Bologna, whose presentations raised a lot of interest and compelling discussions.

We would like to thank all the members of the Program Committee for their excellent work. Moreover, we would like to thank all the members of the Steering Committee of EMAS for their valuable suggestions and support.

August 2015

Matteo Baldoni
Luciano Baresi
Mehdi Dastani

Organization

Workshop Organizers

Matteo Baldoni	University of Turin, Italy
Luciano Baresi	Politecnico di Milano, Italy
Mehdi Dastani	Utrecht University, The Netherlands

Program Committee

Natasha Alechina	University of Nottingham, UK
Matteo Baldoni	University of Turin, Italy
Luciano Baresi	Politecnico di Milano, Italy
Cristina Baroglio	University of Turin, Italy
Jeremy Baxter	QinetiQ, UK
Olivier Boissier	ENS Mines Saint-Etienne, France
Lars Braubach	University of Hamburg, Germany
Rem Collier	University College Dublin, Ireland
Massimo Cossentino	National Research Council, Italy
Fabiano Dalpiaz	Utrecht University, The Netherlands
Mehdi Dastani	Utrecht University, The Netherlands
Louise Dennis	University of Liverpool, UK
Jüergen Dix	Clausthal University of Technology, Germany
Amal El Fallah Seghrouchni	LIP6 - University of Pierre and Marie Curie, France
Aditya Ghose	University of Wollongong, Australia
Paolo Giorgini	University of Trento, Italy
Adriana Giret	Technical University of Valencia, Spain
Jorge Gomez-Sanz	Universidad Complutense de Madrid, Spain
Christian Guttmann	Institute of Value Based Reimbursement System, Sweden
James Harland	RMIT University, Australia
Vincent Hilaire	UTBM/IRYES-SET, France
Koen Hindriks	Delft University of Technology, The Netherlands
Benjamin Hirsch	EBTIC/Khalifa University, UAE
Tom Holvoet	K.U. Leuven, Belgium
Jomi Fred Hubner	Federal University of Santa Catarina, Brazil
Joao Leite	Universidade Nova de Lisboa, Portugal
Yves Lespérance	York University, Canada
Brian Logan	University of Nottingham, UK
Viviana Mascardi	University of Genoa, Italy
Philippe Mathieu	University of Lille 1, France
John-Jules Meyer	Utrecht University, The Netherlands

Frederic Migeon	IRIT, France
Ambra Molesini	Alma Mater Studiourum - Universtà di Bologna, Italy
Pavlos Moraitis	Paris Descartes University, France
Haralambos Mouratidis	University of Brighton, UK
Jörg P. Müller	TU Clausthal, Germany
Andrea Omicini	Alma Mater Studiorum - Università di Bologna, Italy
Juan Pavón	Universidad Complutense de Madrid, Spain
Alexander Pokahr	University of Hamburg, Germany
Enrico Pontelli	New Mexico State University, USA
Alessandro Ricci	Alma Mater Studiorum - Università di Bologna, Italy
Ralph Ronnquist	Real Thing Entertainment Pty Ltd, Australia
Sebastian Sardina	RMIT University, Australia
Valeria Seidita	University of Palermo, Italy
Guillermo R. Simari	Universidad Nacional del Sur in Bahia Blanca, Argentina
John Thangarajah	RMIT University, Australia
Paolo Torroni	Alma Mater Studiorum - Università di Bologna, Italy
M. Birna van Riemsdijk	TU Delft, The Netherlands
Wamberto Vasconcelos	University of Aberdeen, UK
Jørgen Villadsen	Technical University of Denmark
Gerhard Weiss	University of Maastricht, The Netherlands
Danny Weyns	Linnaeus University, Sweden
Michael Winikoff	University of Otago, New Zealand
Wayne Wobcke	University of New South Wales, Australia
Neil Yorke-Smith	American University of Beirut, Lebanon

Steering Committee

Matteo Baldoni	University of Turin, Italy
Rafael Bordini	PUCRS, Brazil
Mehdi Dastani	Utrecht University, The Netherlands
Jürgen Dix	TU Clausthal, Germany
Amal El Fallah Seghrouchni	University Paris 6, France
Paolo Giorgini	University of Trento, Italy
Jörg P. Müller	TU Clausthal, Germany
M. Birna van Riemsdijk	Delft University of Technology, The Netherlands
Tran Cao Son	New Mexico State University, USA
Gerhard Weiss	Maastricht University, The Netherlands
Danny Weyns	Linnaeus University, Sweden
Michael Winikoff	University of Otago, New Zealand

Additional Reviewers

Abushark, Yoosef
Sabatucci, Luca

Contents

Invited Papers

A Future for Agent Programming

Brian Logan[✉]

School of Computer Science, University of Nottingham, Nottingham, UK
bsl@cs.nott.ac.uk

Abstract. There has been considerable progress in both the theory and practice of agent programming since Georgeff & Rao's seminal work on the Belief-Desire-Intention paradigm. However, despite increasing interest in the development of autonomous systems, applications of agent programming are confined to a small number of niche areas, and adoption of agent programming languages in mainstream software development remains limited. This state of affairs is widely acknowledged within the community, and a number of remedies have been proposed. In this paper, I will offer one more. Starting from the class of problems agent programming sets out to solve, I will argue that a combination of Moore's Law and advances elsewhere in AI, mean that key assumptions underlying the design of many BDI-based agent programming languages no longer hold. As a result, we are now in a position where we can rethink the foundations of BDI programming languages, and address some of the key challenges in agent development that have been largely ignored for the last twenty years. By doing so, I believe we can create theories and languages that are much more powerful and easy to use, and significantly broaden the impact of the work we do.

1 Introduction

There is increasing interest in the application of autonomous intelligent systems technology in areas such as driverless cars, UAVs, manufacturing, healthcare, personal assistants, etc. Robotics and autonomous systems have been identified as one of the *Eight Great Technologies* [29] with the potential to revolutionise our economy and society. For example, the UK Knowledge Transfer Network for Aerospace, Aviation & Defence report *Robotics and Autonomous Systems: Challenges and Opportunities for the UK* states: "the economic, cultural, environmental and social impacts and benefits [of autonomous systems] will be unprecedented" [17]. There is also an increasing focus on autonomous systems in artificial intelligence research, with, for example, special tracks on Cognitive Systems and Integrated Systems/Integrated AI Capabilities at AAAI 2015 & 2016. Given the level of interest in both academia and industry, one might expect the agent programming community, which specialises in theories,

---

This paper is a revised and extended version of an invited talk given at EMAS 2015. I am grateful to the workshop organisers for the invitation, and the opportunity to contribute to the post-proceedings.

© Springer International Publishing Switzerland 2015
M. Baldoni et al. (Eds.): EMAS 2015, LNAI 9318, pp. 3–17, 2015.
DOI: 10.1007/978-3-319-26184-3_1

architectures, languages and tools for the development of autonomous systems to be thriving, and the languages and tools they have developed to support the development of autonomous agents to be in widespread use in AI research and perhaps in industry.

However the impact of agent programming in both mainstream AI and in applications is minimal. Surveys suggest that the adoption of Agent-Oriented Programming Languages (AOPL) and Agent-Oriented Software Engineering (AOSE) in both research and industry is limited [7,15,31]. More worrying, the most distinctive outputs of the agent programming community, the Belief-Desire-Intention (BDI)-based approaches which specifically target the development of intelligent or cognitive agents, and which would appear to be best suited to the development of autonomous systems, are least used. A study by Winikoff [31] of applications appearing in the AAMAS Industry/Innovative Applications tracks in 2010 and 2012, reveals that the systems described do not require intelligent goal-based (BDI) agents, and the focus of many applications is at the multi-agent system (MAS) coordination level (e.g., game theory, MDPs). The most recent survey by Müller & Fischer in 2014 [15] reports 46 'mature' applications (out of 152 surveyed applications). They found that:

- 82 % of mature applications focus on the MAS level, while only 9 % focus on 'intelligent agents'
- the majority of mature applications are concentrated in a few industrial sectors: logistics & manufacturing, telecoms, aerospace and e-commerce
- only 10 % of mature applications clearly used a BDI-based platform; of those that did, all used the JACK [30] platform

Müller and Fisher list a number of caveats concerning their study data. In particular, "the large number of applications in the multi-agent systems category certainly reflects the focus towards multi-agent topics in the call for participation rather than a lack of intelligent agent[s]". In addition, they note that some applications used more than one platform, and for some applications the information was not available, so the number of applications using a BDI platform may be higher than 10 %. However even allowing for these factors, it seems hard to argue that BDI agents are having a significant impact in application development.

In this paper I explore the reasons for the apparent lack of interest in agent programming in the broader AI research community and developers of agent-based systems, and make some proposals about what we can (and should) do about it. By 'agent programming' I mean the whole spectrum of agent programming techniques developed to support the implementation of autonomous agents, from more 'object oriented' approaches such as JADE [2] to BDI-based approaches such as Jason [4]. I focus on models, languages and platforms for programming individual agents, as these are most relevant to the implementation of autonomous systems.[1] I will use the term 'agent programming community'

---

[1] Programming frameworks for the development of MAS are an important output of the agent programming community, but are not essential for the implementation of individual autonomous systems.

to refer to the developers of these languages and tools (exemplified by EMAS and its predecessor workshops) rather than their intended users. Except where the distinction is relevant, in the interests of brevity, I often do not distinguish between agent programming languages and the theories on which a language is based or the platform implementing the language specification, and use 'agent programming language' (APL) as a general term to denote the outputs of the agent programming community. My analysis of why agent programming is failing to have an impact applies to all forms of agent programming; however my proposals about what to do about it focus primarily on BDI-based approaches. The tenor of the paper is deliberately polemical, and some steps in the argument may be seen as contentious. However I believe the changes in the context of agent programming in artificial intelligence and computer science I point to, and the opportunities they present, are unassailable. So even if my analysis of the problem is flawed, the opportunities we have to do interesting work are very real.

2 Background

I am not the first to consider the low take-up of agent programming in mainstream software development, or how agent programming languages could or should develop to maximise their adoption. This paper follows in a tradition of talks and panel sessions at agent programming workshops, including the Dagstuhl Seminar on Engineering Multi-Agent Systems [8] and the EMAS 2013 & 2014 workshops. In this section I briefly review some of this work.

In [31] Winikoff identifies a number of challenges for engineering multi-agent systems and proposes directions for future work in engineering MAS. He focusses on the relevance of the AAMAS community to industry, and the relevance of the 'agent engineering' sub-community to the rest of AAMAS, and in particular the extent to which the methodologies, languages and tools developed by this sub-community are used both in the wider AAMAS community, and in industry. I focus here on the latter question, as being more closely related to the topic of the current paper.[2] Drawing on data from [7] and the analysis of papers appearing in the AAMAS Industry/Innovative Applications tracks in 2010 and 2012 mentioned briefly above, he argues that AOPL and AOSE usage is quite limited, and that the applications described focus on coordination aspects and do not require goal-based agents. Based on these observations he recommends that the agent programming community should:

- stop designing AOPLs and AOSE methodologies ... and instead ...
- move to the "macro" level: develop techniques for designing and implementing interaction, integrate micro (single cognitive agent) and macro (MAS) design and implementation

---

[2] The engagement of industry with the AAMAS conference as a whole also does not seem a particularly relevant metric when considering future directions for engineering multi-agent systems. AAMAS is a large conference, and there are typically only a relatively small number of papers on agent programming; even if these papers were very relevant to industry, industrial engagement with the conference as a whole could still be low.

However this recommendation appears to ignore the possibility that the reason current applications focus on coordination of MAS rather than goal-based agents, is that the support provided by current agent programming languages for developing goal-based agents is inadequate. As such, it risks becoming a self-fulfilling prophecy. I will return to this point in the next section. Winikoff also identifies the lack of techniques for the assurance of MAS as a barrier to adoption of agent technology. This is a valid concern, but falls outside the scope of the current paper, which is more narrowly focussed on the design of agent programming languages.

In [13] Hindriks reviews the history of engineering multi-agent systems, including agent programming, and presents a vision of how cognitive agent technology can form a basis for the development of next-generation autonomous decision-making systems. Like Winikoff, he makes a number recommendations and identifies a number of directions for future research, including:

- pay more attention to the kind of support (specifically tools) required for engineering MAS applications
- focus more on issues related to ease of use, scalability and performance, and testing
- facilitate the integration of sophisticated AI techniques into agents
- show that agent-orientation can solve key concurrency and distributed computing issues
- put more effort into integrating agent-based methodologies and programming languages

He concludes that to stimulate the adoption of cognitive agent technology and MAS, the agent programming community must provide "methods and tools that jointly support the agent-oriented mindset". However Hindriks's analysis does not directly address the causes of the low take-up of agent programming in mainstream software development. Rather his proposals can be read as possible or desirable extensions to current APLs rather than features necessary for wider adoption.[3]

Many of the features identified by Winikoff and Hindriks are clearly important for the wider adoption of agent programming languages. However I believe their analyses fundamentally mistake the nature of the problem we face. The key problem lies elsewhere, and has not previously been articulated. I turn to this in the next section.

3   Why Are We Failing to Have an Impact?

I begin by elucidating the problem we are trying to solve. There are many different views of the aims and objectives of 'agent programming' considered as

---

[3] The alternative interpretation, that they are all necessary for the wider adoption of APLs, implies that agent programming as a field *must* progress on a very broad front, and is even more daunting than my analysis below.

a field. As a first approximation, these differing perspectives can be broadly characterised as being either 'AI-oriented' or 'software engineering-oriented'. The AI-oriented view focuses on connections with the broader field of artificial intelligence, and sees agents as 'an overarching framework for bringing together the component AI sub-disciplines that are necessary to design and build intelligent entities' [14]. The software engineering-oriented view on the other hand, focuses on synergies between software engineering and agent research.[4] Each tradition is associated with its own set of research questions and workshops. For example the AI-oriented view is represented by workshops such as Agent Architectures Theories and Languages (ATAL), while the software engineering-oriented view is represented by workshops such as Agent-Oriented Software Engineering (AOSE).

In what follows, I focus on the AI-oriented view. There are several reasons for this choice. The AI-oriented view represents the original motivation for agent programming as a subfield, and I would argue that the most significant contributions of agent programming to the broader AAMAS community have emerged from this tradition, e.g., the 2007 IFAAMAS Influential Paper Award for Rao & Georgeff's work on rational agents [18]. In addition, the agent programming languages and tools developed in this tradition are arguably the most mature software products of the agent programming community, representing approximately thirty years of cumulative development. Lastly, the combination of these two factors (a clear need in the AI community, and the distinctive set of ideas represented by the BDI paradigm) offers the best hope for agent programming to have an impact outside our community.

Perhaps the best characterisation of the AI-oriented view is given in the call for papers for the first ATAL workshop, held in 1994, which states:

> Artificial Intelligence is concerned with building, modeling and understanding systems that exhibit some aspect of intelligent behaviour. Yet it is only comparatively recently — since about the mid 1980s — that issues surrounding the synthesis of intelligent autonomous agents have entered the mainstream of AI. ... The aim of this workshop ... is to provide an arena in which researchers working in all areas related to the theoretical and practical aspects of both hardware and software agent synthesis can further extend their understanding and expertise by meeting and exchanging ideas, techniques and results with researchers working in related areas.
>
> — ATAL 1994 CfP

In this view, agents are a way of realising the broader aims of artificial intelligence. Agents are autonomous systems which combine multiple capabilities, e.g., sensing, problem-solving and action, in a single system. Agent programming is

---

[4] There are, of course, overlaps between the two views. In particular, there is a strand of work in what I am characterising as the AI-oriented view, that focuses on the engineering of intelligent autonomous systems. However the focus of work in the software engineering-oriented tradition is much less on AI and more on distributed systems.

seen as a means of realising and integrating these capabilities to achieve flexible intelligent behaviour in dynamic and unpredictable environments.

Given this characterisation of the goals of agent programming, the reason the agent programming research conducted by the agent programming community has failed to have an impact follows fairly immediately:

> *we can't solve a large enough class of AI problems well enough to be interesting to the wider AAMAS community or application developers*

In the remainder of this section, I will attempt to justify this claim.

3.1   The BDI Model

The Belief-Desire-Intention (BDI) model and its underlying theoretical underpinnings are arguably the main contribution of the agent programming community to the broader field of AI. The BDI approach can be seen as an attempt to characterise how flexible intelligent behaviour can be realised in dynamic environments, by specifying how an agent can balance reactive and proactive behaviour.

In BDI-based agent programming languages, the behaviour of an agent is specified in terms of beliefs, goals, and plans. Beliefs represent the agent's information about the environment (and itself). Goals represent desired states of the environment the agent is trying to bring about. Plans are the means by which the agent can modify the environment in order to achieve its goals. Plans are composed of steps which are either basic actions that directly change the agent's environment or subgoals which are in turn achieved by other plans. Plans are pre-defined by the agent developer, and, together with the agent's initial beliefs and goals, form the program of the agent. For each event (belief change or top-level goal), the agent selects a plan which forms the root of an intention and commences executing the steps in the plan. If the next step in an intention is a subgoal, a (sub)plan is selected to achieve the subgoal and added to the intention.

In most BDI-based agent programming languages, plan selection follows four steps. First the set of relevant plans is determined. A plan is relevant if its triggering condition matches a goal to be achieved or a change in the agent's beliefs the agent should respond to. Second, the set of applicable plans are determined. A plan is applicable if its belief context evaluates to true, given the agent's current beliefs. Third, the agent commits to (intends) one or more of its relevant, applicable plans. Finally, from this updated set of intentions, the agent then selects one or more intentions, and executes one (or more) steps of the plan for that intention. This process of repeatedly choosing and executing plans is referred to the agent's deliberation cycle. Deferring the selection of plans until the corresponding goal must be achieved allows BDI agents to respond flexibly to changes in the environment, by adapting the means used to achieve a goal to the current circumstances.

3.2   Limitations of Current BDI-Based Languages

The BDI approach has been very successful, to the extent that it arguably the dominant paradigm in agent programming [11]. A wide variety of agent languages and agent platforms have been developed which at least partially implement the BDI model, e.g., [4–6,12,30]. A number of these languages and platforms are now reasonably mature in terms of their feature set (if not always in terms of their software engineering). They encompass each of the components of the BDI model in at least rudimentary form, and often have a solid theoretical foundation in the form of a precise operational semantics specifying what beliefs, desires and intentions mean, and how they should be implemented. It is therefore appropriate to consider what the scientific contribution of this work consists of.

The features common to state of the art BDI languages, and which currently define this style of programming, are essentially limited to:

- selecting canned plans at run time based on the current context; and
- some support for handling plan failure (e.g., trying a different plan)

While these features are useful, and are key to implementing agents based on the BDI paradigm, everything else is left to the programmer.

What's left to the programmer is all the hard(er) parts of implementing an autonomous agent. More specifically, some of the things the current generation of agent programming languages can't do (in a *generic* way) includes:

- how to handle costs, preferences, time, resources, durative actions, etc.
- which plan to adopt if several are applicable
- which intention to execute next
- how to handle interactions between intentions
- how to estimate progress of an intention
- how to handle lack of progress or plan failure
- when to drop a goal or try a different approach
- and many others ...

While not all of these capabilities will be required in every agent application, a reasonable argument can be made that many are necessary in most, if not all, cases (e.g., which plan to adopt, which intention to execute next, how to handle plan failure), and each feature is required for a significant class of applications.

There has been some preliminary work on how to implement many of these capabilities, see, for example, [3,16,21–28,32]. However, to date, this work has not been incorporated into the core feature set of popular BDI platforms. One possible explanation for the current state of the art, rests on the observation that, for any particular application, the detailed answers to these questions will differ. The argument that such issues should or must be left to the programmer is reminiscent of the 'New Jersey approach' [9]: do the basic cases well, and leave the programmer to do the hard bits. While this approach may explain the relative popularity of C vs Lisp (the focus of Gabriel's paper), the assumption that the current 'BDI feature set' is a good tradeoff in terms of the kinds of behaviours that can be easily programmed while at the same time being easy for programmers to learn doesn't seem to hold.[5]

It is of course true that for specific applications, the detailed answers to these questions (or even whether a feature is needed at all) will vary. However do we as a community really want to claim that there are *no* general theories or approaches to these questions? If so, developing agents capable of flexible intelligent behaviour in dynamic and unpredictable environments is going to be very hard (and hence very expensive), and the amount that agent programming can contribute will be limited.

In summary, the support currently offered by state of the art APLs is useful, particularly for some problems. However it is not useful enough for most developers to switch platforms, even if we polish our methodologies and tools. I believe we need to answer these questions, and I explain why in the next section.

4   The Broader Context

The analysis presented in the previous section actually underestimates the scale of the problem facing the agent programming community. In this section, I will argue that there is good reason to suppose that the already limited impact of agent programming on the wider AAMAS community and AI generally is likely to decline in the foreseeable future due to changes in the broader AI and CS context. Key assumptions on which the BDI agent programming model are based are not as true as they once were, allowing other AI subfields to colonise the APL space. In addition, some mainstream computing paradigms are starting to look like simple forms of agent programming, potentially limiting the impact of APL technologies on mainstream development. I discuss each of these developments below.

4.1   Reactive Planning

The BDI approach to agent programming is based on early work on reactive planning, e.g., [10]. The underlying rationale for reactive planning rests on a number of key assumptions, including:

- the environment is dynamic, so it's not worth planning too far ahead as the environment will change;
- the choice of plans should be deferred for as long as possible — plans should be selected based on the context in which the plan will be executed.

In their 1987 paper Georgeff & Lansky emphasise the difference between reactive planning and traditional (first principles) planning: "[traditional] planning techniques [are] not suited to domains where replanning is frequently necessary" [10].

---

[5] The argument that an APL should include only basic plan selection features seems spurious for another reason—most widely used programming languages provide support for many more features than will be used in any particular application.

A key implicit assumption underlying this claim is the time required by a traditional planner to find a plan for a given goal. While generative planning remains an NP-hard problem, advances in classical planning and increases in processing power have increased the size of problems that can be solved by a traditional planner in a given amount of time. Since Georgeff & Lansky's paper, available computational power has increased by a factor of approximately 10^5, and by a factor of 10^4 since Rao's classic paper on AgentSpeak(L) [19] which influenced the design of many current state of the art agent programming languages (see Fig. 1).[6]

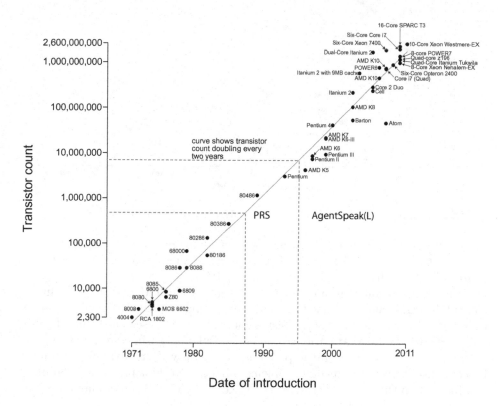

Fig. 1. Microprocessor transitor counts 1971–2011

It is perhaps now time to reconsider whether traditional planning techniques are unsuited to domains where replanning is frequently necessary. Many planning problems can now be solved in less than a second, and some generative planners are approaching the 100ms threshold necessary for agent planning in real time domains. Figure 2 shows the number of solved problem instances with time for all domains of the ICAPS International Planning Competition[7] and a range of

---

[6] Creative Commons 'Transistor Count and Moore's Law' by Wgsimon used under CC-BY-SA-3.0. Transistor counts circa 1987 and 1996 highlighted.

[7] www.icaps-conference.org.

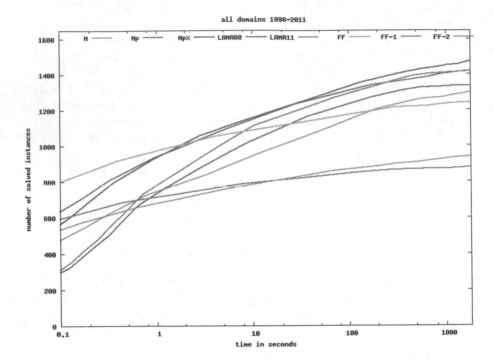

Fig. 2. Number of IPC problem instances solved by different planners with time

generative planners.[8] As can be seen, the best planners (from the point of view of a real time agent) are capable of solving over half the problem instances in < 100 ms. (Note that these results are from 2012.)

While there is some dispute about the extent to which Moore's law continues to hold, it seems safe to assume that available computational power will continue to increase, at least in terms of transistor count, for the foreseeable future. It also seems safe to assume that advances in classical planning will continue. Coupled with an increased interest in the planning community in 'real time' planning,[9] it seems likely that the range of problems amenable to first principles planning will increase in the future. This does not mean the end of reactive planning, but hybrid approaches will become increasingly feasible.

4.2   Reactive Programming

At the same time, work on event-driven and reactive programming[10] (e.g., in robotics) offers similar (or better) functionality to belief triggered plans in agent programming. Such approaches offer:

---

[8] The figure is from http://users.ics.aalto.fi/rintanen/jussi/satplan.html and is reproduced here with the permission of the author. See also [20].

[9] The 2014 edition of the International Planning Competition included a *Sequential Agile* track for the first time. The objective of the Agile track is to 'minimize the CPU time needed for finding a plan'.

[10] See, for example http://rx.codeplex.com.

- a well defined model of streams (immutability, sampling, pull-based computation)
- very fast (microsecond) evaluation of simple SQL-like queries (e.g., LINQ,[11] cqengine[12]) that scale to very large 'belief bases' for evaluation of context conditions

Taken together, these technologies can provide a simple form of event-driven reactive agent behaviour (e.g., if subgoals are seen as a stream of events). These paradigms are now a part of 'mainstream' Computer Science. For example, 'Event Driven and Reactive Programming' is included in the 2013 ACM model curriculum for Computer Science [1].

The developments discussed above do not constitute a comprehensive list of the changes impacting or likely to impact the EMAS community. It is possible to point to similar advances in other subfields of both AI (such as reasoning and scheduling) and CS relevant to agent programming. Together their effect is to erode the niche currently occupied by the current generation of agent programming languages. It follows that agent programming as a discipline will only remain relevant if it is possible to increase the size of the niche it occupies. To do so, agent programming languages must become capable of addressing a wider range of problems in a generic way. The good news is that the same developments which pose a threat to the future of agent programming can enable this transition, as I explain in the next section.

5   The Future

The advances in both hardware and related AI sub-disciplines highlighted in the previous section mean we are now in a position where we can rethink the foundations of agent programming languages. By engaging with cutting edge AI research, we can address some of the key challenges in agent development that have been largely ignored for the last twenty years. Note that this is not just 'more of the same'—the rest of AI has moved on significantly since the early work on the BDI model, creating significant new opportunities that agent programming can exploit.

5.1   Some Ideas

Below, I briefly sketch one possible path such developments could take. The ideas are shaped by my own interests and are not intended to be exhaustive or prescriptive—there are many other ways things could go (for some alternative suggestions, see [13]). However I believe that all feasible futures for agent programming entail a fundamental shift in emphasis: agent programming must become more about describing the problem rather than 'hacking code', with the agent programming language/platform doing (more of) the hard bits currently left to the agent developer.

---

[11] http://msdn.microsoft.com.

[12] http://code.google.com/p/cqengine.

beliefs: how and when beliefs are updated (active sensing, lazy update); handling uncertain and inconsistent beliefs (implications for plan selection)

goals: goals with priorities and deadlines; maintenance and other repeating goals; when to adopt, suspend and drop goals (cf. work on goal life cycles); how to tell if a goal is achieved (e.g., if beliefs are uncertain)

plans: plans with durative and nondeterministic actions; plans with partially ordered steps; when (and how) to synthesise new plans

intentions: how to estimate the time required to execute an intention; which intentions to progress next; how to schedule intentions to avoid interference; how to handle plan failure

MAS level: how to decide when to join an open system/coalition/team; deliberation about roles, norms etc; strategic reasoning about other agents

A key feature common to all these possible research directions, is that they involve the APL rather than the agent developer solving a problem.

5.2   What Counts as Progress

Identifying possible research directions is, on its own, insufficient. To count as progress, future research in agent programming must meet a number of criteria that characterise the unique contribution of agent programming (and agent architectures) as a field, distinct from other subfields of multi-agent systems, and artificial intelligence and computer science more generally. I therefore conclude this section with a set of 'progress metrics' which are rooted in the analysis presented in Sect. 3:

- extensions need to be integrated, e.g., uncertain and inconsistent beliefs have implications for plan selection and determining when a goal is achieved, plans with nondeterministic actions may determine when sensing is required, etc.
- ideally, the agent language/platform needs to be modular, so that an agent developer only needs to master the features necessary for their application
- evaluation of agent programs (and indirectly of APLs) requires richer benchmark problems (or less toy versions of current problems)
- the key evaluation criterion should be whether a developer has to explicitly program something rather than how long it takes them to program it or how many errors they make

The last point is critical. Clearly, the developer will have to write code specific to their particular application. The aim is to raise the level of abstraction offered by the agent programming language, and by doing so address the challenge of integrating the AI sub-disciplines necessary to design and build intelligent entities.[13]

This list of performance metrics is preliminary and can (and should) be improved. However broad consensus around some set of metrics is essential for

---

[13] A similar point is made by Hindriks [13] when he advocates easy access to powerful AI techniques. However Hindriks sees this as a desirable rather than a necessary feature.

EMAS to be coherent as a community, and I would argue that a list something like the above is necessary for our research to have impact in the wider field of multi-agent systems.

6   Conclusion

Agent programming isn't (and can't be for a long while) *primarily* about software engineering. Software engineering is important, but only as a means to an end. The AAMAS community, including EMAS, is primarily a scientific community. It's products are new knowledge about how to achieve flexible intelligent behaviour in dynamic and unpredictable environments, rather than software artefacts or tools. To make progress, we need to focus on solving more interesting AI problems in an integrated, general and tractable way. By doing so, I believe we can create theories and languages that are much more powerful and easy to use, and secure a future for agent programming as a discipline.

References

1. Computer science curricula 2013: Curriculum guidelines for undergraduate degree programs in computer science. ACM/IEEE, December 2013
2. Bellifemine, F.L., Caire, G., Greenwood, D.: Developing Multi-Agent Systems with JADE. Wiley, Chichester (2007)
3. Bordini, R., Bazzan, A.L.C., de O. Jannone, R., Basso, D.M., Vicari, R.M., Lesser, V.R.: AgentSpeak(XL): efficient intention selection in BDI agents via decision-theoretic task scheduling. In: Proceedings of the First International Conference on Autonomous Agents and Multiagent Systems (AAMAS'02), pp. 1294–1302. ACM Press, New York, NY, USA (2002)
4. Bordini, R.H., Hübner, J.F., Wooldridge, M.: Programming multi-agent systems in AgentSpeak using Jason. Wiley Series in Agent Technology. Wiley, New York (2007)
5. Braubach, L., Pokahr, A., Lamersdorf, W.: Jadex: A BDI-agent system combining middleware and reasoning. In: Unland, R., Calisti, M., Klusch, M. (eds.) Software Agent-Based Applications, Platforms and Development Kits. Whitestein Series in Software Agent Technologies, pp. 143–168. Birkhuser, Basel (2005)
6. Dastani, M.: 2APL: a practical agent programming language. Auton. Agent. Multi-Agent Syst. **16**(3), 214–248 (2008)
7. Dignum, V., Dignum, F.: Designing agent systems: state of the practice. Int. J. Agent-Oriented Softw. Eng. **4**(3), 224–243 (2010)
8. Dix, J., Hindriks, K.V., Logan, B., Wobcke, W.: Engineering multi-agent systems (Dagstuhl seminar 12342). Dagstuhl Rep. **2**(8), 74–98 (2012)
9. Gabriel, R.P.: Lisp: good news, bad news, how to win big. In: European Conference on the Practical Applications of Lisp (1990) (Reprinted in the April 1991 issue of AI Expert magazine)
10. Georgeff, M.P., Lansky, A.L.: Reactive reasoning and planning. In: Proceedings of the Sixth National Conference on Artificial Intelligence, AAAI-87, pp. 677–682 (1987)

11. Georgeff, M., Pell, B., Pollack, M.E., Tambe, M., Wooldridge, M.J.: The Belief-Desire-Intention model of agency. In: Papadimitriou, C., Singh, M.P., Müller, J.P. (eds.) ATAL 1998. LNCS (LNAI), vol. 1555, pp. 1–10. Springer, Heidelberg (1999)
12. Hindriks, K.V.: Programming rational agents in GOAL. In: El Fallah, A., Seghrouchni, J.D., Dastani, M., Bordini, R.H. (eds.) Multi-Agent Programming: Languages. Tools and Applications, pp. 119–157. Springer, US (2009)
13. Hindriks, K.V.: The shaping of the agent-oriented mindset. In: Dalpiaz, F., Dix, J., van Riemsdijk, M.B. (eds.) EMAS 2014. LNCS, vol. 8758, pp. 1–14. Springer, Heidelberg (2014)
14. Jennings, N.R.: Agent-oriented software engineering. In: Imam, I., Kodratoff, Y., El-Dessouki, A., Ali, M. (eds.) IEA/AIE 1999. LNCS (LNAI), vol. 1611, pp. 4–10. Springer, Heidelberg (1999)
15. Müller, J.P., Fischer, K.: Application impact of multi-agent systems and technologies: a survey. In: Shehory, O., Sturm, A. (eds.) Agent-Oriented Software Engineering, pp. 27–53. Springer, Heidelberg (2014)
16. Padgham, L., Singh, D.: Situational preferences for BDI plans. In: Gini, M.L., Shehory, O., Ito, T., Jonker, C.M. (eds.) International Conference on Autonomous Agents and Multi-Agent Systems, AAMAS '13, pp. 1013–1020. IFAAMAS (2013)
17. Patchett, C.: Robotics and Autonomous Systems: Challenges and Opportunities for the UK (2014)
18. Rao, A.S., Georgeff, M.P.: Modeling rational agents within a BDI-architecture. In: Proceedings of the Second International Conference on Principles of Knowledge Representation and Reasoning (KR'91), pp. 473–484 (1991)
19. Rao, A.S.: AgentSpeak(L): BDI agents speak out in a logical computable language. In: Perram, J., Van de Velde, W. (eds.) MAAMAW 1996. LNCS, vol. 1038, pp. 42–55. Springer, Heidelberg (1996)
20. Rintanen, J.: Planning as satisfiability: heuristics. Artif. Intell. **193**, 45–86 (2012)
21. Sardiña, S., de Silva, L., Padgham, L.: Hierarchical planning in BDI agent programming languages: a formal approach. In: Nakashima, H., Wellman, M.P., Weiss, E., Stone, P. (eds.) 5th International Joint Conference on Autonomous Agents and Multiagent Systems, pp. 1001–1008. ACM, Hakodate (2006)
22. Sardiña, S., Padgham, L.: Goals in the context of BDI plan failure and planning. In: Durfee, E.H., Yokoo, M., Huhns, M.N., Shehory, O. (eds.) Proceedings of the Sixth International Joint Conference on Autonomous Agents and Multiagent Systems (AAMAS 2007), pp. 1–8. ACM (2007)
23. Singh, D., Hindriks, K.V.: Learning to improve agent behaviours in GOAL. In: Dastani, M., Hübner, J.F., Logan, B. (eds.) ProMAS 2012. LNCS, vol. 7837, pp. 158–173. Springer, Heidelberg (2013)
24. Thangarajah, J., Harland, J., Morley, D., Yorke-Smith, N.: Suspending and resuming tasks in BDI agents. In: Proceedings of the Seventh International Conference on Autonomous Agents and Multi Agent Systems (AAMAS'08), pp. 405–412, Estoril, Portugal, May 2008
25. Thangarajah, J., Harland, J., Morley, D.N., Yorke-Smith, N.: Quantifying the completeness of goals in BDI agent systems. In: Schaub, T., Friedrich, G., O'Sullivan, B. (eds.) ECAI 2014–21st European Conference on Artificial Intelligence, 18–22 August 2014, Prague, Czech Republic - Including Prestigious Applications of Intelligent Systems (PAIS 2014), pp. 879–884. IOS Press (2014)
26. Thangarajah, J., Padgham, L., Winikoff, M.: Detecting & avoiding interference between goals in intelligent agents. In: Gottlob, G., Walsh, T. (eds.) Proceedings of the Eighteenth International Joint Conference on Artificial Intelligence (IJCAI-03), pp. 721–726. Morgan Kaufmann, August 2003

27. Vikhorev, K., Alechina, N., Logan, B.: Agent programming with priorities and deadlines. In: Turner, K., Yolum, P., Sonenberg, L., Stone, P. (eds.) Proceedings of the Tenth International Conference on Autonomous Agents and Multiagent Systems (AAMAS 2011), pp. 397–404, Taipei, Taiwan, May 2011
28. Walczak, A., Braubach, L., Pokahr, A., Lamersdorf, W.: Augmenting BDI agents with deliberative planning techniques. In: Bordini, R.H., Dastani, M., Dix, J., Fallah Seghrouchni, A. (eds.) PROMAS 2006. LNCS (LNAI), vol. 4411, pp. 113–127. Springer, Heidelberg (2007)
29. Willetts, D.: Eight Great Technologies. Policy Exchange (2013)
30. Winikoff, M.: JACK^{TM} Intelligent agents: an industrial strength platform. In: Bordini, R.H., Dastani, M., Dix, J., El Fallah Seghrouchni, A. (eds.) Multi-Agent Programming. Multiagent Systems, Artificial Societies, and Simulated Organizations, pp. 175–193. Springer, Heidelberg (2005)
31. Winikoff, M.: Challenges and directions for engineering multi-agent systems. CoRR, abs/1209.1428 (2012)
32. Yao, Y., Logan, B., Thangarajah, J.: SP-MCTS-based intention scheduling for BDI agents. In: Schaub, T., Friedrich, G., O'Sullivan, B. (eds.) Proceedings of the 21st European Conference on Artificial Intelligence (ECAI-2014), pp. 1133–1134. IOS Press, Prague, Czech Republic (2014)

Towards Agent Aggregates: Perspectives and Challenges

Mirko Viroli$^{(\boxtimes)}$ and Alessandro Ricci

Alma Mater Studiorum – Università di Bologna, Bologna, Italy
{mirko.viroli,a.ricci}@unibo.it

Abstract. Recent works in the context of self-organisation foster the idea of engineering large-scale situated systems by taking an aggregate stance: system design and development are better conducted by abstracting away from individuals' details, rather directly engineering (designing, programming, verifying) the overall system behaviour, as if it were executed on top of a single, continuous-like machine. As a consequence, concerns like interaction protocols, self-organisation, adaptation, and large-scaleness, get automatically hidden "under the hood" of the platform supporting aggregate computing, with notable advantages in raising the abstraction level and scaling with behaviour complexity. This paper provides an initial exploration of potentials and challenges of using aggregate computing techniques in the context of multi-agent systems, considering impact on large-scale reactive MASs, environment engineering and its cognitive exploitation, and on collective team-work by the notion of aggregate plan.

1 Introduction

Self-organisation mechanisms support adaptivity and resilience in complex natural systems at all levels, from molecules and cells to animals, species, and entire ecosystems [25]. A long-standing aim in computer science is to find effective engineering methods for exploiting such mechanisms to bring similar adaptivity and resilience to a wide variety of complex, large-scale computing applications—in smart mobility, crowd engineering, swarm robotics, etc. Practical adoption, however, poses serious challenges, since self-organisation mechanisms often trade efficiency for resilience, and are often difficult to predictably compose to meet more complex specifications.

On the one hand, in the context of multi-agent systems (MASs), self-organisation is achieved relying on a weak notion of agency: following a biology inspiration, agents execute simple and pre-defined behaviour, out of which self-organisation is achieved by emergence [12]—ant foraging being a classical example. This approach however hardly applies to open and dynamic contexts in which what is the actual behaviour to be carried on by a group of agents is to be decided (or even synthesised) at run-time: offline fine-tuning of system parameters often hampers applicability to real-life, non trivial applications.

© Springer International Publishing Switzerland 2015
M. Baldoni et al. (Eds.): EMAS 2015, LNAI 9318, pp. 18–30, 2015.
DOI: 10.1007/978-3-319-26184-3_2

On the other hand, a promising set of results towards addressing solid engineering of open self-organising systems are being achieved under the umbrella of *aggregate programming* [3]. Its main idea is to shift the focus of system programming from the individual's viewpoint to the aggregate viewpoint: one no longer programs the single entity's computational and interactive behaviour, but rather programs the collection. This is achieved by abstracting away from the discrete nature of computational networks, by assuming that the overall executing "machine" is a sort of (space-time) computational continuum able to manipulate distributed data structures: actual self-organisation mechanisms sit below, and are they key for automatically turning aggregate specifications into individual behaviour. Aggregate programming is grounded in the computational field calculus [9], its incarnation in the Protelis programming language [19], on studies focussing on formal assessment of resiliency properties [23], and building blocks and libraries built on top to support applications in the context of large scale situated systems [2].

This paper aims at analysing the potentials and challenges that can arise when combining techniques of aggregate programming in the context of MASs. In Sect. 2 we start recapping the main elements of aggregate computing. Section 3 depicts a methodology for engineering large-scale reactive MASs on top of aggregate computing, based on the construction of layers of resilient composable functions, raising the abstraction level to address system complexity. Section 4 discusses impact on environment engineering: aggregate computing is about manipulation of computational fields [9,14], which can be seen as distributed "traces" or "stigma" that agents leave in the spatial environment as a coordination tool, up to be exploited to externalise true fields of beliefs, goals, and intentions. Section 5 presents early ideas on applying aggregate computing to ground a notion of "aggregate plan", a collective plan shared and cooperatively executed by a dynamic team of agents, developed so as to abstract from participants' number and details. Section 6 concludes providing final remarks.

2   Aggregate Programming

Most paradigms of distributed systems development, there including the multi-agent system approach, are based on the idea of programming each single individual of the system, in terms of its computational behaviour (goals, plans, algorithm, interaction protocol), typically considering a finite number of "roles", i.e., individual classes. This approach is argued to be problematic: it makes it complicated to reason in terms of the effect of composing behaviours, and it forces the programmer to mix different concerns of resiliency and coordination—using middlewares that externalise coordination/social abstractions and interaction mechanisms only partially alleviates the problem [5,24].

These limits are widely recognised, and motivated work toward aggregate programming across a variety of different domains, as surveyed in [1]. Historically such works addressed different facets of the problem: making device interaction implicit (e.g., TOTA [14]), providing means to compose geometric and topological constructions (e.g., Origami Shape Language [16]), providing means for summarising from space-time regions of the environment and streaming these summaries to other regions (e.g., TinyDB [13]), automatically splitting computational behaviour for cloud-style execution (e.g., MapReduce [10]), and providing generalisable constructs for space-time computing (e.g., Proto [15]).

Aggregate computing, based on the field calculus computational model [9] and its embodiment in Protelis programming language [19], lies on top of the above approaches and attempts a generalisation starting from the works on space-time computing, which are explicitly designed for distributed operation in a physical environment filled with embedded devices, but can be extended to work on arbitrary physical/logical environments.

2.1   Computing at the Aggregate Level

The whole approach of aggregate computing starts from the observation that the complexity of large-scale situated systems must be properly hidden "under-the-hood" of the programming model, so that composability of collective behaviour can be more easily supported and better address the construction of complex systems. Aggregate programming is then based on the following three principles:

1. The "machine" being programmed is a region of the computational environment whose specific details are abstracted away (perhaps even to a pure spatio-temporal continuum);
2. The program is specified as a manipulation of data structures with spatial and temporal extent across that region;
3. These manipulations are actually carried out in a robust and self-organising manner by the aggregate of cooperating devices situated in that region, using local interactions.

As an example, consider the problem of designing crowd safety services based on peer-to-peer interactions between crowd members' smart-phones. In this example, smart-phones could interact to collectively estimate the density and distribution of crowding, seen as a distributed data structure mapping each point of space to a real-value indicating the crowd estimation, namely, a *computational field* (or simply *field*) of reals [9,14]. This can be in turn used as input for several other services: warning systems for people nearby dense regions (producing a field of booleans holding true where warning has to be set), dispersal systems to avoid present or future congestion (producing a field of directions suggested to people via their smartphones), steering services to reach points-of-interest (POI) avoiding crowded areas (producing a field of pairs of direction and POI name). Building such services in a fully-distributed and resilient way is very difficult, as it comes to achieve self-* behaviour by careful design of each device's interaction with its neighbours. With aggregate programming, on the other hand, one instead naturally reasons in terms of an incremental construction of computational fields, with the programming platform taking care of turning aggregate programs into programs for the single device.

2.2   Constructs

The *field calculus* [9] captures the key ingredients of aggregate neighbour-based computation into a tiny language suitable for grounding programming and reasoning about correctness – recent works addressed type soundness [9] and self-stabilisation [23] – and is then incarnated into a Java-oriented language called Protelis [19], which we here use for explanation purposes. The unifying abstraction is that of computational field, and every computation (atomic or composite) is about functionally creating fields out of fields. Hence, a program is made of an expression e to be evaluate in space-time (ideally, in a continuum space-time, practically, in asynchronous rounds in each device of the network) and thus producing a field "evolution". Four mechanisms are defined to hierarchically compose expressions out of values and variables, each providing a possible syntactic structure for e:

- **Application:** $\lambda(e_1, \ldots, e_n)$ applies "functional value" λ to arguments $e_1, \ldots,$ e_n (using call-by-value semantics). λ can either be a "built-in" primitive (any non-aggregate operation to be executed locally, like mathematical, logical, or algorithmic functions, or calls to sensors and actuators), a user-defined function (that encapsulates reusable behaviour), or an anonymous function value $(x_1, \ldots, x_n)->e$ (possibly passed also as argument, and ultimately, spread to neighbours to achieve open models of code deployment [9])—in the latter case Protelis ad-hoc syntax is λ.apply$(e_1, \ldots, e_n)$.
- **Dynamics:** `rep(x<-v){e}` defines a local state variable x initialised with value v and updated at each computation round with the result of evaluating the update expression e.
- **Interaction:** `nbr(e)` gathers by observation a map at each neighbour to its latest resulting value of evaluating e. A special set of built-in "hood" functions can then be used to summarise such maps back to ordinary expressions, e.g., `minHood(m)` finds the minimum value in the map m.
- **Restriction:** `if(e){e`$_1$`}else{e`$_2$`}` implements branching by partitioning the network into two regions: where e evaluates to true e_1 is evaluated, elsewhere e_2 is evaluated. Notably, because `if` is implemented by partition, the expressions in the two branches are encapsulated and no action taken by them can have effects outside of the partition.

A simple example using the various constructs (colouring field calculus keywords magenta, built-in functions green, user-defined functions red, and variables green) is:

```
def distance-avoiding-obstacle (source, obstacle){
  if(obstacle) {infinity} else {
    rep(d<-infinity) {
      mux(source, 0, minHood+(nbrRange + nbr(d)))
} } }
```

This code creates a field of estimated distances to devices where `source` is `true`, using a metric that computes such distances by circumventing devices where `obstacle` is `true`. In the region outside the obstacle (by `if`), a distance estimate `d` (established by `rep`) is computed using built-in selector `mux` to set sources to 0 and other devices by the triangle inequality, taking the minimum value obtained by adding the distance to each neighbour to its estimate of `d` (by `nbr`).

3   Impact on Building Large-Scale Self-Organising MASs

Aggregate computing makes weak assumptions on the underlying computing platforms, that well match those of large-scale reactive MASs: asynchronous agent computation, broadcast of messages to neighbours, perception/action on the local part of the physical environment. This paves the way for using aggregate computing techniques for developing large-scale self-organising MASs.

3.1   Raising the Abstraction Level

While the constructs of aggregate computing form an universal set, they are also too low level to be readily used for building complex distributed services like self-organising MASs. To raise the level of abstraction it is fruitful to identify a collection of general combinators (or "building blocks"), which encapsulate reusable coordination mechanisms, and allow one to bypass the trickier aspects of field calculus. Such combinators set is formed by careful selection of coordination mechanisms needed for complex situated MASs, and hence should be *(i)* self-stabilising, meaning that they reactively adjust to changes in environment, *(ii)* scalable to large MASs, and *(iii)* preserve these resilience properties when composed together into more complex coordination services.

Some operators have been identified already, in [2]. Two of them seem particularly relevant for the context of MASs: new operators G and C, to be used along with constructs `if` and built-ins. The two building blocks are defined as:

– G(`source`, `init`, `metric`, `accumulate`) is a "spreading" operation generalising distance measurement, broadcast, and projection. It may be thought of as executing two tasks: it computes a field of shortest-path distances from a `source` region (indicated as a Boolean field) according to the supplied function `metric`, then propagates values along the gradient of the distance field away from source, beginning with value `initial` and accumulating along the gradient with `accumulate`.
– C(`potential`, `accumulate`, `local`, `null`) is complementary to G, accumulating information to the `source` down the gradient of a supplied `potential` field. Beginning with an idempotent `null`, at each device, the `local` value is combined with "uphill" values using a commutative and associative function `accumulate`, to produce a cumulative value at each device in the `source`.

Although there are only a few operators, they are so general as to cover, individually or in combination, a large number of the common coordination patterns used in design of resilient systems. With appropriate implementation in field calculus, this system of operators can thereby provide an expressive programming environment that provides strong guarantees of resilience and scalability, as established in [2].

3.2   Towards Libraries of Collective Distributed Sensing and Action

Key operations of large-scale self-organising MASs involve the need of perceiving events distributed in a whole space region, elaborate them, and properly perform an actuation again into a whole space region. Operators G and C provide a good "lingua franca" for expressing behaviours on top of primitive aggregation/collection operations.

For example, operator G (along with built-ins) can generate a number of interesting functions related to distributed action and information diffusion. One such common computation in spatially embedded systems is estimating the distance from one or more designated "source" devices to others nearby, which can be implemented by a simple application of G, beginning with zero and using estimated device-to-device distance as a metric:

```
def distanceTo(source) {
  G(source, 0, () -> {nbrRange}, (v) -> {v + nbrRange})
}
```

Likewise, another common coordination action, broadcasting a value across the network from a source, can be implemented by another application of G:

```
def broadcast(source, value) {
  G(source, value, () -> {nbrRange}, (v) -> {v})
}
```

Other G-based operations include construction of a Voronoi partition and a "path forecast" that marks paths that cross an obstacle or region of interest.

Similarly, operator C enables functions related to information perception, such as accumulating the sum of all the values of a variable in a region

```
def summarize(sink, accumulate, local, null) {
  C(distanceTo(sink), accumulate, local, null)
}
```

or computing the variable's average or maximum value in that region.

Just as when building any other software library, these API functions can be combined together to create higher level libraries. For example, an average function shared throughout a region can be implemented by applying broadcast to the output of summarize, as follows:

```
def average(sink,value){
  broadcast(sink, summarize(sink,+,value,0) / summarize(sink,+,1,0))
}
```

3.3 Challenges

The main research challenges we identify to foster exploitation of aggregate computing for building large-scale reactive MASs include:

- Extracting from various application contexts general building blocks and APIs to help development of real-life complex systems;
- Designing a platform support for MASs based on aggregate computing, where purely local interactions and cloud-based communications can be dynamically combined;
- Integrating field calculus constructs into agent languages (such as Jason), to streamline combination with existing agent development methodology.

4 Impact on Building MAS Environment

Turning our attention to a stronger notion of agency, how can aggregate programming affect the agent-oriented abstractions rooting MAS engineering? An effective way to do this is by means of the notion of environment as a first-class design and programming abstraction [21,24].

4.1 Coordination Artifacts Enacting Computational Fields

The infrastructural substrate that reifies computational fields, which we can call the *computational fields fabric*, can be modelled as the application environment where agents are logically situated, encapsulating the functionalities that agents can exploit to perform their individual and global tasks. In particular, the computational fields fabric can be characterised as a distributed *coordination artifact* [18], since it can be exploited by agents for coordination and self-organisation purposes. Field calculus and Protelis are the basic tools on top of which we can program such a distributed coordination medium (like in the case of programmable coordination media [11]), making it possible to define the coordination and self-organisation functionalities in a declarative and macro way on the one hand, and execute it in a fully decentralised way on the other hand.

As an example, it can be programmed so as to create a gradient field (with G operator), so that agents willing to advertise an event can inject information in the environment locally, which gets then distributed around, and can be exploited by other agents perceiving the environment, either to just observe information or to move towards its source.

This view generally allows for conceiving in a clean way systems where the environment encapsulates functionalities useful for self-organisation and collective adaptation, still retaining agent full autonomy.

4.2   Cognitive Fields

The integration of aggregate programming and agents lead to consider quite naturally the opportunity of exploiting aggregate coordination functionalities by cognitive agents too, i.e., thinking about computational fields designed in terms of cognitive agents' mental attitudes, such as beliefs and goals. In other words, with cognitive agents, a computational field would represent a kind of distributed, decentralised, and externalised *mental state*, which evolves according to the agent actions and the rules of field evolution specified in the environment program. In that perspective, we envision some strong connection with our previous works exploring the notion of *cognitive stigmergy* [20] and with contributions in the cognitive science literature discussing the idea of the environment as *extended mind* [8]. It is possible to consider three different levels of cognitive fields:

- *Belief fields* – Belief fields are the simplest case, in which a computational field is like a classic partially observable environment whose percepts are modelled as beliefs by the agent situated in it. The aggregate program in this case specifies how some belief should be distributed among the agents depending on their position inside the field. More generally, the aggregate program defines the rule by which the overall distributed "belief" state can evolve and be influenced by each agent and by the environment. As an example, distributed aggregation and then diffusion of information perceived by temperature sensors can be used to automatically create a constant field of the average temperature value across a region of space, which can be interpreted and used as a belief field by the MAS.
- *Goal fields* – In a goal field, the values manipulated by the field are the goals that are meant to be adopted by the agents that are located in some position of the environment. Thus, the aggregate program in this case specifies a *division of labor*, or how tasks are meant to be allocated to agents. For instance, operator G can be used to create a Voronoi partition, dividing the overall space into a set of regions based on proximity to a set of n source agents. Each such agent n_i can be considered as initiator of a distributed goal g_i, diffused to all agents in the region created by n_i. The resulting partition field is hence seen as a goal field, allocating n goals to the MAS.
- *Intention fields* – In an intention field, the values manipulated by the field are the intentions that the agent located in some position of the field has, namely, actions to execute to behave collectively. Thus, the aggregate program in this case specifies a spatial-dependent concept of task. For instance, to steer people towards a POI in a complex pervasive environment, one could establish a gradient field from the POI, on top of which a field of directions towards the source can be created. This can be understood as a field of intentions, feeding e.g. pervasive displays that will use a direction to show a direction sign.

4.3   Tooling

From a technological point of view, enacting computational fields by environment artifacts makes it possible to exploit existing environment-based technologies to integrate aggregate programming with existing MAS programming tools. Main examples are EIS [4] and CArtAgO [21].

In the latter case in particular, we can design a set of *artifacts* [17,21] that make it possible for an agent to perceive and act upon a computational field, as well as to manage the set of computational fields, creating new ones or disposing existing ones. More in detail, in order to work within a computational field, an agent can be equipped with an artifact conceptually representing a piece of field, making it observable (by means of observable properties) both the value of the field in the agent position as well as the values of the neighbourhood. By exploiting CArtAgO with cognitive agent programming languages – such as in the case of JaCaMo [6] based on the Jason agent programming language [7] – this modelling makes it possible to directly implement belief fields, since artifact observable properties are mapped into beliefs of agents observing the artifact. Goal and intention fields can be implemented by using observable properties to represent goals and intentions managed by the field. In this case, using Jason for instance, agents can be equipped with suitable plans to react to changes to the beliefs mapping these observable properties so as to e.g. adopting new goals or adding new plans to the plan library, according to the need.

In this framework, Protelis could be used as high-level language to program the single artifact, to be properly compiled to feed CArtAgO.

4.4   Challenges

Among the many research challenges spawning from the idea of aggregate computing as an environment process, we identify:

- Develop suitable models and infrastructures to support flexible computational fields by environment abstractions;
- Extend the notion of cognitive stigmergy to deal with spatially distributed computational fields;
- Study the consequence of aggregate agent reasoning, in theory, models and implementations of intelligent systems.

5   Impact on Aggregate Plans

Another fruitful idea for the integration between aggregate computing and MASs is that of considering an aggregate program as "an aggregate plan", which an agent can either create or receive from peers, and can deliberate to execute or not in different moments of time.

5.1   Life-Cycle of Aggregate Plans

In our model, aggregate plans are expressed by anonymous functions of the kind ()->e, where e is a field expression possibly calling API functions available as part of each agent's library. One such plan can be created in two different ways, by suitable functions (whose detail we abstract away): first, it can be a sensor `sns-injected-function` to model the plan being generated by the external world (i.e. a system programmer) and dynamically deployed; second, it can model a local planner `plan-creation` that synthesises a suitable plan for the situation at hand. When the plan is created, it should then be shared with other agents, typically by a broadcasting pattern—the full power of field calculus can be used to rely on sophisticated techniques for constraining the target area of broadcasting.

Agents are to be programmed with just a minimal `virtual-machine`-like code [9] that makes it participate to this broadcast pattern, so as to receive all plans produced remotely in the form of a field of pairs of a description of the plan and its implementation by the anonymous function. Among the plans currently available, by the restriction operator if the agent can autonomously decide which one to actually execute, using as condition the result of a built-in deliberation function that has access to the plan's description.

Note that if/when an aggregate plan is in execution, it will make the agent cooperatively work with all the other agents that are equally executing the same aggregate plan. This "dynamic team" will then coherently bring about the social goal that this plan is meant to achieve, typically expressed in terms of a final distributed data structure, used as input for other processes or to feed actuators (i.e., to make agents/devices move). The inner mechanisms of aggregate computing smoothly support entering/quitting the team, making overall behaviour spontaneously self-organise to such dynamism.

5.2   Mapping Constructs, and Libraries

As a plan is in execution, the operations of aggregate programming that it includes can be naturally understood as "instructions" for the single agent, as follows:

- Function application amounts to any pure computation an agent has to execute, there including algorithmic, deliberation, scheduling and planning activities, as well as local action and perception.
- Repetition construct is instead used to make some local result of execution of the aggregate plan persist over time, e.g. modelling belief update.
- Neighbour field construction is the mechanism by which information about neighbour agents executing the same plan can be observed, supporting the cooperation needed to make the plan be considered as an aggregate one.
- Restriction can be used inside a plan to temporarily structure the plan in sub-plans, allowing each agent to decide which of them should be executed, i.e., which sub-team has to be dynamically joined.

As explained in Sect. 3, one of the assets of aggregate programming is its ability of defining libraries of reusable components of collective behaviour, with formally provable resilience properties. Seen in the context of agent programming, such libraries can be used as libraries of reusable aggregate plans, built on top of building blocks:

- Building block G is at the basis of libraries of "distributed action", namely, cooperative behaviour aimed at acting over the environment or sets of agents in a distributed way.
- Building block C conversely supports libraries of "distributed perception", namely, cooperative behaviour aimed at perceiving the environment or information about a set of agents in a distributed way.
- The combination of building blocks G and C, and others [2], allows one to define more complex elements of collective adaptive behaviour, generally used to intercept distributed events and situations, compute/plan response actions, and actuate them collectively.

5.3   Challenges

The notion of aggregate plan suggests several research directions, with the goal of addressing the following challenges:

- study planning techniques for the dynamic creation of aggregate plans;
- experiment the pragmatics of aggregate plans, to explore their abilities of supporting smooth, self-adaptive entering and quitting from the team playing an aggregate plan;
- devise new linguistic constructs for the field calculus to empower its applicability of model for aggregate plans.

6   Conclusions

Aggregate computing is a new metaphor for building distributed systems, with notable impact to the engineering of "complexity", thanks to its ability to: (i) reason in term of field calculus programs to formally derive its behavioural properties [23]; (ii) create reusable combinators of wide applicability, to raise the abstraction layer of system development [2]; (iii) promote a methodology for substitutability of components to improve performance [22]; and (iv) address the problem of platform support in a rather abstract away so as to smoothly support different computation/communication models. All this features are seemingly key for MASs as well.

On the other hand, aggregate programming has also the potential of deeply affecting some aspects of agent theory, fostering a more deep understanding of how "computational fields" can be perceived and exploited by cognitive agents. This can shed light to new methodologies for building intelligent distributed systems, where availability of a huge number of agents can turn from a serious coordination problem to an opportunity for building effective, efficient and resilient systems.

Ultimately, aggregate computing and MASs have the potential of combining into a new powerful notion of "agent aggregate", which this paper only started exploring in its many facets, and which will be matter of our future research investigations.

References

1. Beal, J., Dulman, S., Usbeck, K., Viroli, M., Correll, N.: Organizing the aggregate: languages for spatial computing. In: Mernik, M. (ed.) Formal and Practical Aspects of Domain-Specific Languages: Recent Developments, pp. 436–501. IGI Global, Hershey (2013). http://arxiv.org/abs/1202.5509
2. Beal, J., Viroli, M.: Building blocks for aggregate programming of self-organising applications. In: Workshop on Foundations of Complex Adaptive Systems (FOCAS) (2014)
3. Beal, J., Viroli, M.: Space–time programming. Philos. Trans. R. Soc. Lond A: Math. Phys. Eng. Sci. **373**, 2015 (2046)
4. Behrens, T., Hindriks, K., Dix, J.: Towards an environment interface standard for agent platforms. Ann. Math. Artif. Intell. **61**(4), 261–295 (2011)
5. Boissier, O., Bordini, R.H., Hübner, J.F., Ricci, A., Santi, A.: Multi-agent oriented programming with jacamo. Sci. Comput. Program. **78**(6), 747–761 (2013)
6. Boissier, O., Bordini, R.H., Hübner, J.F., Ricci, A., Santi, A.: Multi-agent oriented programming with jacamo. Sci. Comput. Programm. **78**(6), 747–761 (2013)
7. Bordini, R.H., Hübner, J.F., Wooldrige, M.: Programming Multi-Agent Systems in AgentSpeak using Jason. Wiley Series in Agent Technology. Wiley, Hoboken (2007)
8. Clark, A., Chalmers, D.: The extended mind. Analysis **58**(1), 7–19 (1998)
9. Damiani, F., Viroli, M., Pianini, D., Beal, J.: Code mobility meets self-organisation: a higher-order calculus of computational fields. In: Graf, S., Viswanathan, M. (eds.) Formal Techniques for Distributed Objects, Components, and Systems. LNCS, vol. 9039, pp. 113–128. Springer, Heidelberg (2015)
10. Dean, J., Ghemawat, S.: MapReduce: simplified data processing on large clusters. Commun. ACM **51**(1), 107–113 (2008)
11. Denti, E., Natali, A., Omicini, A.: Programmable coordination media. In: Garlan, D., Le Métayer, D. (eds.) COORDINATION 1997. LNCS, vol. 1282, pp. 274–288. Springer, Heidelberg (1997)
12. Fernandez-Marquez, J.L., Serugendo, G.D.M., Montagna, S., Viroli, M., Arcos, J.L.: Description and composition of bio-inspired design patterns: a complete overview. Nat. Comput. **12**(1), 43–67 (2013)
13. Madden, S.R., Szewczyk, R., Franklin, M.J., Culler, D.: Supporting aggregate queries over ad-hoc wireless sensor networks. In: Workshop on Mobile Computing and Systems Applications (2002)
14. Mamei, M., Zambonelli, F.: Programming pervasive and mobile computing applications: the tota approach. ACM Trans. Softw. Eng. Methodol. **18**(4), 1–56 (2009)
15. MIT Proto. Software available at http://proto.bbn.com/. Accessed 1 January 2012
16. Nagpal, R.: Programmable self-assembly: constructing global shape using biologically-inspired local interactions and origami mathematics. Ph.D. thesis, MIT (2001)
17. Omicini, A., Ricci, A., Viroli, M.: Artifacts in the A&A meta-model for multi-agent systems. Auton. Agent. Multi-Agent Syst. **17**(3), 432–456 (2008)
18. Omicini, A., Ricci, A., Viroli, M., Castelfranchi, C., Tummolini, L.: Coordination artifacts: environment-based coordination for intelligent agents. In: Jennings, N.R., Sierra, C., Sonenberg, L., Tambe, M. (eds.) Proceedings of AAMAS 2004, vol. 1, pp. 286–293. ACM, 19–23 July 2004
19. Pianini, D., Beal, J., Viroli, M.: Practical aggregate programming with protelis. In: ACM Symposium on Applied Computing (SAC 2015) (2015) (To appear)

20. Ricci, A., Omicini, A., Viroli, M., Gardelli, L., Oliva, E.: Cognitive stigmergy: towards a framework based on agents and artifacts. In: Weyns, D., Van Dyke Parunak, H., Michel, F. (eds.) E4MAS 2006. LNCS (LNAI), vol. 4389, pp. 124–140. Springer, Heidelberg (2007)
21. Ricci, A., Piunti, M., Viroli, M.: Environment programming in multi-agent systems: an artifact-based perspective. Auton. Agents Multi-Agent Syst. **23**(2), 158–192 (2011)
22. Viroli, M., Beal, J., Damiani, F., Pianini, D.: Efficient engineering of complex self-organising systems by self-stabilising fields. In: IEEE Conference on Self-Adaptive and Self-Organising Systems (SASO 2015) (2015)
23. Viroli, M., Damiani, F.: A calculus of self-stabilising computational fields. In: Kühn, E., Pugliese, R. (eds.) COORDINATION 2014. LNCS, vol. 8459, pp. 163–178. Springer, Heidelberg (2014)
24. Weyns, D., Omicini, A., Odell, J.: Environment as a first class abstraction in multiagent systems. Auton. Agents Multi-Agent Syst. **14**(1), 5–30 (2007)
25. Zambonelli, F., Viroli, M.: A survey on nature-inspired metaphors for pervasive service ecosystems. Int. J. Pervasive Comput. Commun. **7**(3), 186–204 (2011)

Contributed Papers

Designing a Knowledge Representation Interface for Cognitive Agents

Timea Bagosi$^{(\boxtimes)}$, Joachim de Greeff, Koen V. Hindriks,
and Mark A. Neerincx

Delft University of Technology, Delft, The Netherlands
{T.Bagosi,J.deGreeff,K.V.Hindriks,M.A.Neerincx}@tudelft.nl

Abstract. The design of cognitive agents involves a knowledge representation (KR) to formally represent and manipulate information relevant for that agent. In practice, agent programming frameworks are dedicated to a specific KR, limiting the use of other possible ones. In this paper we address the issue of creating a flexible choice for agent programmers regarding the technology they want to use. We propose a generic interface, that provides an easy choice of KR for cognitive agents. Our proposal is governed by a number of design principles, an analysis of functional requirements that cognitive agents pose towards a KR, and the identification of various features provided by KR technologies that the interface should capture. We provide two use-cases of the interface by describing its implementation for Prolog and OWL with rules.

Keywords: Knowledge representation technology · Agent programming framework · Generic interface design

1   Introduction

In cognitive agents, knowledge representation (KR) is used to store, retrieve and update information. In principle, knowledge can be represented in many different ways, but in practice programmers tend to be limited to a specific KR approach that a particular agent programming framework offers. We consider an agent programming framework to be a set of tools for developing or creating cognitive agents. Cognitive agents are entities or pieces of software that percieve and act in an environment, as it is explained more in detail in Sect. 3.2. In many agent frameworks (e.g. Jason [5], 2APL [7] and GOAL [15]), Prolog (or a variant) has become the de-facto standard. There are several reasons why a programmer might prefer to use a different KR from Prolog. A negotiating agent, for example, might need some legislative information, that would need to be encoded when using Prolog. On the other hand, when using OWL, it is possible for the agent to access large amounts of readily available information on the semantic web. However, most agent programming frameworks are committed to a specific KR, and switching to another is not supported.

© Springer International Publishing Switzerland 2015
M. Baldoni et al. (Eds.): EMAS 2015, LNAI 9318, pp. 33–50, 2015.
DOI: 10.1007/978-3-319-26184-3_3

1.1 Motivation

A generic interface for connecting different KRs to cognitive agents is useful for several reasons. Our main motivations are described next.

Knowledge representation languages differ in the *expressivity* that they offer. It is well-known, for example, that negation in logic programming has a semantics based on the Closed World Assumption whereas the family of web ontology languages support the Open World Assumption. Depending on the task, domain, or scenario, one language might be more appropriate than another.

An *agent programmer*, may have a personal preference based on, e.g., ease of use, familiarity, or other factors. An ontology enginner could model a domain of interest easily, but might find other languages difficult.

The Dagstuhl report on "Engineering Multi-Agent Systems" [10] advocates a *component-based* agent design, as this would provide flexibility, reduce overhead, bridge the gap to other architectures and could facilitate more widespread adoption of agent frameworks in real-world applications. A separation of the agent framework and the KR it uses – that is agnostic with respect to the underlying agent programming language – subscribes to this component-based approach, that our interface aims to support.

When using agent programming as part of real-world applications, one commonly has to access existing infrastructure, which typically may include industry-standard approaches for data storage (e.g. Oracle database). Rather than implementing some kind of bridge between these *legacy databases* and the knowledge representation language used in the agent framework on an ad-hoc basis, a much better approach would be the use of a generic interface, so that the agent framework can use the available technology directly. The semantic web offers a wide range of information in RDF standard format, that could be accessed by OWL-knowledgeable agents.

An agent may need to combine knowledge from *multiple sources*, that are either distributed or not. A generic interface supporting a variety of KR languages, allowing the use of several KR sources from several locations is useful in this context. A particular case is when dealing with large multi-agent systems that may include different manifestations of the agents, such as embodied in robots, software agents and modeling users, where they might be of different technologies.

A wide range of agent frameworks could benefit from providing a flexible choice of various logic-based KR formalisms. *Reusability* prevents the need for reinventing the wheel, as the effort to support this interface for a particular agent framework or a particular KR is a one time investment.

1.2 Scope and Methodology

In this paper we propose a design for a *Knowledge Representation Interface* (KRI) that facilitates an easy choice of KR for cognitive agents. Currently, this interface presupposes the adoption of the chosen KR by all agents in an agent programming framework. In principle, it is conceivable that a single agent would use multiple KRs, or multiple interacting agents would each utilize different KRs. The combination of multiple KRs into a single agent framework poses a number of issues that are investigated by [8]. This work is orthogonal to our work, as our aim is to facilitate the easy integration of an arbitrary *single* KR technology into a cognitive agent. Investigating issues relating to multiple interacting agents that each may use a different KR technology is therefore outside the scope of this work.

Our proposed interface design is applicable to a range of agent frameworks that facilitate agents with mental states, and all classes of KR that comply to the definition of [8], as described in detail in Sect. 3. By supporting the interface, an agent framework facilitates the choice of a technology that provides the required expressivity or other feature, and the choice of a preferred knowledge technology by its user.

Creating a generic KRI poses a number of challenges. For instance, it is important to identify the right abstraction level for the KRI specification. Striking the right balance between a high level description (to be as inclusive as possible) and a low level description that may be close to a particular KR language (to be able to specify the details) is essential for the interface design. Careful consideration is needed when identifying where an agent needs some form of KR, such as to represent the contents of its plans, skills, goals, etc.

We use the following methodology to derive the interface. First, we explore related literature, describing the various approaches of how each agent framework incorporates a specific KR. Usually the choice of representing knowledge through a certain language is implicitly integrated within a given framework, rather than being explicitly considered, let alone providing users with any sort of choice. To the best of our knowledge, no work has yet been done on the design and development of a generic interface that facilitates the use of a range of KRs.

Having identified the need for such a KRI (based on the motivations described above), and given the apparent lack of such a construct in related work, we then present the design of the KRI, governed by the following three aspects: (1) a number of design principles serving as guidelines, (2) the concept of cognitive agents and the functionality requirements they pose towards a KR, and (3) the identification of features provided by various KR technologies that the KRI should be able to provide.

After having presented the KRI, we describe its application with two implementation: in the first implementation the KRI is instantiated with SWI Prolog (representing a logic programming KR language), and in the second it is instantiated with the ontological web language OWL with SWRL rules (a description logics language), with Pellet [31] as the reasoning engine. After that we assess the KRI usability for these two cases, and based on this draw conclusions regarding the interface's effectiveness and limitations.

The remainder of this paper is organized as follows. Section 2 discusses related work on the usage of knowledge representation technologies into agent frameworks with a focus on the agent programming literature. In Sect. 3 we introduce a number of design principles and present a structural analysis of agents and features of KR technologies that guide the design of the proposed interface.

Section 4 presents the design of the KR interface itself and motivates the choices that we have made. In Sect. 5 we discuss two instantiations of the interface (Prolog and OWL). Section 5.3 briefly discusses a preliminary analysis of the interface that was implemented for Prolog, and OWL with rules. Finally, we conclude the paper with future work in Sect. 6.

2 Related Work

In this section we discuss related work with respect to the choice and possible use of KR languages in agent frameworks. It is useful to note here that some agent frameworks such as JACK [33] and Jadex [28] have taken a more pragmatic road, and use object oriented technology in combination with, e.g., XML, to implement the beliefs and goals of an agent, rather than using a knowledge technology in the sense that we use it here (cf. Davis [9]). The focus of our paper is more on generic *logic-based* agent frameworks that use an existing technology for representing an agent's environment.

Most work on logic-based agent programming frameworks has built on top of logic programming or some kind of variant thereof, e.g. 2APL [7], GOAL [15], Jason [5]. Alternatively, several works have described approaches towards the integration of semantic web technologies (such as OWL) into agent-based frameworks. For example, for Jason there exist the JASDL extension [19], which allows for integration with OWL, and as such lets agents incorporate OWL knowledge into their belief base. The Java-based agent framework, JIAC [16], also uses OWL for representing agent knowledge. While comparable in the sense that these systems allows for the use of OWL in the agent framework, the KR interface that we propose here is aimed to provide a practical solution to the more general problem, and to allow a range of KRs to be used in an agent framework.

The work in [22] defines a version of the BDI agent-oriented programming language AgentSpeak based on description logic, rather than one based on predicate logic (e.g. Prolog). The work reported in [12] proposes the use of a semantic web language as a unifying framework for representing and reasoning about agents, their environment, and the organizations they take part in. The work is presented as a first step towards the use of ontologies in the multi-agent framework JaCaMo, but does not discuss the particulars to achieve this.

Probabilistic approaches have also been considered as KRs in conjunction with multi-agent systems. E.g. [32] propose an extension of the 3APL language based on a probabilistic logic programming framework, while [30] discuss the use of Bayesian networks for representing knowledge in agent programs.

Access to external data sources by agents in the IMPACT agent framework [11] is achieved through an abstraction layer, dubbed *body of software code*, that specifies a set of all data-types and functions the underlying data source provides.

DyKnow [13] is a stream-based approach to knowledge processing middleware, supporting knowledge sharing and processing within a single platform. It focuses more on the dynamics of knowledge, and such is orthogonal to our work.

The work described in [8] investigated the issue of integrating multiple KR technologies into a single agent. The paper proposes techniques for combining knowledge represented in different knowledge representation languages. This is orthogonal to our work as our aim is to facilitate the easy use of an arbitrary *single* KR within a cognitive agent framework.

The usefulness of facilitating the use of a particular KR in other frameworks has been recognized in the literature, and has driven several efforts in defining an Application Programming Interface (API) for several technologies. [3,17] for instance, have proposed an API for description logics and OWL respectively, and [6] proposes an API for a Fuzzy Logic inference engine. These APIs are facilitating all aspects of a specific KR. In contrast, in this paper we aim at a generic KRI to connect arbitrary agent frameworks with arbitrary KRs that comply to our minimal assumptions.

Although most work has focused on the integration of logic programming and semantic web technologies and Bayesian networks, we are not aware of any work that has investigated the use of these technologies in agent frameworks in a generic manner.

3 Dimensions of the KRI Design

Our aim is to design a standardized, extensible and easy to use interface that allows for a flexible choice of KR languages in agent frameworks. To this end, we first present our **design approach**. In Sect. 4 we propose an interface specification as a Java-based API. Three design dimensions are taken into account to cover all aspects that can have influence on the design of such an interface. The first dimension concerns the *design principles*, which we discuss in Sect. 3.1. The second dimension concerns the concept of a *cognitive agent* and related assumptions that we make about agent frameworks. In Sect. 3.2 we present a structural and generic analysis of the features and components that are typically required by agent frameworks. The third dimension concerns the *features* that are made available by existing KR technologies that can be supported by the proposed interface. In Sect. 3.3 we analyze and identify these features. Taken together, these three dimensions define the design space of the proposed interface.

3.1 Design Principles

For creating a generic KR interface for agent frameworks, reuse is a key concern. We want the interface to serve all agent frameworks that could benefit from an easy choice of KRs. To this end, we present and briefly discuss various *reuse design principles* that we have taken into account in the design of the interface.

One of the most important reuse principles in the design of a well-defined interface concerns **abstraction**. Abstraction plays a central role in software reuse, and is essential for the reuse of software artifacts [20]. By means of abstraction, important aspects are put in focus while unimportant details are ignored [1,20]. Each KR technology introduces a specific language, and a key issue for our interface specification is how to abstract from differences in the grammar between KR languages. We want to be largely agnostic about the particular type of agent framework that a knowledge representation is used in. We will only assume, for example, that an agent decides what to do next based on a state representation expressed in some KR language, and will make no stronger assumptions about the particular structure of the mental state of an agent (see for a more detailed discussion Sect. 3.2). Similarly, we want to be largely agnostic about the particular type of KR languages. We assume, for example, that a KR language provides variables, but will not assume that such a language provides rules (which would exclude, e.g., SWRL and PDDL without axioms; see for a more detailed discussion Sect. 3.3). The interface that we propose here provides an abstraction in the sense that it is a *high-level, succinct, natural, and useful specification* that facilitates easy use of KRs in agent frameworks.

Two closely related design principles that are very important when designing for reuse are the principles of **generality** and **genericity** [1]. Generality is achieved by the abstraction of commonalities and ignoring the (detailed) differences that relate to how, when, or where things are done by a technology. Generality is important when looking at different KR technologies, as our aim is to be as general as possible and support any KR class that fits our assumptions. An obvious example is to abstract from the particulars of how a reasoning engine made available by a technology answers a query; an interface should only assume that some engine is made available. Genericity refers to the abstraction of specific parameters of a technology and the introduction of generic parameters that represent generic types. The use of generic parameters is an aid to reusability, because it allows to define generic functionality instead of functionality that is tight to technology specific features.

The principle of **modularity** refers to considerations of size and number of a reusable software components. The general principle dictates to split large software components into smaller subcomponents; the basic idea being that adequate modular design increases reusability. In order to obtain a loosely coupled system, we design a modular interface whose components are determined by the functional requirements it has to fulfill.

3.2   Cognitive Agent Frameworks: Functional Requirements

In this section we examine which features are required for using a KR within an agent programming framework. Importantly, an interface only provides an effective specification if it includes all of the information that is needed to realize its purpose. In other words, the KRI needs to provide support for all of the functions that an agent is supposed to be able to implement. To identify these *functional requirements*, we discuss and make explicit the notion of a cognitive agent that has been used for the interface specification.

Because we do not want to commit to any particular agent concept, we start from the very abstract concept of an agent as an entity that *perceives* and *acts* in its environment of [29]. Starting from this notion of agent, we assume that an agent *maintains a state* in order to represent its environment by means of

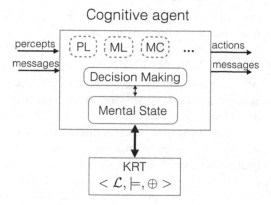

Fig. 1. A cognitive agent architecture, consisting of a mental state and decision making module. Optional components are automated planning (PL), machine learning (ML) model checking (MC), and other modules. Mental states are realized with a KR, accessed through an interface.

a knowledge representation language. As is usual in most agent literature on cognitive agents, we call this agent state a *mental state*, even though we do not make any additional assumptions on the structure of this state. Mental states in agent frameworks differ significantly, and we do not want to commit to any particular framework. A state of a Jason agent, for example, consists of events, beliefs, and plans [4], whereas a state of a GOAL agent consists of knowledge, beliefs, and declarative goals [15].

A cognitive agent (cf. Fig. 1) maintains a mental state in order to be able to evaluate whether certain conditions hold, by *querying* its state. Querying is one of the most important uses of a KR technology, as it provides an essential capability required for effective decision making of an agent, which we identify here as the main functional component of an agent. Another reason for an agent to maintain a mental state is to maintain an accurate and up to date representation of the state of its environment by *updating* its state with information received through percepts or other events. The basic notion of agent of [29] already implies that an agent is connected to an environment. Such an agent needs to be able to align *percepts* it receives from an environment with its mental state. An agent also needs to be able to evaluate when it can perform an action, and represent what the effects of an action are. In other words, an agent needs some kind of *action specification* to be able to interact with its environment. Finally, we also assume that an agent can be part of a multi-agent system, and is able to *exchange messages* with other agents. Figure 1, which represents the basic agent architecture that is used in the design of the interface, illustrates this.

Summarizing, we identify the following list of minimum capabilities that are required for creating a functional cognitive agent in a multi-agent framework:

1. *represent* the contents of a *mental state*
2. *store* the contents of a mental state
3. *query* the contents of a mental state in order to evaluate conditions by means of some form of reasoning

4. *update* the contents of a mental state to reflect changes in an environment
5. *process percepts* received from an environment
6. *process actions* by evaluating *preconditions* and reflecting *postconditions*
7. *process messages* exchanged between agents

Next, we discuss the functional requirements that these items introduce towards the KR language and technology, and its consequences regarding the design of a generic interface.

Item 1 above does not introduce any requirements as representing is the main purpose of a knowledge representation language. We do not assume, for example, that an agent's state must be consistent in a specific sense. **Item 2** requires that a KR provides support for the (temporary) storage of the contents of an agent's state. This item does not require such a store to be persistent. **Item 3** requires support from a KR technology to evaluate queries on the mental state of an agent. Without any additional assumptions on the structure of a mental state, this item does not introduce new requirements, as querying is a common feature provided by the KR. **Item 4** requires support from a KR technology to update, i.e., to add and remove, contents of a mental state. This is a basic requirement, that only requires that a KR makes available the capabilities of adding and removing content from a store. **Item 5** requires support in principle for representing any information that an agent receives from its environment, and updating the representation of the environment that the agent maintains, these functionalities being already mentioned in Item 1 and 4. **Item 6** requires that the knowledge representation language can also be used to represent the actions that the agent can perform. We assume an action can be expressed as a list of preconditions and postconditions. It is essential to be able to evaluate whether an action can be performed, processing preconditions being fulfilled by the querying functionality of Item 3. The ability to process the effects of an action, i.e. its postconditions, is fulfilled by item 4 that requires support for updating a mental state. **Item 7** requires support for representing and processing the content of a message that agents exchange. We assume here that communication between agents does not introduce any additional requirements besides those already introduced by previous items 1–4.

Apart from very generic features and components of cognitive agents such as mental state, we also take into account that agent frameworks might support additional optional components that are only available in some frameworks, but not all. The components drawn with dotted lines in Fig. 1 represent these components. For example, an agent framework might support automated planning (PL), model checking (MC), and even learning mechanisms, such as, for example, reinforcement learning (RL). These components do not exhaust the possible optional components as indicated by the three dots. It is likely that such optional components introduce additional demands on the interface, since they provide support to an agent framework through the interface.

3.3 Features of Knowledge Representation Technologies

Figure 1 includes an abstract definition of a knowledge representation technology as a tuple $\langle \mathcal{L}, \models, \oplus \rangle$, where $\mathcal{L}$ is a language, $\models$ is an inference relation, and $\oplus$ is an update operator (definition taken from [8] and based on [9]). The inference relation evaluates a subset $L_q \subseteq L$ of expressions of the language called *queries* on a store or set of language elements. We consider our interface to be applicable to the classes of KR that comply to this definition.

This notion of a KR technology covers most, but not all existing technologies, including, for example, logic programming (Prolog), database languages (e.g., SQL, Datalog), semantic web languages (e.g., OWL, SWRL), description logic programming (DLP), planning domain definition language (PDDL), and fuzzy logic. Answer set programming (ASP) provides a computational model that we do not support, even though the pure reasoning support of ASP could be integrated using the proposed interface. Using this abstract definition as a starting point, we identify more concrete features and functions that are supported by KR technologies that can be included in an interface specification.

Having described KR technologies in a general sense above, we now define those modules that have an impact on the design of a generic KR interface, either on its structure or its provided functionality.

Language. Although expressivity is a very important aspect of any knowledge representation language, we do not consider it here, as it does not appear to be useful to control expressivity by means of a KR interface. It is essential for a KR to provide a *parser*, necessary to be able to operate with the textual representation of the language, and perform syntax checking. Syntax highlighting is an extra feature that the parser can provide.

Support for *data types* may widely differ between KRs, but it is important for the engineering of practical agent frameworks. Typically, basic data types such as (big) integers, floats, booleans, strings, and lists are distinguished from more complex data structures such as stacks in programming languages.

Storage. The main purpose of a storage is to store knowledge. As a basic feature of any KRT is a knowledge base, *creating a store* is an important requirement towards a generic abstraction. In addition, *modifying a store* poses the requirement to be able to insert into and delete from a knowledge store.

Even though we did not identify a functional requirement for stores to be *persistent* in Sect. 3.2, still, a knowledge technology may provide support for persistence, and a KR interface may make this capability available to an agent. An example for such a knowledge technology is persistent triple stores for ontologies. This feature should be included in order to create a knowledge base that needs to be preserved for a later use.

Integrating knowledge from other sources can be realized in many forms, such as accessing existing (legacy) databases, or accessing information on the web. One example is the linked open data repositories of the Semantic Web. This feature, however favorable, cannot be considered as a general requirement.

Reasoning. *Querying* is the basic operation to retrieve information from a knowledge base. We can assume the basic form of querying is to retrieve ground data that matches a query pattern with free variables. Without querying there can be no interaction with a knowledge base, hence it is a main requirements towards a KR interface.

Parallel querying is to be able to ask multiple queries simultaneously. This feature is available for some technologies only (like triplestores), but not for others (such as Prolog), where one needs to first exhaust all solutions of a query at a time, hence it is considered an extra feature, and not a basic requirement.

We assume that a substitution based *parameter instantiation mechanism* is supported, as is usual for logic-based languages for all practical purposes. Note that this does not mean that we make any strong assumptions about the domains of computation. Query results are in the form of bindings between variables and some arbitrary terms. A substitution to represent a variable to term binding therefore is the basic form of expressing a query result.

Other. *Error handling* provides support for errors that might occur during parsing, knowledge base creation, modification, or other language-related operations. Some form of error handling is indispensable from an interface.

A knowledge technology that supports *modularization* facilitates the structuring of knowledge into different modules. This feature may greatly enhance the simultaneous development of knowledge by a team of developers. A modular architecture might greatly influence our design of interface, as mappings between the modules of the knowledge and the interface might be identified.

Three forms of *logical validation* can be supported by a KR: consistency, satisfiability and validity checking. As these validation forms are either provided by the technology or not, we cannot generalize it into a feature requirement.

Summarizing the above, we identified the following list of basic features and extra features:

Basic Features

1. Parsing
2. Data types (including checking)
3. Creating a store
4. Modifying a store
5. Querying
6. Parameter instantiation
7. Error handling

Extra Features

1. Persistent storage
2. Integrate other knowledge sources
3. Parallel querying
4. Modularization
5. Logical validation

4   The KR Interface

Next, we describe the KR Interface (KRI) designed, a Java-based API to address the issues of creating a generic, a specific KR-independent abstraction. The link to our repository, where the interface is located, can be found at [14]. Throughout the description of the interface we show how each design choice was based on the generic features of KRTs, described in Sect. 3.3, and how it fulfills the functionality requirements that an agent programming framework poses in Sect. 3.2.

Based on the principle of modularization, we want to ensure a separation of concerns related to *language*, *storage*, *reasoning*, and *others*. We propose a structured interface design, such that it facilitates these sub-interfaces, as described next in detail.

Language. The language module of the interface contains the abstract grammatical constructs of a KRT. This fulfills the requirement of being able to express all items on the list of Sect. 3.2, since the language concepts need to be able to represent the contents of an agent's mental state, queries and updates, percepts of the environment, and agent messages.

Our generic language proposal, shown as a conceptual hierarchy in Fig. 2, abstracts any language construct into the higher level `Expression` concept, corresponding to a well-formed sentence or formula in the knowledge representation language. An expression can be of type: `Term`, `Update`, `Query` and `DatabaseFormula`. A `Term` can be simple: `Var`, and `Constant` or complex: a `Function`.

From a KR language's point of view, differentiation between the concepts of *querying* and *updating* is dictated by the syntax, and hence can differ per language. From an agent programming's perspective such a distinction is necessary to require that performing a query never results in an update. It would be difficult to understand the behavior of a system that can change the state as a side-effect of performing a query.

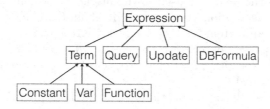

Fig. 2. Language concepts architecture

The `Term` concept represents a language construct of a formula or sentence (ground formula, i.e. without free variables). It can be simple or complex. A variable is a simple term expressed with the concept `Var`. The interface does not enforce variables to be present, however, most languages that support parameter instantiation and querying, need to represent variables. Another simple term is a `Constant`, which is a basic unstructured name that refers to some object or entity, e.g. a number. A `Function` is the representation of a complex term, with a functor and arguments. No restriction on the type or the number of arguments is imposed.

A `Substitution` is a mapping of distinct variables to terms. A substitution binds the term to the variable if it maps the variable to the term. A substitution may be empty. Its functionality includes the usual map operations. It fulfills Item 6 of the language features' list, namely, to have some form of substitution-based parameter mechanism, as we have assumed a set of substitutions to be also the result of a query.

An `Expression` is any grammatically correct string of symbols of a KR language, fulfilling the responsibility of Item 1 of Sect. 3, to be able to represent the contents of an agent's mental state. Every expression has a different signature, a definition of the form *operatorname/arity*, where the operator name is the functor, and the arity is the number of arguments associated with the operator. In case we need to unify two expressions, the most general unifier method returns a substitution that makes two expressions equal. To apply a substitution to an expression means to substitute variables in the expression that are bound by the substitution with the term bound to the variable, or, only rename it in case the substitution binds a variable to another one.

It is important for an agent to be able to understand which expressions it can use to query, put in a database, and to update a database with. A `DatabaseFormula` stands for an expression that can be inserted into a storage facility. Usually, this is a formula with all ground terms, and no operator that needs more processing, e.g.: conditionals. The `Query` concept is used to query the database, and hence it should contain at least one free variable. An `Update` is semantically equivalent with the combination of a delete and an insert operation. To reflect this, it offers two methods to retrieve the list of database formulas to be added and to be deleted from the knowledge base. For example, in Prolog these classes are different, but may overlap: database formulas are facts (positive literals), a query is an arbitrary conjunction of literals, and an update is a conjunction of basic literals, where basic means the predicate used in the literal is not defined by a rule.

Based on the assumption that every KR should provide its own parsing mechanism identified in Item 1 of the identified KR features' list, the interface should provide a parser for parsing the source (files) represented in the KR language. In case a parser initialization error occurs, proper error handling should be defined and provided.

The `Parser` class fulfills the functionality of a KR to provide its own parser, Item 1 of Sect. 3.3. We abstract a parser to receive an input source file, and return language constructs of our KR interface; database formulas, queries, updates, terms, etc. In case an error occurs during parsing, a method to get the errors returns the source object, which can be inspected for error handling purposes.

Basic *data types*, such as numbers (integers, floats), strings, booleans, are provided together with the functionality of returning the data type of a constant, and data type checking, thus fulfilling the requirement mentioned as Item 2 of Sect. 3.3.

Storage. To create a storage, the main class of the interface provides the way to create a database in the specific KR it hides away. Using the `getDatabase(Collection<DatabaseFormula> content)` method, it creates a new `Database` with the provided content, that is a list of database formulas to be inserted in the database before it being returned. Thus it fulfills the requirement of creating a store by Item 3 of Sect. 3.3.

The `Database` class fulfills the second item of the functional requirements listed in Sect. 3.2. It holds the content represented in the KR language, viewed as a set of `DatabaseFormula`-s. It provides the functionality to store new information in the database by inserting a formula in it, deleting a formula from it, fulfilling the update operation, listed as Item 4 of Sect. 3.2, and Item 4 of Sect. 3.3. Upon insertion of a formula or an update, the database should entail the information added. The converse applies to deleting a formula, after removal of the formula, in principle, the database should no longer entail the information removed from the database. Any occurring error during insertion, deletion, or destruction of the database is signaled by throwing a database exception.

Reasoning. In order for an agent to inspect its knowledge base, querying functionality has to be provided by the KR, as we mentioned in our assumptions sections, Item 3, and our KR features section, Item 5. The query(Query query) method fulfills that functionality, and returns as a result a set of Substitutions. In case of an error, a query failed exception is thrown.

Other. The *KRException* and its more specific classes capture the several different types of exceptions, and take the responsibility of error reporting, Item 7 of KR features support list. Separate error types are differentiated for parsing, database operations, failed query errors. In case of parsing, error handling is capable to refer to the source (file) where the error occurred.

5   KR Interface Implementations

In this section we describe the two use cases we studied in depth, and implemented the interface with: Prolog and OWL with SWRL rules. Implementing the KR interface with a new language puts our design choices to the test. We want to investigate how much the interface fits other, different logic-based languages, and provide a first proof of concept for our proposal.

5.1   Prolog Implementation

Prolog was the default logic used for knowledge representation in the GOAL agent framework, as it is a first natural choice for cognitive agent programming, due to its computational powers and the features of logic programming.

Next we describe how we instantiated the interface with SWI-Prolog using the JPL API. The high-level API's class hierarchy consists of the top-level classes: Term, Query, JPLException. The abstract superclass Term consists of subclasses for variables, compounds, atoms as a specialization of compounds, integers and floats. A Query is a wrapper around a term, but it also has a mechanism to hold the retreived results and much more.

A clear match of terminology could be found between the way the KRI captures language constructs and the hierarchy of the JPL API. An Expression is a JPL term representing a Prolog expression, the most general language construct in Prolog. The Var is mapped to a JPL variable, Constants to integers, floats, and strings, and a Function is matched to a Compound term. A JPL term is the representation of both a Term, a DBFormula, and a Query. We chose not to map the JPL's query class to the KRI's Query. The former attaches more functionality of the querying process to the class than what the representation a query formula would necessitate. The solution to use a term as a query conveniently matches the JPL idea. Then, performing the check if a term is valid to be inserted in a database, or can be used as a query is delegated to the parser for efficiency reasons (to avoid such checks at runtime).

An Update is a term that is assumed to be a conjunction that can be split into a list of conjuncts. We needed to separate the literals to be added or deleted, so we distinguished the positive from the negative literals (with a preceding not operator) to denote the two lists. A Substitution is a mapping of distinct variables to terms. We do not use JPL variables as keys, because it has no implementation for hash code, and therefore putting these in a map will fail. Thus, we were forced to using strings.

The main issue encountered during the implementation was the question of a parser. Existing Prolog implementations do not completely conform to the ISO/IEC 13211-1 International Standard. We created our own lexer and parser, following the standard in most cases. Our reasons for deviating have been pragmatically motivated: we wanted to keep our grammar simple, and we did not want it to support certain options that quickly lead to unreadable code, such as using graphic tokens as predicate names, or redefine operators' precedence.

The module feature of Prolog has been used to implement different types of stores. As a conclusion of this choice, modules cannot be made available to an agent programmer any more, as it would potentially clash with the modules that are introduced automatically by the interface.

SWI-Prolog has one fast database to hold all formulas. To be able to differentiate different Databases for various mental state construction, we need to specify for each clause which database it belongs to. Our solution was to prefix each database formula with the database name.

Destroying a database removes all predicates and clauses from the SWI-Prolog database, but this is not fully implementable in SWI-Prolog. The JPL interface does not support removing the dynamic declarations. The suggested practice is to reset a database to free up some memory, but after resetting not to re-use this database, but to make a new one.

SWI-Prolog needs access to various libraries at runtime and to load these dynamically. If many agents try to do this at the same time, this creates access errors. A possible solution is to load these libraries upfront when we need them, that implies a check whether we need a library of course. The benefit is that we only need to synchronize the creation of databases and not all query calls. As a pragmatic choice, we solved this issue by adding synchronized querying.

5.2   Ontological Language Implementation

We implemented the proposed KR interface using the OWL ontological language with DL-safe SWRL rules, such an agent being considered a novelty in the field of agent programming. The web ontology language standard (OWL) is a W3C standard recommendation [21] for formalizing an ontology. It is based on the underlying logic called: Description Logic (DL) [2], which has become one of the main knowledge representation formalism. The Semantic Web Rule Language (SWRL) [18] is an OWL-based rule language, and is an extension to the existing ontology language OWL, to provide more expressivity through rules. In order to preserve decidability, SWRL rules are restricted to so called DL-safe rules [23], which requires each variable in a rule to occur in a data atom in the rule body. A data atom is one that refers to existing named individuals in the ontological knowledge base.

In order to instantiate the interface, two APIs are available for the ontological language: the OWL API [17], that contains representation for SWRL rules as well, or the SWRL API [25] of Protégé-OWL, which is built on top of the OWL API, but extends it further with a query language and provides a parser.

In the following we describe the identified matching between the KRI constructs and the ontological rule language. The higher level concept **Expression** was mapped to **SWRLRule**, that consists of a head and a body. The **Function** concept was mapped to **SWRLAtom**, since atoms are the building blocks of rules, a **Constant** to a **SWRLArgument**, representing a data object or an individual object. A variable is corresponding to **SWRLVariable**.

In order to create a shared, persistent storage, and to access the Semantic Web, a **Database** is mapped to an RDF repository (or triple store). The Resource Description Framework (RDF) is a serialized representation of an ontology, in triple format [26]. The most performant reasoners are available for triple store technologies, and can be queried using the query language SPARQL [27], the adopted standard by the community.

The choice of query language for OWL and SWRL was not a straightforward decision. Query languages for Semantic Web ontologies are categorized into two: RDF-based and DL-based. The default and mostly used querying mechanism is the RDF-based SPARQL, but since it operates on the RDF serialization of OWL, it has no semantic understanding of the language constructs that those serializations represent. On the other hand, the Semantic Query-enhanced Web Rule Language (SQWRL) [24] is a DL-based query language designed on top of the SWRL rule language, with a working implementation provided by the Protégé-OWL API, which would be a very convenient choice in our case.

Faced with the decision between using two different languages for representing knowledge and querying on one hand, or not benefiting from the available advanced triplestore technologies on the other hand, we decided to try to keep the advantages of both. We created a transformation from SWRL rules into SPARQL queries, by treating them as query bodies, with all free variables being considered as part of the query pattern. Having established a querying mechanism, an **Update** then consists of an addition and a deletion operation, provided by the SPARQL Update syntax's insert and delete.

5.3   Discussion of the KRI Implementation

In this section we reflect on the outcomes of our work: the KRI, and how well it performed when put to the test by implementing it with two different KRTs. We reflect on the implementation process, and complement our discussion with extra features that the KRI makes available for the agents. Revisiting the creation of mental states for agents, GOAL poses a difficult requirement: it should be possible to query the combination of a knowledge and belief base (and knowledge and goal base), i.e., query the union of two bases. It was possible to do this with the proposed KRI, since most KRTs provide either some mechanism to import knowledge from one base into another (e.g., modules in SWI-Prolog) or allow for multi-base querying (federated SPARQL queries for OWL).

An implementation of a specific KR with the interface was highly dependent on the available Java API for the technology. In case several APIs for a language were available, we assessed which one fits best our needs, and can provide most features. Then, the concept hierarchy had to be matched to the interface's corresponding elements, and the functionality correspondence validated. In general the proposed KRI turns out to be generic enough to be implemented for different KR technologies. Following the design principles described in Sect. 3.1 and incorporating features identified in Sect. 3.3, the KRI satisfies all requirements deemed fundamental to represent mental states for cognitive agents (Sect. 3.2); moreover, different types of states (cf. Jason vs GOAL, Sect. 3.2) can be implemented.

The KRI can make use of the extra features that come along with the two languages, e.g., it allows for ontological language with rules to use triple store technologies existing on the web, accessing the Semantic Web thus becoming implicitly available to agents. Another example is parallel querying, that again, agents are at liberty to perform using OWL and SWRL, which comes from exploiting the benefit of a triple store for an agent's mental database. A third benefit of OWL agents that the interface makes possible, is the creation of a shared database, so multiple agents can operate on the same set of knowledge, incrementing data reuse and sharing. On the other hand, when chosing Prolog as the KR, the agent is powerful in computational tasks, and can work easily with lists. This support that would not have been available when chosing OWL, since lists are not by default present in OWL, and are not supported by reasoners that can handle rules. The major benefits of the two languages could be exploited through the instantiation of the interface, which shows that our proposal does not limit the use of a KR for agents.

6   Conclusions and Future Work

In conclusion, this paper introduced a generic KRI that is reusable across a range of agent frameworks that can benefit from the use of different KR languages. Our contribution is a methodological analysis of the features and requirements between knowledge representation technologies and cognitive agent programming frameworks. We proposed and implemented a generic interface to create an abstraction layer and a modular setup to how agents can use a KR. The need for such a KR interface and the apparent lack of such a construct in related work has motivated the design of the interface, governed by the following three aspects (as described in Sect. 3): (1) a number of design principles serving as guidelines, (2) the concept of cognitive agents and related assumptions that we make about agent frameworks, and (3) the identification of features provided by various KRs that are considered as requirements for a KRI. We put this interface to the test with two knowledge representations, namely Prolog and OWL with SWRL rules, in the agent programming framework GOAL. Based on these two cases we conclude that the KRI is generic enough to support a variety of KR languages, and could be easily applied in the GOAL agent framework.

In the future we will focus on the improvement points identified during the process, and move to a next step of trying different knowledge representation technologies and other agent programming frameworks, to discover the full extent of applicability of, and any modifications needed to our proposed interface.

References

1. Anguswamy, R., Frakes, W.B.: Reuse design principles (2013)
2. Baader, F.: The Description Logic Handbook: Theory, Implementation, and Applications. Cambridge University Press (2003)
3. Bechhofer, S., Horrocks, I., Patel-Schneider, P.F., Tessaris, S.: A proposal for a description logic interface. In: Proceedings of Description Logics, pp. 33–36 (1999)
4. Bordini, R.H., Hübner, J.F.: Jason-A Java-based interpreter for an extended version of AgentSpeak (2007)
5. Bordini, R.H., Hübner, J.F., Wooldridge, M.: Programming multi-agent systems in AgentSpeak using Jason, vol. 8. Wiley (2007)
6. Cingolani, P., Alcala-Fdez, J.: jfuzzylogic: a robust and flexible fuzzy-logic inference system language implementation. In: 2012 IEEE International Conference on Fuzzy Systems (FUZZ-IEEE), pp. 1–8, June 2012
7. Dastani, M.: 2APL: a practical agent programming language. Auton. Agent. Multi-Agent Syst. **16**(3), 214–248 (2008)
8. Dastani, M., Hindriks, K.V., Novák, P., Tinnemeier, N.A.M.: Combining multiple knowledge representation technologies into agent programming languages. In: Baldoni, M., Son, T.C., van Riemsdijk, M.B., Winikoff, M. (eds.) DALT 2008. LNCS (LNAI), vol. 5397, pp. 60–74. Springer, Heidelberg (2009)
9. Davis, R., Shrobe, H., Szolovits, P.: What is a knowledge representation? AI Mag. **14**(1), 17 (1993)
10. Dix, J., Hindriks, K.V., Logan, B., Wobcke, W.: Engineering multi-agent systems (dagstuhl seminar 12342) (2012)
11. Dix, J., Zhang, Y.: IMPACT: A multi-agent framework with declarative semantics. In: Multi-Agent Programming, pp. 69–94 (2005)
12. Freitas, A., Schmidt, D., Panisson, A., Meneguzzi, F., Vieira, R., Bordini, R.H.: Integrating multi-agent systems in JaCaMo using a semantic representations. In: Workshop on Collaborative Agents, CARE for Intelligent Mobile Services (2014)
13. Heintz, F.: Dyknow: A stream-based knowledge processing middleware framework (2009)
14. Hindriks, K.V.: The GOAL Agent Programming Language hub. https://github.com/goalhub/krTools/tree/master/krInterface
15. Hindriks, K.V.: Programming rational agents in GOAL. In: El Fallah Seghrouchni, A., Dix, J., Dastani, M., Bordini, R.H. (eds.) Multi-Agent Programming: Languages, Tools and Applications, pp. 119–157. Springer (2009)
16. Hirsch, B., Konnerth, T., Heßler, A.: Merging agents and services the JIAC agent platform. In: Multi-Agent Programming: pp. 159–185. Springer (2009)

17. Horridge, M., Bechhofer, S.: The OWL Api: A Java Api for OWL ontologies. Semant. Web **2**(1), 11–21 (2011)
18. Horrocks, I., Patel-Schneider, P.F., Boley, H., Tabet, S., Grosof, B., Dean, M., et al.: SWRL: A semantic web rule language combining OWL and RuleML. W3C Member Submission **21**, 79 (2004)
19. Klapiscak, T., Bordini, R.H.: JASDL: a practical programming approach combining agent and semantic web technologies. In: Baldoni, M., Son, T.C., van Riemsdijk, M.B., Winikoff, M. (eds.) DALT 2008. LNCS (LNAI), vol. 5397, pp. 91–110. Springer, Heidelberg (2009)
20. Krueger, C.W.: Software reuse. ACM Comput. Surv. **24**(2), 131–183 (1992)
21. McGuinness, D.L., Van Harmelen, F., et al.: OWL web ontology language overview. W3C Recommendation **10**(10), 2004 (2004)
22. Moreira, A.F., Vieira, R., Bordini, R.H., Hübner, J.F.: Agent-oriented programming with underlying ontological reasoning. In: Baldoni, M., Endriss, U., Omicini, A., Torroni, P. (eds.) DALT 2005. LNCS (LNAI), vol. 3904, pp. 155–170. Springer, Heidelberg (2006)
23. Motik, B., Sattler, U., Studer, R.: Query answering for OWL-DL with rules. Web Semant.: Sci., Serv. Agents World Wide Web **3**(1), 41–60 (2005)
24. O'Connor, M.J., Das, A.K.: SQWRL: a query language for OWL. In: OWLED, vol. 529 (2009)
25. O'Connor, M.J., Shankar, R.D., Musen, M.A., Das, A.K., Nyulas, C.: The SWR-LAPI: a development environment for working with SWRL rules. In: OWLED (2008)
26. Pan, J.Z.: Resource description framework. In: Handbook on Ontologies, pp. 71–90. Springer (2009)
27. Pérez, J., Arenas, M., Gutierrez, C.: Semantics and Complexity of SPARQL. ACM Trans. Database Syst **34**(3), 16:1–16:45 (2009)
28. Pokahr, A., Braubach, L., Lamersdorf, W.: Jadex: A BDI reasoning engine. In: Multi-agent programming, pp. 149–174. Springer (2005)
29. Russell, S., Jordan, H., O'Hare, G.M.P., Collier, R.W.: Agent factory: a framework for prototyping logic-based AOP languages. In: Klügl, F., Ossowski, S. (eds.) MATES 2011. LNCS, vol. 6973, pp. 125–136. Springer, Heidelberg (2011)
30. Silva, D.G., Gluz, J.C.: AgentSpeak (PL): A new programming language for BDI agents with integrated bayesian network model. In: 2011 International Conference on Information Science and Applications (ICISA), pp. 1–7. IEEE (2011)
31. Sirin, E., Parsia, B., Grau, B.C., Kalyanpur, A., Katz, Y.: Pellet: A practical OWL-DL reasoner. Web Semant.: Sci., Serv. Agents World Wide Web **5**(2), 51–53 (2007)
32. Wang, J., Ju, S.E., Liu, C.N.: Agent-oriented probabilistic logic programming. J. Comput. Sci. Technol. **21**(3), 412–417 (2006)
33. Winikoff, M.: JACK intelligent agents: An industrial strength platform. In: Multi-Agent Programming, pp. 175–193. Springer (2005)

A Probabilistic BPMN Normal Form to Model and Advise Human Activities

Hector G. Ceballos[1]([✉]), Victor Flores-Solorio[1], and Juan Pablo Garcia[2]

[1] Tecnologico de Monterrey, Campus Monterrey, Monterrey, Mexico
ceballos@itesm.mx, vmfsolorio@gmail.com
[2] Universidad Autonoma de Baja California, Mexicali, Mexico
pablo.garcia@uabc.edu.mx

Abstract. Agent-based technologies, originally proposed with the aim of assisting human activities, have been recently adopted in industry for automating business processes. Business Process Model and Notation (BPMN) is a standard notation for modeling business processes, that provides a rich graphical representation that can be used for common understanding of processes but also for automation purposes. We propose a normal form of Business Process Diagrams based on Activity Theory that can be transformed to a Causal Bayesian Network, which in turn can be used to model the behavior of activity participants and assess human decision through user agents. We illustrate our approach on an Elderly health care scenario obtained from an actual contextual study.

Keywords: BPMN · Agent-based systems engineering · Bayesian networks · Activity theory

1 Introduction

BPMN is a standard notation for modeling business processes that provides a rich graphical representation that can be used for common understanding of processes [13]. Furthermore, BPMN has been used for process automation with support of agent technologies [10].

BPMN uses gateways for representing decisions, which are usually labeled with textual descriptions indicating the criterion followed. These decisions are based on information that is available at the moment of decision making and may refer to information of the process in course or to historical information (*data-based decisions*).

But when the BPMN workflow describes a human activity in terms of user tasks this decision criterion might be unknown or inaccessible to the modeler, e.g. the buying decision of a customer. For dealing with the uncertainty introduced by human intervention, approaches like [6] have proposed annotating edges with the probability of each alternative. Nevertheless, this approach does not permit to determine if the cause of such variability comes from some part of the process under the control of some participant, i.e. capture causal relationships between

© Springer International Publishing Switzerland 2015
M. Baldoni et al. (Eds.): EMAS 2015, LNAI 9318, pp. 51–69, 2015.
DOI: 10.1007/978-3-319-26184-3_4

non-consecutive nodes. And despite BPMN has been recently used for agent-based software engineering, decision making under uncertainty has not been addressed in current approaches [3,7,10,12].

For these reasons, we propose a normal form of BPMN Process Diagrams for modeling human activities suitable for generating a probabilistic representation of activity's dynamic suitable for discovering causal relationships. Possible scenarios specified in the BPMN workflow can be used for predicting the behavior of human participants based on observable events. The BPMN normal form is inspired by Activity Theory [4], providing goal-oriented BPMN Process Diagrams capable of representing collective human activities.

This paper is organized as follows. In Sect. 2, we present other applications of BPMN for agent-based software engineering and introduce probabilistic formalisms traditionally used for agent decision making. In Sect. 3 we discuss the pertinence of using BPMN for modeling human activities and propose a BPMN normal form suitable for its transformation to a Bayesian Network. We provide an automatic transformation procedure that produces a probabilistic representation of activity's dynamics that can be used for agent decision making based on previous activity developments. In Sect. 4, we present other probabilistic approaches to BPMN and compare our selection of BPMN elements with other agent engineering approaches. Finally, in Sect. 5, we present our conclusions and future work.

2   Background

We revise current applications of BPMN for agent-based system engineering, and review probabilistic graphic models used for decision making.

2.1   Business Process Diagrams for Agent Engineering

Business Process Model and Notation (BPMN) is a standard notation used by organizations for understanding internal business procedures in a graphical notation. Due to its expressivity and its growing adoption by industry, it has been also used as a tool for modeling MultiAgent Systems [3,7,10,12].

Endert et al. [3] proposed a mapping of Business Process Diagram (BPD) elements to agent concepts. In particular they considered a BPMN fragment constituted by: event nodes (start, intermediate and end), activity nodes, subprocess nodes, split and merge gateways (XOR, OR, AND), and pools. They map each pool to an agent and the process itself constitutes a plan; properties of start (and end) events constitute inputs (respectively outputs) for the plan. Independent subprocesses are mapped to goals and embedded subprocesses are mapped to plans. Activity nodes are represented by plan operations, whereas control flows are mapped to sequences, if-else blocks and loops. Data flow, i.e. arguments passed to messages and operations, is captured in node attributes and it is used for modeling agent beliefs.

Hinge and colleagues developed a tool for annotating BPMN in order to provide a semantic description of events and actions [7]. Actions are described by their direct effects: the observable conditions that hold immediately after action execution. These annotations are used for calculating the current development of a process, this is, determining which events and actions have occurred by observing the accumulation of effects on a knowledge base. The knowledge base is considered non-monotonic as long as this approach counts with a procedure for detecting the removal of facts.

Muehlen and Indulska evaluated the combination of modeling languages for business processes and business rules [12]. Their overlap analysis look for the minimization of redundancy on constructors and the maximization of modeling expressivity. Modeling constructors were grouped in four categories: sort of things, states, events and systems. They conclude that the highest representation power is given by the combination of BPMN for representing the business process and SWRL [8] for representing business rules. Nevertheless, their analysis reveals that this combination, despite it is the most complete, lacks of a representation of states.

Jander and colleagues proposed Goal-oriented Process Modeling Notation (GPMN), a language for developing goal-oriented workflows [9]. The process is initially modeled by decomposing a main goal into subgoals, and then each subgoal is linked to a BPMN diagram that represents the plan to achieve that goal. This graphical language includes *activation plans* which decide subgoal parallelization or serialization, replicating the functionality of gateways in the goal hierarchy tree. A goal can be connected to multiple plans, enabling means-end reasoning.

Finally, Kuster and colleagues provide a full methodology for process oriented agent engineering that complements BPMN process diagrams with: declaration of data types (ontology engineering), a model for agent organization and distribution, low-level algorithms for activity nodes (service engineering), and use cases diagrams that link roles and process diagrams [10]. This framework implements the mapping of BPMN to agents described in [3] for agent engineering.

These approaches show how BPMN workflows can be used for designing agent specifications from the description of their interactions in a process. Nevertheless they assume that all the information needed by agent for making a decision is available, which in turn produces reactive agent specifications but is not sufficient for coping with uncertainty.

2.2 Decision Making Based on Bayesian Networks

Bayesian Networks (BNs) have been used for quite a while for representing decision making under uncertainty and learning through observation/experience. BNs are suitable for identifying causal dependencies between random variables representing events and actions occurred at different time steps. Despite Markovian Decision Processes (MDPs) have gained popularity for their capacity for providing efficient probabilistic inference in long term processes, their representation lacks of memory, i.e. it only captures conditional dependencies between contiguous time steps. Nevertheless, MDPs are suitable for capturing causal dependencies in cyclic sequences of events where the final outcome is the result of numerous attempts or iterations.

Bayesian Networks. A *Bayesian Network* is a probabilistic graphical model that represents a set of events denoted by random variables, and their conditional dependencies via a directed acyclic graph (DAG), denoted:

$$M = \langle V, G_V, P(v_i|pa_i) \rangle$$

where V is a set of random variables, G_V is the graph consisting of variables in V and directed arcs between them, and $P(v_i|pa_i)$ is a conditional probabilistic distribution where the probability of v_i depends on the value of its parents (pa_i) in G_V.

A random variable V_i is a numerical description of the outcome of an experiment, and can be either discrete or continuous. The set of possible values a discrete random variable may hold, or *domain* $Dom(V_i) = \{v_{i1}, ..., v_{in}\}$, represents the possible outcomes of a yet-to-be-performed experiment, or the potential values of a quantity whose already-existing value is uncertain.

The *realization* of a random variable V_i to the value $v_{ij} \in Dom(V_i)$ is represented as $V_i = v_{ij}$, or v_i if the realization value is not relevant in a given context.

Random variables satisfy the probability theory requisite which dictates that in an experiment, a random variable can be realized to a single value of its domain. This means that all events represented by a random variable are disjoint.

G_V is an independence map (I-Map), i.e. a minimal graph where the presence of an arc from V_i to V_j indicates conditional dependence whereas its absence indicates conditional independence. An I-Map is called minimal because indirect dependencies are not included.

Bayesian Networks can be modeled from two distinct perspectives: evidential or causal. If arrows go from effects to causes the perspective is *evidential*, e.g. determining the disease based on the patient symptoms. A network is modeled from a *causal* perspective if arcs go from causes to effects. For instance, in *Dynamic Bayesian Networks* a different set of random variables represents the state of the system at time $t, t+1, ... , t+n$; arcs can go from a variable in t to another in $t + i$, but the opposite is not allowed.

Bayesian networks are used to find out updated knowledge of the state of a subset of variables $\bar{v}_1$ when another variables $\bar{v}_2$ (evidence) are observed, denoted $P(\bar{v}_1|\bar{v}_2)$. This process of computing the posterior distribution of variables given certain evidence is called *probabilistic inference*.

Influence Diagrams. An *Influence Diagram* is a generalization of a Bayesian Network devised for modeling and solving decision problems using probabilistic inference. Nodes may represent decisions (rectangles), uncertain conditions (ovals) or the utility obtained in a given scenario (diamond).

Arcs ending in decision nodes denote the information taken into account for making the decision. Arcs between uncertain nodes propagate uncertainty or information like in Bayesian Networks.

Decision nodes and their incoming arcs determine the *alternatives*. Uncertainty nodes and their incoming arcs model the *information*. Value nodes and their incoming arcs quantify the *preference* on the outcome. An alternative is chosen based on the maximum expected utility in the given scenario, calculated by the a posteriori probability of all nodes (including unknown values).

Causal Bayesian Networks. Judea Pearl introduced the notion of Causality on Bayesian Networks under the concept of *intervention*, where the value of a variable could be subject to alteration through a mechanism F or let its value being freely set [15]. Pearl and Robins proposed that nodes in a Bayesian network can be classified into purely observable variables, or *Covariates* (Z), and controllable variables (X) which are subject to intervention, denoted by $do(x_i)$ [16]. From this distinction they establish a graphical method for identifying the set of covariates $(W_k \subset Z)$ that must be observed for determining the *causal effect* of a sequence of interventions $do(x_1), ..., do(x_k)$ on Y, i.e. $P(y|do(x_1), ..., do(x_k), w_k)$. This sequence of interventions constitutes a plan, which probability of success can be evaluated a priori and be revised once that the network is updated with information.

3 Probabilistic Decision Making on Business Process Diagrams

An Activity of Daily Living (ADL) modeled as a BPMN workflow is used for illustrating the proposed normal form. Then a procedure for transforming this workflow to a Bayesian Network is provided and some examples of probabilistic inference are given to validate the model.

The subset of graphical elements of the BPMN 2.0 specification [13] we use in our example and in our normal form is shown in Fig. 1. BPMN Business Process Diagrams (BPDs) basically describe a process in terms of *events* and *actions* connected through *control flows* that indicate valid sequences in the process development. *Gateways* are special nodes connected through control flows that indicate whether the process develops in parallel (AND), alternatively (XOR) or optionally (OR). The beginning of the process is denoted by an *initial event* node and its conclusion by a set of *end event* nodes.

3.1 An Example of an ADL Modeled in BPMN

We motivate the discussion using as example the medical consultation of an elder person, taken from an actual contextual study based on Activity Theory [5]. In this activity, the *subject* is an older adult who has a medical appointment (the *object*). The *objective* of the activity is having a medical appraisal and its

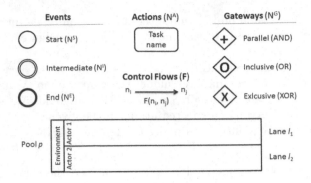

Fig. 1. BPMN graphical notation.

outcome includes getting a prescription, supply medicines and schedule a next appointment. The *community* involved in the activity includes a family member (optionally) and the doctor.

This diagram is used for compensating the lack of a formal representation of the activity's dynamic in Activity Theory (AT) [4]. At some extent, control flows and gateways formalize the set of rules specified in the AT specification.

Figure 2 shows the activity diagram modeled with BPMN. It illustrates two alternative ways the elder may choose for getting to the hospital: going by himself, or being carried out by a family member. It also shows five possible outcomes for the activity: (1) treatment finished, (2) taking new medication, (3) taking medication and follow up, (4) medication not available at the hospital's pharmacy, and (5) missing the appointment (failure outcome).

3.2   A Probabilistic BPMN Normal Form

The proposed normal form has the purpose of illustrating alternative sequences of actions performed by activity participants, mediated by intermediate events that the subject or other participants can observe. XOR gateways are used for representing disjoint alternatives. Activity's development has a triggering condition (initial event) and a set of successful or failure outcomes (end events). The resulting graph must be acyclic for facilitating its translation to a Bayesian Network through a graphical procedure. A BPMN BPD satisfies the probabilistic normal form if it observes the following constraints:

1. A Business Process Diagram **W** is represented by a set of pools (**P**), lanes (**L**), nodes (**N**) and control flows (**F**).

$$\mathbf{W} = \{\mathbf{P}, \mathbf{L}, \mathbf{N}, \mathbf{F}\}$$

2. Nodes (**N**) allowed in the diagram are: start events (N^S), intermediate events (N^I), end events (N^E), atomic actions (N^A) and gateways (N^G).

$$\mathbf{N} = N^S \cup N^I \cup N^E \cup N^A \cup N^G$$

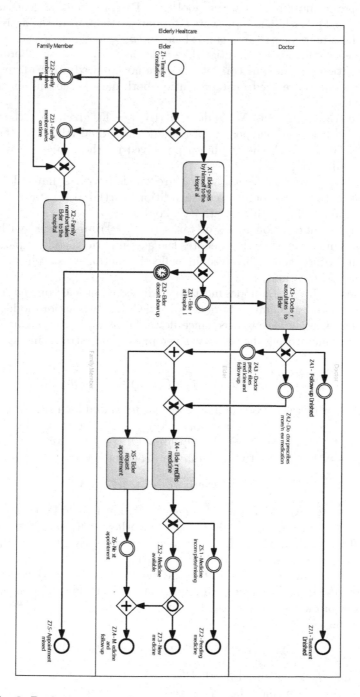

Fig. 2. Business process diagram of the medical consultation activity.

3. The diagram must have a single pool ($p \in \mathbf{P}$) containing at least one lane ($l_i \in \mathbf{L}, i \geq 1$). Each lane represents a human participant in the activity, and nodes must be allocated in a single lane ($in(n, l_i), n \in \mathbf{N}$).
4. All sequence flows are unconditional, denoted as $F(n_i, n_j) \in \mathbf{F}$ where $n_i, n_j \in N$. Conditional or default control flows are not allowed; instead, intermediate event nodes are used for representing both data-based and event-based control flow.
5. A single start event $s \in N^S$ is defined ($|N^S| = 1$), given that the activity is modeled from the perspective of a single individual (the subject), and it must be labeled with the condition perceived by the subject that triggers activity's development.
6. Intermediate event nodes ($i \in N^I$) are labeled with a natural language description that corresponds to the condition (partial world state) that must hold for proceeding with the activity's course.
7. Similarly, atomic action nodes or tasks ($a \in N^A$) are labeled with a verb expressed in active voice that denotes the action performed by a participant, indicating other actors involved in collective actions, as well as required artifacts and locations.
8. Two consecutive action nodes must be mediated by at least one intermediate event node and as many gateways as needed, i.e. two action nodes are not connected directly through sequence flows. Observable intermediate events will permit monitoring the activity development and introducing agent assistance [2].

$$\forall a \in N^A, (F(n, a) \in \mathbf{F} \vee F(a, n) \in \mathbf{F}) \rightarrow n \notin N^A$$

9. Each split or merge of control flows must be mediated by a splitting gateway ($N_S^G \subseteq N^G$) or a merging gateway ($N_M^G \subset N^G$), respectively. Gateways can be of type Parallel-AND (A), Optional-OR (O), or Exclusive-XOR (X). Gateways with both multiple incoming and outgoing flows are not permitted.

$$\forall g \in N^G, type(g, t) \rightarrow t \in \{A, O, X\}$$

10. Splitting gateways XOR ($g \in N_S^G, type(g, X)$) must be followed by intermediate event nodes ($F(g, i) \in \mathbf{F}, i \in N^I$) or other XOR gateways, denoting alternative ways on which the activity can develop. Event node labels indicate the reason for selecting each alternative.
11. The diagram might have multiple end nodes, but two end nodes cannot represent the same outcome; their labels must reflect some difference. Control flows and gateways must be used for connecting all possible workflows ending in the same outcome.

$$\forall e_1, e_2 \in N^E \rightarrow Label(e_1) \not\equiv Label(e_2)$$

12. The graph G_N constituted by all $F(n_i, n_j) \in \mathbf{F}$ must not have any directed cycle or loop, i.e. it must be a Directed Acyclic Graph (DAG).
13. All other nodes, gateways and control flows are disallowed in the diagram. BPMN artifacts (associations, groups and text annotations) are ignored.

3.3 Translating BPDs to Bayesian Networks

Next we describe the rules and the procedure used for translating a BPD satisfying the previous normal form to a Bayesian Network. In short, events and actions are mapped to observable and controllable random variables, respectively, whereas control flows and gateways are used for building the conditional dependency graph and the probabilistic distribution of the model.

Events. Events represent partial world states in the activity context, hence their representation is associated to observable random variables (Z_i), whereas their occurrence is represented probabilistically by the realization of these variables $(Z_i = z_i)$.

The *start event* is detected by the activity subject and it is represented by the boolean variable Z_S, which realization to $True$ holds on any process execution. Z_S has no parents and it is used for start process monitoring. In our example, the start event is the doctor's appointment time $(Z_S = Z_1)$.

$$s \in N^S \rightarrow define(Z_S), Dom(Z_S) = \{True, False\}, map(s, Z_S = True) \quad (1)$$

The function $define(V_i)$ is used for declaring random variables, whereas the function $map(n, V_i = v_i)$, $n \in \mathbf{N}$, establishes the correspondence between elements of both representations.

A BPD might include multiple *end nodes* as shown in our example. Given that each end node corresponds to different outcomes of the activity, all of them are represented by a single random variable Z_E. Each outcome node e represents a possible realization of Z_E. In our example Z_7 represents Z_E, with $Dom(Z_7) = \{7.1, 7.2, 7.3, 7.4, 7.5\}$.

$$\forall e \in N^E \rightarrow e \in Dom(Z_E), map(e, Z_E = e) \quad (2)$$

Intermediate event nodes are used in the BPD for two reasons: (1) observing the evidence of actions performed by people in the real world (event-based control flow), and (2) controlling the workflow based on data produced during process execution (data-based control flow). Additionally to *generic intermediate event nodes* that can be expressed with expressions in First Order Logic, *timeout nodes* are introduced for representing temporal reasoning for process monitoring.

Intermediate event nodes are classified as subgoals or alternative events. *Subgoal events* are event nodes that must be performed in order to continue with process execution in a given workflow. A subgoal event is represented by a boolean random variable, where its realization to $True$ indicates that the condition/event was met and $False$ if it did not occurred during process execution. The node representing the scheduling of the *Next appointment* (Z_6) is an example of a *subgoal event*.

$$\forall i \in N^I, F(n, i) \in \mathbf{F}, (n \notin N^G \land (n \in N^G, \neg type(n, X)))) \rightarrow \quad (3a)$$
$$define(Z_i), Dom(Z_i) = \{True, False\}, map(i, Z_i = True) \quad (3b)$$

Alternative events are mutually exclusive world states denoted by intermediate event nodes preceded by a XOR gateway, and are represented by a single
observable random variable. We define the set *Alt* for identifying these gateways in further steps of the transformation. For instance, the events *Follow up
finished* ($Z_{4.1}$), *Doctor prescribes more/new medication* ($Z_{4.2}$), and *Doctor prescribes medicine and follow up* ($Z_{4.3}$), are represented by the random variable
Z_4. Successor intermediate events mediated exclusively by XOR gateways are
included in the set of disjoint events as well (see 4c–4e).

$$\forall g \in N_S^G, type(g, X), F(g, i) \in \mathbf{F}, i \in N^I \rightarrow \qquad (4a)$$

$$define(Z_g), i \in Dom(Z_g), map(i, Z_g = i), g \in Alt \qquad (4b)$$

$$\forall g \in N_S^G, type(g, X), F(g, g_1) \in \mathbf{F}, g_1 \in N^G, type(g_1, X), ..., \qquad (4c)$$

$$F(g_{k-1}, g_k) \in \mathbf{F}, g_k \in N^G, type(g_k, X), F(g_k, i) \in \mathbf{F}, i \in N^I \rightarrow \qquad (4d)$$

$$define(Z_g), i \in Dom(Z_g), map(i, Z_g = i), g \in Alt \qquad (4e)$$

Observable random variables Z_i representing intermediate events are considered *mandatory* if Z_i is included in all paths connecting the start variable Z_S
with the end variable Z_E. And it is considered *optional* if other alternative paths
exist that connect Z_S and Z_E that do not pass through it. All optional random
variables include the value *False* in their domain for considering those cases
where the process develops through an alternative path. This rule is applied
after having obtained the conditional dependence graph G_V as explained next.
Z_3 is an example of a mandatory variable with $Dom(Z_3) = \{3.1, 3.2\}$, whereas
Z_4 is optional given the alternative path through $Z_{3.2}$, making $Dom(Z_4) = \{4.1, 4.2, 4.3, False\}$.

$$\exists p_i = path(Z_S, Z_E) \in G_V, Z_j \notin p_i \rightarrow False \in Dom(Z_j) \qquad (5)$$

Actions. Action nodes in BPDs might represent atomic actions or subprocesses.
In this analysis we only consider *atomic actions*, which correspond to the definition of action given by Leontiev [11], i.e. something that the person makes
consciously to achieve a goal. This action might require the participation of
other actors, like in the auscultation made by the doctor to the elder (X_3), or be
performed individually, like when the elder going by himself to the hospital (X_1).

Similarly to subgoal events, *atomic actions* are represented by boolean random variables, denoted X_i, where the value *True* denotes the execution of the
action, and *False* represents its omission. If the action is not performed, the
value of the variable is set to *False* at the end of activity's monitoring.

$$\forall a \in N^A \rightarrow define(X_a), Dom(X_a) = \{True, False\}, map(a, X_a = True) \quad (6)$$

Control Flows. Control flows encode necessary conditions for the development
of a process, this is, the occurrence of previous events or actions enables event
observation or action execution. For instance, medical consultation (X_3) requires

the patient being at the hospital ($Z_3 = 3.1$), and the next appointment (Z_6) requires that the elder had request it (X_5).

A control flow $V_i \rightarrow V_j$ indicates: (1) temporal precedence of the action/event V_i with respect to another action/event V_j, and (2) conditional dependence of V_j on V_i. For this reason, the equivalent representation of the BPD is a Bayesian Network modeled from a causal perspective.

In order to identify conditional dependencies between events and actions, we use control flows incoming and outgoing to their corresponding random variables. A copy of the DAG constructed with these control flows, denoted $G'_N : N \times N$, is modified according to rules (7a) – (7d) in Fig. 3 for removing unnecessary gateways and unifying end nodes in a single one. In these rule we use graph operations such as adding/removing arcs and absorbing nodes. Absorbing n consists on adding control flows $F(n_i, n_j)$ for the cross product given by every pair $F(n_i, n) - F(n, n_j)$, and then removing the node n and those arcs connected to it.

$$\forall i \in N^I, F(g, i) \in G'_N, g \in Alt \rightarrow absorbe(i, G'_N) \quad (7a)$$

$$\forall g \in N_M^G \rightarrow absorbe(g, G'_N) \quad (7b)$$

$$\forall g \in N_S^G, g \notin Alt \rightarrow absorbe(g, G'_N) \quad (7c)$$

$$\forall e_i \in N^E, i > 1, F(n, e_i) \in G'_N \rightarrow remove(F(n, e_i), G'_N), add(F(n, e_1), G'_N) \quad (7d)$$

Fig. 3. Transformation of G_N to G'_n.

The resulting DAG G'_N and those mappings generated in the first stage of the process are used for defining the arcs that constitute the conditional dependence graph between random variables $G_V : V \times V$.

$$\forall F(n_i, n_j) \in G'_N, map(n_i, V_i = v_i), map(n_j, V_j = v_j) \rightarrow add(Arc(V_i, V_j), G_V) \quad (8)$$

At this point, the conditional dependence graph G_V of the medical consultation activity is shown in Fig. 4. Random variables labeled Z_i represent observable variables, whereas X_i denote atomic actions. Note that alternative event nodes are grouped in random variables Z_2, Z_3, Z_4 and Z_5.

Gateways. Gateways, on the other hand, codify how likely is that two or more events/actions occur during process execution, which corresponds to the definition of the Conditional Probabilistic Distribution (CPD), i.e. $P(v_i|pa_i)$.

The different process developments (scenarios) that can be generated according to gateway constraints provide the joint probabilistic distribution of the process. This distribution assumes that all scenarios are equally likely and it is used for learning the CPDs of random variables using the dependencies given by the graph in Fig. 4. Figure 5 shows the 15 scenarios that can be generated from

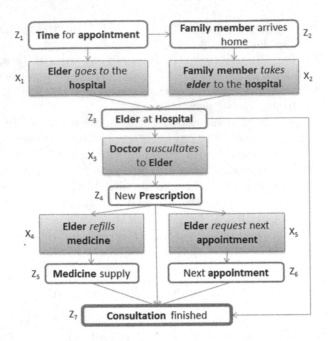

Fig. 4. The medical consultation activity's conditional dependence graph

Z1	X1	Z2	X2	Z3	X3	Z4	X4	Z5	X5	Z6	Z7
T	F	2.1	T	3.1	T	4.1	F	F	F	F	7.1
T	F	2.1	T	3.1	T	4.2	T	5.1	F	F	7.2
T	F	2.1	T	3.1	T	4.2	T	5.2	F	F	7.3
T	F	2.1	T	3.1	T	4.3	T	5.2	T	T	7.4
T	F	2.1	T	3.2	F	F	F	F	F	F	7.5
T	F	2.2	T	3.1	T	4.1	F	F	F	F	7.1
T	F	2.2	T	3.1	T	4.2	T	5.1	F	F	7.2
T	F	2.2	T	3.1	T	4.2	T	5.2	F	F	7.3
T	F	2.2	T	3.1	T	4.3	T	5.2	T	T	7.4
T	F	2.2	T	3.2	F	F	F	F	F	F	7.5
T	T	F	F	3.1	T	4.1	F	F	F	F	7.1
T	T	F	F	3.1	T	4.2	T	5.1	F	F	7.2
T	T	F	F	3.1	T	4.2	T	5.2	F	F	7.3
T	T	F	F	3.1	T	4.3	T	5.2	T	T	7.4
T	T	F	F	3.2	F	F	F	F	F	F	7.5

Fig. 5. Valid process developments.

the process in Fig. 2, where columns indicate the realization of random variables in each scenario.

Table 1 shows the structures supported by our normal form, aligned with the corresponding transformation rules. The column Mappings shows the correspondence between BPD nodes and random variables, indicating the rule applied, and the last column indicates which nodes prevail in the reduced graph G'_N, indicating the rule that makes the reduction.

Table 1. Valid structures in the BPD normal form.

Structure			Constraint	Mappings	In G'_N
Trigger		$s \longrightarrow n_i$	$n_i \in N \setminus N^S$	map(s, Z_s=True) (1)	s
Outcome		$n_i \longrightarrow e$	$n_i \in N \setminus N^E$	map(e$_i$, Z_E=e$_i$) (2)	e$_1$ (7d)
Event		$n_i \longrightarrow i \longrightarrow n_j$	$i.\ \ n_i \notin N^G$ $ii.\ \ n_i \in N^G \wedge \neg type(n_i, X)$	map(i, Z_i=True) (3)	i
Actions		$n_i \longrightarrow a \longrightarrow n_j$	$n_i, n_j \in N \setminus N^A$	map(a, X_a=True) (6)	a
Split gateways	Decision	$n_i \longrightarrow g \longrightarrow \begin{smallmatrix} n_{j\text{-}1} \\ n_{j\text{-}2} \end{smallmatrix}$	$type(g, X), n_i \in N,$ $i.\ \ n_j \in N^I$ $ii.\ \ n_j \in N^G \wedge type(n_j, X)$	map(i, Z_g=i) (4)	g (7a)
	Alternative	$n_i \longrightarrow g \longrightarrow \begin{smallmatrix} n_{j\text{-}1} \\ n_{j\text{-}2} \end{smallmatrix}$	$type(g, A) \vee type(g, O)$ $n_i, n_j \in N$	n$_i$, n$_j$ (see above)	n$_i$, n$_j$ (7c)
Merge gateways		$\begin{smallmatrix} n_{i\text{-}1} \\ n_{i\text{-}2} \end{smallmatrix} \longrightarrow g \longrightarrow n_j$	$n_i, n_j \in N$	n$_i$, n$_j$ (see above)	n$_i$, n$_j$ (7b)

3.4   The Activity Causal Bayesian Network

The Bayesian Network produced by the transformation process described above is defined as follows.

Definition 1. *An Activity Causal Bayesian Network (ACBN) is represented by*

$$D = \langle G_V, X, Z, Z_S, Z_E, P(v_i | pa_i) \rangle$$

where G_V is a minimal DAG which arcs denote temporal precedence and conditional dependence between observable events (Z) and actions (X), $P(v_i | pa_i)$ encodes conditional probabilistic dependencies between random variables $V = Z \cup X$, and G_V has at least one directed path from the initial condition $Z_S \in Z$ to the outcome variable $Z_E \in (Z \setminus Z_S)$.

The Causal Bayesian Network of the activity modeled in Fig. 2 has seven observable conditions or events ($Z_1 - Z_7$) and five human actions ($X_1 - X_5$). The initial condition is the appointment time (Z_1) and the outcome variable is Z_7. Its graph G_V is shown in Fig. 4 and the corresponding $P(v_i | pa_i)$ is learned from the process instances shown in Fig. 5.

Probabilistic Inference. Figure 6 shows an example of probabilistic inference for a partially observed activity instance where the observed evidence (e) is: the family member arrived late to elder's house ($Z_2 = 2.2$), the elder arrived to the hospital on time ($Z_3 = 3.1$), and the doctor prescribed new medication only ($Z_4 = 4.2$). Posterior probabilities for the other variables are shown in Fig. 6.

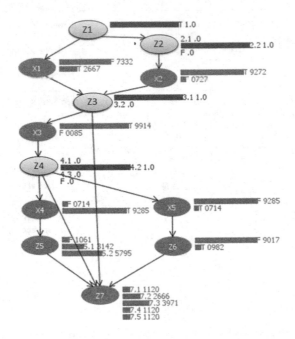

Fig. 6. Probabilistic inference on a valid scenario.

The probabilistic model can be used with two purposes: (1) predicting the most plausible world, and (2) deciding between alternative actions based on desirable outcomes.

In a general form, the posterior probability $P(v_i|e)$ indicates how likely is that an event or action v_i had occurred or will occur, given observed evidence e. Posterior probabilities of human actions (X_i) indicate how likely is their execution despite the model is only feed with information of observable events. For instance, it predicts that the elder will refill medicine ($P(X_4 = True|e) = 0.9285$) but he will not request a new appointment ($P(X_5 = False|e) = 0.9285$), which is consistent with the BPMN workflow. On the other hand, the probability of the elder going to the hospital alone ($X_1 = True$) is slightly higher than he being carried out by his family member ($X_2 = True$), which can be explained by the fact that the last arrived late to elder's home but the elder arrived on time at the hospital.

In the example of Fig. 6, the probability of the elder getting all the medicine ($Z_7 = 7.3$) or part of it ($Z_7 = 7.2$) are slightly higher than the other outcomes.

Both probabilities increase if more evidence is given (e.g. Z_5 and Z_6). Given that the Bayesian network was trained with valid process developments only, it predicts well the outcome on similar scenarios (see $P(z_7|e)$ in Fig. 6), but it assigns the same probability to all the five outcomes in invalid scenarios, which represents an uncertain outcome.

On the other hand, the probabilistic model can be used for decision making when the activity reaches a splitting exclusive gateway and the activity's subject must decide between alternative actions. In our example, the elder must decide between going to the hospital by himself or being taken by a family member. Assuming that the probabilistic distribution is obtained from real activity developments it is quite likely to observe that a late arrival of the family member provokes missing the appointment. A proper representation of this causal dependency can be encoded in the Bayesian Network by an arc from Z_2 to Z_3, which is not possible in the BPMN diagram.

The probability of observing a successful outcome would then be represented by $\sum_i P(z_{Fi}|x_j, e)$, where z_{Fi} represents all the successful outcomes, x_j the action to choose, and e is the observed evidence. Going alone to the hospital would be recommended when the family member is known to arrive late ($Z_2 = 2.2$), if:

$$\sum_i P(z_{Fi}|X_1 = True, Z_2 = 2.2) > \sum_i P(z_{Fi}|X_2 = True, Z_2 = 2.2)$$

4   Discussion

First we analyze other probabilistic approaches to BPMN. Then we compare our selection of BPMN elements with other approaches that transform BPDs to agent-based system specifications. Finally we discuss the applications of probabilistic workflows as agent engineering tool.

4.1   Probabilistic Approaches to BPMN

In 2008, Prandi and colleagues [17] proposed a formal semantics for BPMN based on the process calculus COWS. Each BPD node is considered as a COWS service and the translation describes the message flow between them. They provide a COWS formula for each node-centered structure supported by their normal form and produce a single composite formula that represents the flow of tokens across the BPD. BPDs are formalized as Continuous Time Markov Chains, a model used for automated verification of Web Service composition. Thanks to the implementation of COWS in the probabilistic model checker PRISM, the probability of observing certain event or condition at a time t can be estimated. Tasks, annotated with a duration range, occur at a different time in each alternative workflow produced by gateways present in the workflow; hence the probability of observing an event or action at a time t is expressed probabilistically.

Herbert and Sharp [6] proposed *stochastic BPMN workflows*, an extension of Core BPMN that includes: probabilistic flows (sequence flows with a given probability) and rewards associated to the execution of tasks. Using PRISM, authors transform BPMN workflows into Markovian Decision Processes (MDPs). A PRISM module is generated for each task based on a structure supported by their normal form; code templates codify transitions between states (represented by tasks), mediated by actions (represented by gateway conditions and task completion). PRISM is then used for generating all valid action sequences and calculating: (1) transitory and steady state probabilities of process conditions, (2) the probability of occurrence of an event (at a time t), (3) best and worst scenarios, and (4) the average time of process execution.

On the other hand, Bobek and colleagues [1] proposed a transformation of BPMN workflows to Bayesian Networks (BNs). The translation is straightforward, each node (action, event or gateway) is translated into a Boolean random variable whereas control flows are used for constructing the conditional dependency graph. The Bayesian Network is trained with BPMN workflows obtained from a process library, producing CPTs that indicate how likely is to observe a node N_1 followed by another node N_2. The resulting BN is used for recommending missing nodes during a new process specification. This approach lacks of a mechanism for recognizing disjoint events and detecting equivalent events/tasks across different BPDs.

4.2   Translatable Fragments of BPMN Workflows

The BPMN fragment of our approach differs from the one used in the translation of BPMN to BPEL [14] in two aspects. First, in [14] exist two types of end events, one for indicating that the participation of a component has finished, and another for indicating process termination. Given that we model the process from the perspective of the activity's subject, end events represent the different ways on which the process might terminate, successfully or on failure for the subject. Second, in our approach we don't consider data/event-based XOR gateways as long as an equivalent expressivity is provided by XOR gateways followed by intermediate events that might represent the event to observe for deciding which branch is followed during process execution.

Unlike the mapping of BPMN to agents proposed in [3], we only consider a single pool on which every lane represents a role. The use of multiple pools forces to specify illocutions between agents as part of the activity description, which produces a low-level specification which is not the purpose of our approach at this point. In contrast, BPEL, used for specifying systems based on Web Services, does not capture the attribution of agent capabilities (perceptions and actions) grouped around roles, which is evidenced on that it does not consider BPMN pools and lanes on its translation [14].

A limitation of our normal form is that we do not permit the representation of cycles in the BPMN workflow as long as it would produce non-acyclic graphs. This can be solved by replacing the feedback arc by a subprocess that replicates the cyclical section and it is called recursively until reaching the stop condition.

Another approach would be translating the cyclic section to a MDP, as proposed by [6,17].

Another limitation is that the definition of random variables from intermediate events relies in a single fixed structured (XOR gateways). This mechanism can be generalized by calculating the different ways on which the graph can be traversed and determining which events never occur together, establishing a criterion for grouping proximate disjoint nodes.

4.3 Probabilistic Workflows as Agent Engineering Tool

Modeling human activities using BPMN from an Activity Theory perspective provides a goal-oriented plan representation for the User agent representing to the activity's subject in a MAS. The corresponding ACBN can be used for modeling other participants and providing recommendations to the user. Given that human actions are not directly observable, observable events between them can be used for estimating what happened or what will occur next.

As we show in [2], the causal network can be further used for introducing the participation of software agents and generating Prometheus scenarios. As shown in Fig. 7, agent actions can facilitate the occurrence of an event, e.g. a reminder, or they can be used for monitoring the occurrence of human actions, e.g. the arrival of the elder to the hospital. BPMN workflows provide a user-friendly way of specifying the activity dynamics and its probabilistic distribution.

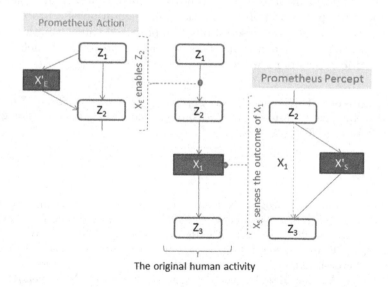

Fig. 7. Introducing agent assistance in ACBNs.

In this paper we illustrate how the BPD can be modeled from the perspective of a single actor (the subject) meanwhile it captures his interactions with other participants. Modeling a complex system where other actors should achieve their own goals requires capturing in a single BPD the perspective of other participants, or modeling their perspectives in separate BPDs and calculating their intersections. For instance, the participation of the Doctor is conditioned to his presence at the hospital previous to the appointment time; this is not represented in Fig. 2, but such precondition should be available in the Doctor's consultation workflow.

5 Conclusions

We introduced a BPMN Business Process Diagram (BPD) normal form based on Activity Theory that can be used for representing the dynamics of a collective human activity from the perspective of a subject. We introduce a novel automatic procedure that transforms this workflow into a Causal Bayesian Network that can be used for modeling human behaviors and assessing human decisions.

The resulting Bayesian Network is not only consistent with the valid process developments encoded in the BPD, but it can be further complemented with causal dependencies discovered by algorithms like Pearl's Inferred Causation [15] from actual process developments in order to improve goal achievement's prediction.

Providing a semantic representation of event and action nodes will permit to overcome the limitations of other approaches for detecting equivalent nodes and will provide the platform for the composition of workflows, the generation of agent role descriptions and plans, and the implementation of a process monitoring procedure. Using these descriptions, the proposed transformation can be extended with a proper translation of loops and subprocesses, which in turn could be used for providing a work around for cycles.

Acknowledgments. This research was supported by Tecnologico de Monterrey through the "Intelligent Systems" research group, and by CONACyT through the grant CB-2011-01-167460.

References

1. Bobek, S., Baran, M., Kluza, K., Nalepa, G.J.: Application of bayesian networks to recommendations in business process modeling. In: Proceedings of the Workshop AI Meets Business Processes 2013, CEUR, vol. 1101, pp. 41–50 (2013)
2. Ceballos, H., García-Vázquez, J.P., Brena, R.: Using activity theory and causal diagrams for designing multiagent systems that assist human activities. In: Castro, F., Gelbukh, A., González, M. (eds.) MICAI 2013, Part I. LNCS, vol. 8265, pp. 185–198. Springer, Heidelberg (2013)
3. Endert, H., Kuster, T., Hirsch, B., Albayrak, S.: Mapping BPMN to agents: An analysis. Agent, Web Services, and Ontologies Integrated Methodologies. In: International Workshop MALLOW-AWESOME 2007, pp. 43–58 (2007)

4. Engeström, Y., Miettinen, R., Punamäki, R.: Perspectives on Activity Theory. Learning in Doing: Social, Cognitive and Computational Perspectives, Cambridge University Press, New York (1999)
5. Garcia-Vazquez, J.P., Rodriguez, M.D., Tentori, M.E., Saldana, D., Andrade, A.G., Espinoza, A.N.: An agent-based architecture for developing activity-aware systems for assisting elderly. J. Univ. Comput. Sci. **16**(12), 1500–1520 (2010)
6. Herbert, L., Sharp, R.: Precise quantitative analysis of probabilistic business process model and notation workflows. J. Comput. Inf. Sci. Eng. 13(1), 011007(1–9) (2013)
7. Hinge, K., Ghosey, A., Koliadisz, G.: Process seer: A tool for semantic effect annotation of business process models. In: Proceedings of 13th IEEE International Enterprise Distributed Object Computing Conference, EDOC 2009, pp. 54–63 (2009)
8. Horrocks, I., Patel-Schneider, P., Boley, H., Tabet, S., Grosof, B., Dean, M.: SWRL: A semantic web rule language combining OWL and RuleML. W3C Member Submission, 21 May 2004
9. Jander, K., Braubach, L., Pokhar, A., Lamersdorf, W., Wack, K.J.: Goal-oriented processes with GPMN. Int. J. Artif. Intel. Tools **20**, 1021–1041 (2011)
10. Kuster, T., Lutzenberger, M., Hessler, A., Hirsh, B.: Integrating process modelling into multi-agent systems engineering. In: Multiagent and Grid Systems, pp. 105–124 (2012)
11. Leont'ev, A.: Activity, Consciousness, and Personality. Prentice-Hall, Englewood Cliffs (1978)
12. zur Muehlen, M., Indulska, M.: Modeling languages for business processes and business rules: A representational analysis. Inf. Syst. **35**(4), 379–390 (2010)
13. OMG: Business Process Model and Notation (BPMN), Version 2.0, January 2011. http://www.omg.org/spec/BPMN/2.0
14. Ouyang, C., van der Aalst, W., Dumas, M., Hofstede, A.: Translating BPMN to BPEL. BPM Center Report BPM-06-02, BPMcenter.org (2006)
15. Pearl, J.: Causality. Models, Reasoning, and Inference. Cambridge University Press, New York (2000)
16. Pearl, J., Robins, J.: Probabilistic evaluation of sequential plans for causal models with hidden variables. In: Besnard, P., Hanks, S. (eds.) Uncertainty in Artificial Intelligence, vol. 11, pp. 444–453 (1995)
17. Prandi, D., Quaglia, P., Zannone, N.: Formal analysis of BPMN via a translation into COWS. In: Lea, D., Zavattaro, G. (eds.) COORDINATION 2008. LNCS, vol. 5052, pp. 249–263. Springer, Heidelberg (2008)

ACE: A Flexible Environment for Complex Event Processing in Logical Agents

Stefania Costantini[⊠]

Department of Information Science and Engineering, and Mathematics (DISIM),
University of L'Aquila, L'Aquila, Italy
stefania.costantini@univaq.it

Abstract. In this paper we propose the general software engineering approach of transforming an agent into an Agent Computational Environment (ACE) composed of: (1) the "main" agent program; (2) a number of Event-Action modules for Complex Event Processing, including generation of complex actions; (3) a number of external contexts that the agent is able to access in order to gather information. In our view an ACE is composed of heterogeneous elements: therefore, we do not make assumptions about how the various components are defined, except that they are based upon Computational Logic. In order to show a concrete instance of ACE, we discuss an experiment based upon the DALI agent-oriented programming language and Answer Set Programming (ASP).

1 Introduction

Event processing (also called CEP, for "Complex Event Processing") has emerged as a relevant new field of software engineering and computer science [1,2]. In fact, a lot of practical applications have the need to actively monitor vast quantities of event data to make automated decisions and take time-critical actions (the reader may refer to the Proceedings of the RuleML Workshop Series). Several products for event processing have appeared on the market, provided by major software vendors and by start-up companies. Many of the current approaches are declarative and based on rules, and often on logic-programming-like languages and semantics: for instance, [3] is based upon a specifically defined interval-based Event Calculus [4].

Complex Event Processing is particularly important in software agents. Naturally most agent-oriented languages, architectures and frameworks are to some extent event-oriented and are able to perform event-processing. The issue of Event Processing Agents (EPAs) is of growing importance in the industrial field, since agents and multi-agent systems are able to manage rapid change and thus to allow for scalability in applications aimed at supporting the ever-increasing level of interaction.

This paper is concerned with logical agent-oriented languages and frameworks, i.e., those approaches whose semantics is rooted in Computational Logic. There are several such approaches, some mentioned below (for a recent survey cf., e.g., [5]). For lack of space, we are not able here to discuss and compare

© Springer International Publishing Switzerland 2015
M. Baldoni et al. (Eds.): EMAS 2015, LNAI 9318, pp. 70–91, 2015.
DOI: 10.1007/978-3-319-26184-3_5

their event-processing features. Rather, we recall only the ones that have more strongly influenced the present work.

A recent but well-established and widely used approach to CEP in computational logic is ETALIS [6,7], which is an open source plug-in for Complex Event Processing implemented in prolog which runs in many Prolog systems (available at URL http://code.google.com/p/etalis/). ETALIS is in fact based on a declarative semantics, grounded in Logic Programming. Complex events can be derived from simpler events by means of deductive rules. ETALIS, in addition, supports reasoning about events, context, and real-time complex situations, and has a nice representation of time and time intervals aimed at stream reasoning. Relations among events can be expressed via several operators, reminiscent of those of causal reasoning and Event Calculus.

In the realm of logical agents, some work about CEP is presented in [8,9], which discuss the issue of complex reactivity by considering the possibility of selecting among different applicable reactive patterns by means of simple preferences. In [10], more complex forms of preferences among possible reactive behaviors are introduced. Such preferences can be also defined in terms of "possible worlds" elicited from a declarative description of a current or hypothetical situation, and can depend upon past events, and the specific sequence in which they occurred. [11–13] discuss event-based memory-management, and temporal-logic-based constraints for complex dynamic self-checking and reaction.

Teleo-Reactive Computing by Kowalski and Sadri [14,15] is an attempt to reconcile and combine conflicting approaches in logic programming, production systems, active and deductive databases, agent programming languages, and the representation of causal theories in AI, also considering complex events. In this approach, enhanced reactive rules determine the interaction of an agent with the environment in a logical but not necessarily "just" deductive way. The semantics relies upon an infinite Herbrand-like model which is incrementally constructed.

In this paper, we propose a novel conceptual view of Complex Event Processing in logical agents and a formalization of the new approach. We observe that a complex event cannot always result from simple deterministic incremental aggregation of simple events. Rather, an agent should be able to possibly interpret a set of simple events in different ways, and to choose among possible interpretations. We also consider complex actions, seen as agent-generated events. To this aim, we propose to equip agents with specific modules, that we call *Event-Action modules* (whose first general idea was provided in [16,17]), describing complex events and complex actions. Such modules are activated by a combination of simple events, and may return: (i) possible interpretations of a set of simple events in terms of complex events; (iii) detection of anomalies; (iv) (sets of) actions to perform in response. An Event-Action module is re-evaluated whenever new instances of the "triggering" events become available, and may adopt any reasoning technique, including preferences, to identify plausible scenarios and make a choice in case of several possibilities.

Each agent can be in principle equipped with a number of such modules, possibly defined in different languages/formalisms. Also, in order to reason about events an agent may have to resort to extracting knowledge from heterogeneous external sources, that in general cannot be "wrapped" and considered as agents. We draw inspiration from the Multi-Context Systems (MCS) approach, which has been proposed to model information exchange among several knowledge sources [18–20]. MCSs are purposely defined so as to avoid the need to make such sources in some sense homogeneous: rather, the approach deals explicitly with their different representation languages and semantics. Heterogeneous sources are called "contexts" and in the MCS understanding are fundamentally different from agents: in fact, contexts do not have reactive, proactive and social capabilities, while it is assumed that they can be queried and updated. MCSs have evolved from the simplest form [18] to managed MCS (mMCS) [21], and reactive mMCS [20] for dealing with external inputs such as a stream of sensor data. MCSs adopt "bridge rules" for knowledge interchange, which are special rules assumed to be applied whenever applicable, so that contexts are constantly "synchronized".

In this paper we propose the software engineering approach of transforming an agent into an Agent Computational Environment (ACE) composed of: (1) the "main" agent program, or "basic agent"; (2) a number of Event-Action modules; (3) a number of external contexts that the agent is able to access. We assume the following. (i) Agents and modules can query (sets of) contexts, but not vice versa. (ii) Agents and modules are equipped, like contexts in MCSs, with bridge rules for knowledge interchange. Their application is however not only aimed at extracting knowledge from contexts, but also at knowledge interchange among the basic agent and Event-Action modules. On the one hand modules can access the agent's knowledge base, on the other hand the agent can access modules' conclusions. (iii) We do not make assumptions about how the various components are defined, except that they are based upon Computational Logic. We propose a full formalization with a semantics, where again we draw inspiration from MCSs' equilibrium semantics, on which we make necessary non-trivial enhancements. However, we devise a smooth extension which introduces as little additional technical machinery as possible. The approach proposed here introduces substantial advancements with respect to preliminary work presented in [16,17]. The formalization and the semantics are fully novel.

To demonstrate practical applicability of ACEs, we discuss a prototypical example that we have experimented by using the DALI agent-oriented language [22,23]. In the experimental setting we have adopted Answer Set Programming (ASP) for implementing Event-Action modules. In fact, Answer Set Programming (cf., among many, [24–27]) is a well-established logic programming paradigm where a program may have several (rather than just one) "model", called "answer set", each one representing a possible interpretation of the situation described by the program. We show how ASP-based Event-Action modules can be defined in a logic-programming-like fashion (we adopt in particular a DALI-like syntax) and then translated into ASP and executed via an ASP plugin integrated into the DALI interpreter. We define precise guidelines for the translation, and provide a practical example.

The paper is organized as follows. In Sect. 2 we provide the necessary background on MCSs. In Sect. 3 we present the proposal, its formal definition and its semantics. In Sects. 4 and 5 we discuss one particular instance, based upon DALI and ASP modules. Finally, in Sect. 6 we discuss some related work and conclude.

2 Background

Managed Multi-Context systems (mMCS) [19–21]) model the information flow among multiple possibly heterogeneous data sources. The device for doing so is constituted by "bridge rules", which are similar to prolog or, more precisely, datalog rules (cf., e.g., [28] a for survey about datalog and prolog and the references therein for more information) but allow for knowledge acquisition from external sources, as in each element of their "body" the "context", i.e. the source, from which information is to be obtained is explicitly indicated. In the short summary of mMCS provided below we basically adopt the formulation of [20], which is simplified w.r.t. [21].

Reporting from [19], a logic L is a triple $(KB_L; Cn_L; ACC_L)$, where KB_L is the set of admissible knowledge bases of L, which are sets of KB-elements ("formulas"); Cn_L is the set of acceptable sets of consequences, whose elements are data items or "facts" (in [19] these sets are called "belief sets"; we adopt the more neutral terminology of "data sets"); $ACC_L : KB_L \rightarrow 2^{Cn_L}$ is a function which defines the semantics of L by assigning each knowledge-base an "acceptable" set of consequences. A managed Multi-Context System (mMCS) $M = (C_1, \ldots, C_n)$ is a heterogeneous collection of contexts $C_i = (L_i; kb_i; br_i)$ where L_i is a logic, $kb_i \in KB_{L_i}$ is a knowledge base (below "knowledge base") and br_i is a set of bridge rules. Each such rule is of the following form, where the left-hand side $o(s)$ is called the *head*, also denoted as $hd(\rho)$, the right-hand side is called the *body*, also denoted as $body(\rho)$, and the comma stand for conjunction.

$$o(s) \leftarrow (c_1 : p_1), \ldots, (c_j : p_j),$$
$$not\,(c_{j+1} : p_{j+1}), \ldots, not\,(c_m : p_m).$$

For each bridge rule included in a context C_i, it is required that $kb_i \cup o(s)$ belongs to KB_{Li} and, for every $k \leq m$, c_k is a context included in M, and each p_k belongs to some set in KB_{L_k}. The meaning is that $o(s)$ is added to the consequences of kb_i whenever each atom p_r, $r \leq j$, belongs to the consequences of context c_r, while instead each atom p_w, $j < w \leq m$, does not belong to the consequences of context c_s. While in standard MCSs the head s of a bridge rule is simply added to the "destination" context's knowledge base kb, in managed MCS kb is subjected to an elaboration w.r.t. s according to a specific operator o and to its intended semantics: rather than simple addition. Formula s itself can be elaborated by o, for instance with the aim of making it compatible with kb's format, or via more involved elaboration.

If $M = (C_1, \ldots, C_n)$ is an MCS, a data state or, equivalently, belief/ knowledge state, is a tuple $S = (S_1, \ldots, S_n)$ such that each S_i is an element of Cn_i. Desirable data states are those where each S_i is acceptable according to ACC_i. A bridge rule ρ is applicable in a knowledge state iff for all $1 \leq i \leq j : p_i \in S_i$ and for all $j + 1 \leq k \leq m : p_k \notin S_k$. Let $app(S)$ be the set of bridge rules which are applicable in a data state S.

For a logic L, $F_L = \{s \in kb \,|\, kb \in KB_L\}$ is the set of formulas occurring in its knowledge bases. A *management base* is a set of operation names (briefly, operations) OP, defining elaborations that can be performed on formulas, e.g., addition of, revision with, etc. For a logic L and a management base OP, the set of operational statements that can be built from OP and F_L is $F_L^{OP} = \{o(s) \,|\, o \in OP, s \in F_L\}$. The semantics of such statements is given by a management function, which maps a set of operational statements and a knowledge base into a modified knowledge base. In particular, a management function over a logic L and a management base OP is a function $mng : 2^{F_L^{OP}} \times KB^L \to 2^{KB_L} \setminus \emptyset$. The management function is crucial for knowledge incorporation from external sources, as it is able to perform any elaboration on the knowledge base given the acquired information.

Semantics of mMCS is in terms of *equilibria*. A data state $S = (S_1, \ldots, S_n)$ is an equilibrium for an MCS $M = (C_1, \ldots, C_n)$ iff, for $1 \leq i \leq n$, $kb'_i = S_i \in ACC_i(mng_i(app(S), kb_i))$. Thus, an equilibrium is a global data state composed of acceptable data states, one for each context, encompassing inter-context communication determined by bridge rules and the elaboration resulting from the operational statements and the management functions.

Equilibria may not exist (where conditions for existence have been studied, and basically require the avoidance of cyclic bridge-rules application), or may contain inconsistent data sets (local inconsistency, w.r.t. *local consistency*). A management function is called *local consistency (lc-) preserving* iff, for every given management base, kb' is consistent. It can be proved that a mMCS where all management functions are lc-preserving is locally consistent. Algorithms for computing equilibria have recently been proposed (see, e.g., [29] and the references therein). Notice that bridge rules are intended to be applied whenever they are applicable. In [20], where mMCS are adapted so as to continuous reasoning in dynamic environments, where contexts' contents are updated by external input, the notion of a "run" is in fact introduced. A run of mMCS M under a sequence $Obs^0, Obs^1, \ldots$ of observations is a sequence $R = \langle S^0, KB^0 \rangle, \langle S^1, KB^1 \rangle \ldots$ such that $\langle S^0, KB^0 \rangle$ is a *full equilibrium* of M under Obs^0, and for $i > 0$ $\langle S^i, KB^i \rangle$ is a full equilibrium of M under Obs^i, where a full equilibrium is obtained by taking the observations into consideration in every context for bridge rules application: in fact, observation literals can occur in bridge rule bodies.

3 Agents as Computational Environments

In the approach that we present here, an agent is equipped with a number of *Event-Action modules* for performing Complex Event Processing, and with a number of contexts which are known to the agent and to which the agent may resort for gathering information. We assume the agent to be based upon its own underlying logic, and so are the Event-Action modules and the contexts. Different Event-Action modules may be based on different logics, depending upon the task they are supposed to perform: for instance, some modules might be aimed at event interpretation, some others at learning patterns from event occurrences, some others at evaluating possible courses of action, etc.

In order to finalize an agent's operation, we assume that each Event-Action module admits just one acceptable sets of consequences, differently from MCSs where each context may in principle admit several. In such case, we assume to choose one by means of some kind of selection function. In [20] the problem is mentioned in the conclusions, referring to unwanted sources of non-determinism that may arise. They thus suggest to adopt a global preference criteria to fix the problem, and also mention some existing preference functions that might be exploited. However, as seen below we will take the problem as solved for contexts to which agents are able to refer to, so we will care only about consequences selection for Event-Action modules.

Let a logic L be defined as reported in previous section.

Definition 1. *Let a* Logic with Preferences $L^{\mathcal{P}}$ *be a quadruple* $(KB_{L^{\mathcal{P}}}; Cn_{L^{\mathcal{P}}};$ $ACC_{L^{\mathcal{P}}}; \mathcal{P})$ *where* $ACC_{L^{\mathcal{P}}}$ *is a function which extends the one defined before for a logic L since it selects the "preferred" one among acceptable set of consequences of the given knowledge base, according to the preference criterion $\mathcal{P}$.*

As seen, we leave the preference criterion as an open parameter, as each module may in principle employ a different one. In general, a preference criterion is some kind of device which induces a total order on $Cn_{L^{\mathcal{P}}}$. On one extreme it can even be random choice, though in general domain/application-dependent criteria will be better suited.

Similarly to what is done in Linear Time Logic (LTL), we assume a discrete, linear model of time where each state/time instant can be represented by an integer number. States $t_0, t_1, \ldots$ can be seen as time instants in abstract terms. In practice we will have $t_{i+1} - t_i = \delta$, where δ is the actual interval of time after which we assume a given system to have evolved. In particular, agent systems usually evolve according to the perception of events (among which we include communications with other agents).

Definition 2. *Let $\Pi = \Pi_1, \Pi_2, \ldots$ be a sequence of sets of events, where Π_i is assumed to have been perceived by given agent at time $i > 0$. Each event in Π, say E, can be denoted as $E : t_i$ where t_i is a time-stamp indicating time i, and meaning that $E \in \Pi_i$. By $E : [t_i, t_j]$ with $1 \leq i \leq j$ we mean that E persists during an interval, i.e., we have $E : t_s$ for every $i \leq s \leq j$.*

A number of expressions can be defined on events, for instance: $E_1, \ldots, Ek :$ $[t_i, t_j]$ to mean that all the E_is, $i \leq k$, persist in given interval; $E_1, \ldots, Ek \setminus E :$ $[t_i, t_j]$ intending that all the E_is persist in given interval, where E does not occur therein. We do not go into the detail, but we assume that some syntax is provided for defining *Event Expressions*, where each such expression can be evaluated to be true or false w.r.t. Π.

Definition 3. *Let $\mathcal{H}$ be a set of sequences of sets of events as defined above, i.e., $\Pi \in \mathcal{H}$ is of the form $\Pi = \Pi_1, \Pi_2, \ldots$ Let $\mathcal{E}$ be a set of event expressions and let $ev^{\mathcal{E}} : \mathcal{E}, \mathcal{H} \to \{true, false\}$ be an evaluation function which establishes whether an event expression $\epsilon \in \mathcal{E}$ is true/false w.r.t. $\Pi \in \mathcal{H}$.*

Below we define Event-Action modules, which include an event expression that functions as a trigger, meaning that the module is evaluated whenever the given event expression is entailed by the present event sequence. Event-Action modules may resort to bridge rules for obtaining knowledge from both external contexts, and from the agent's knowledge base. They elicit, by means of some kind of reasoning, complex events that may have occurred and/or actions that the agent might perform. In case several possibilities arise, preferences are employed to finalize the reasoning.

Definition 4. *We let an Event-Action module be defined as $M = (L_M{}^{\mathcal{P}}; kb_M; br_M; mng_M; tr_M)$ where $L_{M_i}{}^{\mathcal{P}}$ is a Logic with Preferences (as defined above) and $kb_M \in KB_{L_M{}^{\mathcal{P}}}$ is a knowledge base. br_M is a set of bridge rules of the form defined for mMCS (seen in previous section), and mng_M is the management function adopted by the module. tr_M is an event expression which triggers the module evaluation, where tr_M belongs to a given set $\mathcal{E}$ associated to evaluation function $ev^{\mathcal{E}}$.*

Definition 5. *An Event-Action module M is active w.r.t. sequence Π of sets of events (or simply "active" if leaving Π implicit) iff $ev^{\mathcal{E}}(tr_M, \Pi) = true$, i.e., if Π enables the module evaluation.*

Complex events and/or actions derived from the evaluation of an active Event-Action module will be included in its set of consequences, whose contents will also depend upon bridge-rules application.

An agent program can be defined in any agent-oriented computational-logic-based programming language, such as, e.g., DALI (cf. [22,23]), AgentSpeak (cf. [30,31] and the references therein), GOAL (cf. [32] and the references therein) 3APL (cf. [33] and the references therein), METATEM (cf. [34] and the references therein), KGP (cf [36] and the references therein), or any other (cf. [35] for a survey). So, to our purposes we provide a very simple general definition of a basic agent, able to encompass any of the mentioned approaches. Only, we add bridge rules, in a form which allows an agent to access contexts, and to incorporate Event-Action modules results that can be either complex events or complex actions.

Definition 6. *We let a basic agent be defined as $A = (L_A; kb_A; br_A, mng^A)$ where L_A is a logic, $kb_A \in KB_{L_A}$ is a knowledge base (encompassing the agent program), and br_A is a set of bridge rules of the form:*

$$o(s) \leftarrow B_1, \ldots, Bj,$$
$$not\, C_{j+1}, \ldots, not\, C_k.$$

where, for $j > 0$, $k \geq 0$, each of the Bs and Cs can be in one of the following forms, where p is an atom: (i) $(c : p)$ where c is a context. (ii) $(m : ce : p)$ or $(m : act : p)$ where m is an Event-Action module, ce is a constant meaning "complex event" and act is a constant meaning "complex action". mng^A is the management function which, analogously to what seen before for mMCSs, incorporates the conclusion $o(s)$ of bridge rules into the agent's knowledge base.

Thus, agent A can update its knowledge base according to what can or cannot be concluded by a set of contexts and Event-Action modules and according to its own knowledge management policies.

Definition 7. *An Agent Computational Environment (ACE) $\mathcal{A}$ is a tuple*

$$\langle A, M_1, \ldots, M_r, C_1, \ldots, C_s \rangle$$

where, for $r, s \geq 0$, A is a basic agent, the M_is are Event-Action modules and the C_is are contexts in the sense of MCSs[1]. All components can include bridge rules. For the basic agent A they are of the form just seen above. For the other components they are of the form seen for mMCSs, with the following restrictions on bridge rule bodies: both contexts and the basic agent A can be mentioned in bodies of bridge rules in the M_is; only contexts can be mentioned in bodies of bridge rules in the C_is.

That is, contexts can only query other contexts; Event-Action modules can query contexts, but also the basic agent (thus, they have some access to its knowldedge base); the basic agent can query every component (and will in general interact with the environment and with other agents).

Definition 8. *Let $\mathcal{A} = \langle A_1, \ldots, A_h \rangle$ be an ACE, defined as above (i.e., the A_is include the basic agent, and, possibly, Event-Action modules and contexts). A data state of $\mathcal{A}$ is a tuple $S = (S_1, \ldots, S_h)$ such that each of the S_is is an element of Cn_i, according to the logic in which S_i is defined.*

As for MCSs, desirable data states are those where each S_i is acceptable according to ACC_i, taking bridge rules application into account. However, bridge rules applicability here is different. In fact, it is required that each Event-Action module which is queried is also active. So, the *app* function must be extended w.r.t. mMCSs, as for determining which bridge rules can be applied in a certain data state it will have to take into consideration also the sequence of sets of events occurred so far.

Definition 9. *Let S be a data state of ACE $\mathcal{A}$, and let Π be a sequence of sets of events. A bridge rule ρ is applicable in S given Π iff every Event-Action module mentioned in the body is active w.r.t. Π, and for every positive literal in the body referring to component A_i the atom occurring therein belongs to S_i*

---

[1] The acronym "ACE" emerged by chance: nevertheless, with the occasion the author wishes to dedicate the ACE approach to the memory of Alan Turing.

and for every negative literal in the body referring to component A_i the atom occurring therein does not belong to S_i. Let $app(S, \Pi)$ be the set of bridge rules which are applicable in a data state S w.r.t. sequence of sets of events Π.

We can extend to ACEs the definition of equilibrium already provided for mMCSs.

Definition 10. *A data state $S = (S_1, \ldots, S_n)$ of ACE $\mathcal{A}$ is an equilibrium w.r.t. sequence of sets of events Π, and is then denoted as $\Xi_{\mathcal{A}}{}^{\Pi}$, iff for $1 \leq i \leq n$, $kb'_i = S_i \in ACC_i(mng_i(app(S, \Pi), kb_i))$.*

For every component which based upon a preferential logic (i.e., at least Event-Action modules) ACC_i is, as said before, univocal. It is easy to see that if the set of contexts included in ACE $\mathcal{A}$ constitutes in itself an mMCS which admits equilibria, then also $\mathcal{A}$ does so. As soon as the sequence of set of events acquires more elements over time, this determines new equilibria to be formed.

Definition 11. *Given ACE $\mathcal{A}$ and sequence of sets of events $\Pi = \Pi_1, \Pi_2, \ldots, \Pi_k, \ldots$, the corresponding ACE-Evolution is the sequence of equilibria $\Xi_{\mathcal{A}}{}^{\Pi_1}$, $\Xi_{\mathcal{A}}{}^{\Pi_1, \Pi_2}, \ldots, \Xi_{\mathcal{A}}{}^{\Pi_1, \Pi_2, \ldots, \Pi_k}, \ldots$*

This implies that each Event-Action module is either evaluated or not in different stages of an ACE's evolution. In case a bridge rule queries a module which at that stage is not active, no result will be returned. This is a departure from MCSs, where each literal in a bridge rules is supposed to always evaluate to either true or false. In case of ACEs, some bridge rules will be "idle" at some evolution stages, i.e., unable to return results. Results may anyway have been returned previously or may be returned later, whenever the involved modules become active. Event-Action modules might be for instance defined in ETALIS, or in Reactive Answer Set Programming [37], or in Abductive Logic Programming or in many other formalisms.

For lack of space we cannot discuss verification. However we may notice that via LTL (Linear Temporal Logic), interesting properties of an ACE can be defined and verified. For instance, for proposition φ it can be checked whether φ holds for agent A in some equilibrium reached at a certain time or within some time interval.

4   Event-Action Modules in DALI

The ACE framework is especially aimed at designing agent-based computational environments involving heterogeneous components. Purposely, the proposal does not make assumptions about the logics and the preference rules the various component are based upon. In order to make the proposal less abstract by demonstrating its practical applicability, in this section we however report about an experiment that we have been developing in DALI, where: the basic agent is a DALI agent; contexts are simply prolog knowledge bases; Event-Action modules are defined in a DALI-like syntax, and are then translated into Answer Set Programming (ASP), and thus executed by means of the ASP plugin which has been integrated into the DALI interpreter. ASP is in fact quite suitable for obtaining plausible scenarios from a set of constraints. Several approaches to preferences have been defined for ASP: cf., e.g., [20] and the references therein, and also [38–41] and [42,43]). The translation is discussed in the next section.

In the examples below syntax is reminiscent of DALI, which is a prolog-like language with predicates in lowercase and variables in uppercase. Postfix E designs a predicate as an event, postfix A as an action, and postfix P an event which has occurred in the past. Special keywords indicate, for the convenience of programmers and readers, different parts of each module. However, there is no special reason for adopting these keywords rather than any other syntax.

4.1 Examples of Event-Action Modules

Deriving Complex Events. The following example illustrates an *Event-Action module* evaluating symptoms of either pneumonia, or just flu, or both (clearly, we do not aim at medical precision). The Event-Action module will be activated whenever its *triggering events* occur within a certain time interval, and according to specific conditions: in the example, the module is evaluated whenever in the last two days both high temperature and intense cough have been recorded. For the sake of conciseness the example is propositional, thus referring to an unidentified single patient. In general, it might, by means of introducing variables, refer to a generic patient/person.

EVENT-ACTION-MODULE diagnosis

```
TRIGGER
(high_temperatureE AND intense_coughE) : [2days]
COMPLEX_EVENTS
suspect_flu OR suspect_pneumonia
    suspect_flu :- high_temperatureP.
    suspect_pneumonia :- high_temperatureP : [4days], intense_coughP.
    suspect_pneumonia :-
            diagnosis(clinical_history, suspect_pneumonia) : diag_knowledge_base.
PREFERENCES
suspect_flu :- patient_is_healty.
suspect_pneumonia :- patient_is_at_risk.
ACTIONS
stay_in_bedA :- suspect_flu.
take_antibioticA :- suspect_flu,
                high_temperatureP : [4days], not suspect_pneumonia.
take_antibioticA :- suspect_pneumonia.
consult_lung_doctorA :- suspect_pneumonia.
MANDATORY
suspect_preumonia :- high_temperatureP : [4days],
                suspect_fluP, take_antibioticP : [2days].
```

From given symptoms, either a suspect flu or a suspect pneumonia or both can be derived. This is stated in the *COMPLEX_EVENTS* section, which in general lists the complex events that the module might infer from the given definition. For suspecting pneumonia high temperature should have lasted for at least four days, accompanied by intense cough. Pneumonia is also suspected if the patient's clinical history suggests this might be the case. This is an example of a bridge rule, as the analisys of clinical history is demanded to an external context, here indicated as *diag_knowledge_base*. Notice that, in our implementation, every predicate not defined within the module is obtained from the agent's knowldge base via a standard bridge rule, that might look, for agent Ag, of the form $A :- A : Ag$. As stated before in fact, in an ACE every Event-Action module has access, via bridge rules, to the basic agent knowledge base.

Explicit preferences are expressed in the *PREFERENCES* section. A conclusion is preferred if the conditions are true: therefore, in this case it is stated that hypothesizing a flu should be preferred in case the patient is healthy, while pneumonia is the preferred option for risky patients. Actions to undertake in the two cases are specified, and the agent can access them via bridge rules. In this case, if a flu is suspected then the patient should stay in bed, and if the high temperature persists then an antibiotic should also be assumed (even if pneumonia is not suspected). In case of suspect pneumonia, an antibiotic is mandatory, plus a consult with a lung doctor.

The *MANDATORY* section of the module includes constraints, that may be of various kinds: in this case, it specifies which complex events must be mandatorily inferred in module (re)evaluations if certain conditions occur. Specifically, pneumonia is to be assumed *mandatorily* whenever flu has been previously assumed, but high temperature persists despite at least two days of antibiotic therapy.

Monitoring the Environment. The next Event-Action-module models an agent's behavior if encountering a traffic light. The triggering events are the presence of the traffic light, and the color of the traffic light as perceived by the agent. The objective of the module is to assess whether the observed color is correct (*CHECK* section), to detect and manage possible anomalies, and to determine what to do then. The module evaluates as correct any color which is either red or yellow or green. Section *ANOMALIES* detects violations to the expected color or color sequence which is, namely, yellow after green, red after yellow and green after red. Actions for both the normal and anomalous case are specified. Postfix P indicates the last previous value of an event.

Thus, if the agent meets a traffic light which is, say, red, then the agent stops, and the event $colorE(tl, red)$ is recorded as a *past event* in the form $colorP(tl, red)$. If, after some little while, the event $colorE(tl, green)$ arrives, then the module is re-evaluated and the agent passes. The *ANOMALIES* section copes with two cases: (i) the color is incorrect, e.g., the traffic light might be dark or flashing; (ii) the agent has observed the traffic light for a while, and the color sequence is incorrect. This is deduced by comparing the present color $colorE(tl, c1)$ with previous color $colorP(tl, c2)$. Actions to undertake in case of anomaly are defined, that in the example imply passing with caution and reporting to the police in the former case, and choosing another route and reporting to the police in the latter. Anomaly detection is in our opinion relevant, as anomalies in event occurrence may be considered themselves as particular (and sometimes important) instances of complex events.

EVENT-ACTION-MODULE traffic

$TRIGGER$ $traffic\_lightE(tl)$ AND $colorE(tl, C)$
$CHECK$
$color\_ok(tl, C), C = red$ XOR
$color\_ok(tl, C), C = green$ XOR
$color\_ok(tl, C), C = yellow :\text{-} colorE(tl, C)$
$ANOMALIES$
$anomaly1(tl) :\text{-}$ $colorE(tl, C), not\ color\_ok(tl, C).$
$anomaly2(tl) :\text{-}$ $colorE(tl, red), not\ colorP(tl, yellow).$
$anomaly2(tl) :\text{-}$ $colorE(tl, yellow), not\ colorP(tl, green).$
$anomaly2(tl) :\text{-}$ $colorE(tl, green), not\ colorP(tl, red).$
$ACTIONS$
$stopA :\text{-} color\_ok(tl, red).$
$stopA :\text{-} color\_ok(tl, yellow).$
$passA :\text{-} color\_ok(tl, green).$
$ANOMALY\_MANAGEMENT\_ACTIONS$
　　　$pass\_with\_cautionA,$
　　　$report\_to\_policeA(tl) :\text{-} anomaly1(tl).$
　　　$stopA,$
　　　$change\_wayA,$
　　　$report\_to\_policeA(tl) :\text{-} anomaly2(tl)$

Generating Complex Actions. The last example is related to what happens when two persons meet. In such a situation, it is possible that the one who first sees the other smiles, and then either simply waves or stops to shake hands: section $RELATED\_EVENTS$ specifies, as a boolean combination, events that may occur contextually to the triggering ones. Some conditions are specified on these events, for instance that one possibly smiles and/or waves if (s)he is neither in a bad temper nor angry at the other person. Also, one who is in a hurry just waves, while good friends or people who meet each other in a formal setting should shake hands. In this sample formulation, actions simply consist in returning what the other one does, and it is anomalous not doing so (e.g., if one smiles and the other does not smile back). The expression $meet\_friend(A, F)$ means that agent A meets agent F: then, each one will possibly make some actions and the other one will normally respond. This module is totally revertible, in the sense that it manages both the case where "we" meet a friend and the case where vice versa somebody else meets us. This is the reason why in some module sections events have no postfixes. In fact, $meet\_friend(A,F)$, $smile$, $wave$ and $shake\_hands$ are present events if a friend meets "us", and are actions if "we" meet a friend.

Postfixes appear in the $ACTIONS$ and $ANOMALY$ sections, where all elements (whatever their origin) have become past events to be coped with.

The *PRECONDITIONS* section expresses action preconditions, via connective : <. Section *MANDATORY* defines obligations, here via a rule stating that it is mandatory to shake hands in a formal situation. The anomaly management section may include counter-measures to be taken in case of unexpected behavior, that in the example may go from asking for explanation to getting angry, etc.

EVENT-ACTION-MODULE meet

TRIGGER meet_friend(A, F),
RELATED_EVENTS
smile(A, F) *OR* (*wave*(A, F) *XOR* *shake_hands*(A, F))
PRECONDITIONS
smileA(A, F) :< *not angry*(A, F), *not bad_temper*(A).
waveA(A, F) :< *not angry*(A, F).
shake_handsA(A, F) :<
    good_friends(A, F), *not angry*(A, F), *not in_a_hurry*(A), *not in_a_hurry*(F).
MANDATORY
shake_handsA(A, F) :- *formal_situation*(A, F).
ACTIONS
smiled(X, Y) :- *smileP*(X, Y).
waved(X, Y) :- *waveP*(X, Y).
shaken_hands(X, Y) :- *shake_handsP*(X, Y).
smileA(A, F) :- *smiled*(F, A).
waveA(A, F) :- *waved*(F, A).
shake_handsA(A, F) :- *shaken_hands*(F, A).
ANOMALY
anomaly1(*meet_friend*(A, F)) :- *smileP*(A, F), *not smileA*(F, A).
anomaly2(*meet_friend*(A, F)) :- *waveP*(A, F), *not waveA*(F, A).
anomaly3(*meet_friend*(A, F)) :- *shake_handsP*(A, F), *not shake_handsA*(F, A).
ANOMALY_MANAGEMENT_ACTIONS
...

5   ASP Representation of DALI Event-Action Modules

The examples that we have illustrated above have been presented in a DALI-like syntax. However, DALI (being a prolog-like language with a minimal model semantics [44]) cannot account for the different scenarios outlined by Event-Action modules. In fact, each module can perform a selection (according to conditions and preferences) among different complex events or complex actions that might result from the given simple events and the available complex events/ actions description. In order to suitably implement such intended behavior, we have devised a prototypical implementation where Event-Action modules are translated into Answer set programs. Answer set programming (ASP) is nowadays a well-established and successful programming paradigm based upon answer set semantics [24,45–47], with applications in many areas (cf., e.g., [25–27] and the references therein). An answer set program may have several answer sets, each one representing a solution of the problem encoded in the program. As seen below, each Event-Action module can be translated in a fully automated way into an ASP module.

The way of evaluating Event-Action modules within a DALI ACE basic functioning is the following.

– At each agent's evolution step, i.e., when new events have been perceived, ASP modules corresponding to Event-Action modules are (re-)evaluated given the history of all events perceived, and the agent's current knowledge base. It is required to re-evaluate a module whether the condition in the *TRIGGER* headline is satisfied. As seen, this condition is specified in terms of a boolean combination of present and/or past events. DALI is equipped with timestamps and time intervals and is thus able to perform such evaluation.
– A module will admit as a result of evaluation none, one or more answer sets. Non-existence of answer sets can result from constraint violation, and implies that no reaction to triggering events can be determined at present.
– If the module admits answer sets, one answer set among the available ones must be selected. Answer set selection is performed according to the preferences expressed in section *PREFERENCES*. If there are answer sets which are equally preferred, the current solution in the prototypical implementation is random choice. Methods for choosing answer sets according to preferences are discussed for instance in [38, 48].

5.1 Answer Set Programming (ASP) in a Nutshell

Answer Set Programming (ASP) is a logic programming paradigm based upon logic programs with default negation under the *answer set semantics*, which [24, 45]. This semantics considers logic programs as sets of inference rules (more precisely, default inference rules). In fact, one can see an answer set program as a set of constraints on the solution of a problem, where each answer set represents a solution compatible with the constraints expressed by the program. The reader may refer, among many, to [24, 25, 27, 45] for a presentation of ASP as a tool for declarative problem-solving.

Syntactically, an answer set program (or, for short, just "program") Π is a collection of *rules* of the form $H \leftarrow L_1, \ldots, L_m, not\ L_{m+1}, \ldots, not\ L_{m+n}$ where H and each L_is, $m \geq 0$ and $n \geq 0$, are atoms. Symbol $\leftarrow$ is usually indicated with :- in practical systems. An atom L_i and its negative counterpart $not\ L_i$ are called *literals*. The left-hand side and the right-hand side of the clause are called *head* and *body*, respectively. A rule with empty body is called a *fact*. A rule with empty head is a *constraint*, where a constraint of the form $\leftarrow L_1, ..., L_n$. states that literals $L_1, \ldots, L_n$ cannot be simultaneously true in any answer set.

A program may have several answer sets, each of which represents a solution to the given problem which is consistent w.r.t. the problem description and constraints. If a program has no answer set, this means that no such solution can be found. and the program is said to be *inconsistent* (w.r.t. *consistent*).

In practical terms, a problem encoded by means of an ASP program is processed by an ASP solver which computes the answer set(s) of the program, from which the solutions can be easily extracted by abstracting away from irrelevant details. Several well-developed answer set solvers [49] can be freely downloaded by potential users. All solvers provide a number of additional constructs and features useful for practical programming, that for simplicity we do not consider here. Solvers are periodically checked and compared over well-established benchmarks, and over challenging sample applications proposed at the yearly ASP competition (cf. [50]). The expressive power of ASP and its computational complexity have been deeply investigated [51].

5.2 Translation Guidelines

The answer set programming (module) Π corresponding to a given Event-Action module is obtained by translating into ASP the contents of sections *COM-PLEX_EVENTS*, *CHECK*, *RELATED_EVENTS*, *ANOMALIES* and *MANDA-TORY*. The translation can be fully defined and automated. Sections *ACTIONS*, *ANOMALY_MANAGEMENT_ACTIONS* and *PRECONDITIONS* do not need translation, as they are in fact composed of logic programming rules which by definition are ASP rules. So, these sections are just copied (with some minor modifications seen below) into the ASP version of the given Event-Action module. Notice that we do not need stream or reactive answer set programming, as triggers and time intervals are coped with by the underlying DALI interpreter. Each module resulting from the translation is evaluated in the standard ASP fashion whenever the conditions for doing so occur. The translation can be in particular performed by exploiting the following ASP patterns. Please consider that ASP solvers provide sophisticated and flexible programing constructs for expressing many of these patterns. However, for the sake of clarity we consider only the basic simple forms listed below.

conj In ASP, the conjunction among a number of elements $a_1, \ldots, a_n$ is simply expressed as $conj \leftarrow a_1, \ldots, a_n$.

or-xor Disjunction between two elements a and b is expressed by the cycle $a \leftarrow not\, b$ $b \leftarrow not\, a$. This disjunction is not exclusive, since either a or b or both might be derived elsewhere in the program. To obtain exclusive disjunction, a constraint $\leftarrow a, b$ must be added. A constraint in ASP can be read as *it cannot be that all literals in the body are true*. In the case of the exclusive disjunction of a and b, it cannot be that both a and b belong to the same answer set. Disjunction can also be expressed on several elements.

choice Choice, or possibility, or hypothesis, expressing that some element a may or may not be included in an answer set, can be expressed by means of a cycle involving a fresh atom, say na. The cycle is of the form $a \leftarrow not\, na$ $na \leftarrow not\, a$. Therefore, an answer set will contain either a or na, the latter signifying the absence of a.

choyf Makes the *choice* pattern stronger: element a can be in fact chosen only if certain conditions *Conds* are satisfied, is expressed by a choice pattern plus a rule $c \leftarrow Conds$ and a constraint $\leftarrow a, not\, c$. The constraint states that a cannot be hypothesized in an answer set if c does not hold, i.e., if *Conds* are not implied by that answer set.

mand Mandatory presence in an answer set of atom a defined by rule $a \leftarrow Body$ whenever *Body* is implied by that answer set can be obtained as follows.

In addition to the defining rule $a \leftarrow Body$, a constraint must be added of the form $\leftarrow not\, a, Body$ stating that it cannot be that an answer set implies $Body$ but does not contain a. The constraint is necessary for preventing a to be ruled out by some other condition occurring elsewhere in the program.

Specifically, the translation can be performed by means of the following guidelines (a full and formal definition of the translation is not possible here for lack of space).

- Sections *COMPLEX_EVENTS* and *RELATED_EVENTS* are basically coped with by the *conj* and *choice* patterns. More involved combinations of events may require the *choyf* and *or-xor* patterns.
- Constraints in the *MANDATORY* section can be expresses by means of the *mand* pattern.
- Sections *CHECK* and *ANOMALIES* can be either translated by a plain transposition of their rules into ASP, or by exploiting the *conj* and *or-xor* patterns.

5.3   Translation Example

We provide below an example of translation, considering the Event-Action module 'diagnosis' that we have presented before. Notice preliminarly that, for each past event evP, it is possible to specify atoms of the form $evP(N, M)$ where M is a unit of time (specifically, M can be seconds, minutes, days) and N is a number of units of time. Such an atom is evaluated by means of a plugin, and returns true (succeeds) in case event ev has been recorded at least once for each of the N time units. E.g., $evP(4, days)$ succeeds whenever event ev has occurred, and has consequently been recorded as a part event, at least once a day for four days. A plugin is also provided for bridge rules: in fact, each atom $p(args) : c$ occurring in the body of such a rule is transformed into $p(args, c)$ and evaluates to true (with suitable instantiations of the arguments) if context c returns the corresponding answer.

Concerning the *Complex Events* section, the translation procedure exploits the **or** pattern for the expression:

suspect_flu OR suspect_preumonia

and then just copies the remaining rules of the section, with suitable syntactic rearrangements. The result is the following:

suspect_flu :- not suspect_pneumonia.
suspect_pneumonia :- not suspect_flu.
suspect_flu :- high_temperatureP.
suspect_pneumonia :- high_temperatureP(4, days), intense_coughP.
suspect_pneumonia :-
        diagnosis(clinical_history, suspect_pneumonia, diag_knowledge_base).

Translation of the *MANDATORY* section, i.e.:

suspect_preumonia :-
        high_temperatureP : [4days], suspect_fluP, take_antibioticP : [2days].

exploits the **mand** pattern, with result

:- *not suspect_preumonia,*
           high_temperatureP(4, days), suspect_fluP, take_antibioticP : (2, days).

Rules in the *ACTIONS* section are just copied (modulo minor rearrangements), with result:

stay_in_bedA :- suspect_flu.
take_antibioticA :- suspect_flu,
                      high_temperatureP(4, days), not suspect_pneumonia.
take_antibioticA :- suspect_pneumonia.
consult_lung_doctorA :- suspect_preumonia.

Adapting the notation of [42], the *PREFERENCES* section

suspect_flu :- patient_is_healty.
suspect_pneumonia :- patient_is_at_risk.

would be translated into the *conditional p-lists*:

suspect_flu > suspect_pneumonia :- patient_is_healty.
suspect_pneumonia > suspect_flu :- patient_is_at_risk.

The (prototypical) *Raspberry* inference engine [52] would then be able to execute the resulting program, thus returning the preferred answer set. The recent *aspirin* system [38] might also be used.

6   Related Work Concluding Remarks

In this paper we have proposed ACE, as a framework for the design of component-based agent-oriented environments where a "main" agent program, the basic agent, is enriched with a number of Event-Action modules for Complex Event Processing and complex actions generation, and with a number of external data sources that can accessed via bridge rules, borrowed from MCSs. Components of an ACE are in principle heterogeneous, though we assume them to be based upon Computational Logic. The only condition for employing any computational-logic-based language for defining ACE agents or Event-Action modules is that such language must be extended with the possibility of defining bridge rules: this improvement should not however imply either semantic or technical difficulties. We have proposed a formalization and a semantics for ACE. We have also discussed a prototypical experimentation of the approach in the DALI agent-oriented programming language, employing ASP as an implementation tool.

A research work which is related to the present one is DyKnow [53], which is a knowledge processing middleware framework providing software support for creating streams representing high-level events concerning aspects of the past, current, and future state of a system. Input is gathered from distributed sources, can be processed at many different levels of abstraction, and finally transformed into suitable forms to be used by reasoning functionalities. A knowledge process specification is understood as a function. DyKnow is fully implemented, and has been experimented in UAVs (Unmanned Aerial Vehicles) applications.

ACE can be considered as a generalization of such work, in that ACE: (i) is agent-oriented; (ii) is aimed at managing heterogeneity in the definition/description of knowledge sources, that moreover can interact among themselves and with external sources; (iii) is aimed at providing a uniform semantics of single components and of the overall system; (iv) is aimed at allowing for verification of properties.

Several future directions are ahead of us. First, simple preferences are just one possible way of selecting among plausible alternatives. More generally, we plan to consider also informed choice deriving from a learning process: i.e., an agent should learn from experience what is the "best" interpretation to give to a situation, or which are the preference criteria to (dynamically) adopt. Learning should be a never-ending process, as different outcomes might be more plausible in different contexts and situations. Verification of ACE systems is a very relevant aspect to be coped with. We believe that both a priori verification and run-time assurance (cf., e.g., [54]) should be combined for ensuring desirable properties of this kind of systems. Formalization and verification of MASs (Multi-Agent Systems) composed of ACE agents is a further important issue that we intend to consider. ACE agent systems can in principle be part of DACMACSs ("Data-Aware Commitment-based MASs"). The approach of DACMACS, recently proposed in [55,56] as an extension of DACMAS [57], includes (like in DACMAS) the element of logical ontologies within Multi-Agent systems, but also allows agents of the MAS to query heterogeneous external contexts, possibly with bi-directional interchange of ontological definitions.

References

1. Chandy, M.K., Etzion, O., von Ammon, R.: 10201 executive summary and manifesto - event processing. In: Chandy, K.M., Etzion, O., von Ammon, R. (eds.) Event Processing. Number 10201 in Dagstuhl Seminar Proc., Dagstuhl, Germany, Schloss Dagstuhl - Leibniz-Zentrum fuer Informatik, Germany (2011)
2. Etzion, O., Niblett, P.: Event Processing in Action. Manning Publications Co., Greenwich (2010)
3. Paschke, A., Kozlenkov, A.: Rule-based event processing and reaction rules. In: Governatori, G., Hall, J., Paschke, A. (eds.) RuleML 2009. LNCS, vol. 5858, pp. 53–66. Springer, Heidelberg (2009)
4. Kowalski, R., Sergot, M.: A logic-based calculus of events. New Gener. Comput. 4, 67–95 (1986)
5. Fisher, M., Bordini, R.H., Hirsch, B., Torroni, P.: Computational logics and agents: a road map of current technologies and future trends. Comput. Intell. J. 23(1), 61–91 (2007)
6. Anicic, D., Rudolph, S., Fodor, P., Stojanovic, N.: Real-time complex event recognition and reasoning - a logic programming approach. Appl. Artif. Intell. 26(1–2), 6–57 (2012)
7. Anicic, D., Rudolph, S., Fodor, P., Stojanovic, N.: Stream reasoning and complex event processing in ETALIS. Semant. Web 3(4), 397–407 (2012)

8. Costantini, S., Dell'Acqua, P., Tocchio, A.: Expressing preferences declaratively in logic-based agent languages. In: Proceedings of Commonsense 2007, the 8th International Symposium on Logical Formalizations of Commonsense Reasoning. AAAI Spring Symposium Series (2007). (a special event in honor of John McCarthy)
9. Costantini, S.: Answer set modules for logical agents. In: de Moor, O., Gottlob, G., Furche, T., Sellers, A. (eds.) Datalog 2010. LNCS, vol. 6702, pp. 37–58. Springer, Heidelberg (2011)
10. Costantini, S., De Gasperis, G.: Complex reactivity with preferences in rule-based agents. In: Bikakis, A., Giurca, A. (eds.) RuleML 2012. LNCS, vol. 7438, pp. 167–181. Springer, Heidelberg (2012)
11. Costantini, S., De Gasperis, G.: Memory, experience and adaptation in logical agents. In: Casillas, J., Martínez-López, F.J., Vicari, R., De la Prieta, F. (eds.) Management Intelligent Systems. AISC, vol. 220, pp. 17–24. Springer, Heidelberg (2013)
12. Costantini, S.: Self-checking logical agents. In: Gini, M.L., Shehory, O., Ito, T., Jonker, C.M. (eds.) Proceedings of AAMAS 2013, 12th International Conference on Autonomous Agents and Multi-Agent Systems, IFAAMAS/ACM, pp. 1329–1330 (2013). (Extended Abstract)
13. Costantini, S., De Gasperis, G.: Meta-level constraints for complex event processing in logical agents. In: Online Proceedings of Commonsense 2013, the 11th International Symposium on Logical Formalizations of Commonsense Reasoning (2013)
14. Kowalski, R.A., Sadri, F.: Reactive computing as model generation. New Gener. Comput. **33**(1), 33–67 (2015)
15. Kowalski, R.A., Sadri, F.: Teleo-reactive abductive logic programs. In: Artikis, A., Craven, R., Kesim Çiçekli, N., Sadighi, B., Stathis, K. (eds.) Sergot Festschrift 2012. LNCS, vol. 7360, pp. 12–32. Springer, Heidelberg (2012)
16. Costantini, S., Riveret, R.: Event-action modules for complex reactivity in logical agents. In: Bazzan, A.L.C., Huhns, M.N., Lomuscio, A., Scerri, P. (eds.) Proceedings of AAMAS 2013, 13th International Conference on Autonomous Agents and Multi-Agent Systems, IFAAMAS/ACM, pp. 1503–1504 (2014). (Extended Abstract)
17. Costantini, S., Riveret, R.: Complex events and actions in logical agents. In: Giordano, L., Gliozzi, V., Pozzato, G.L. (eds.) Proceedings of the 29th Italian Conference on Computational Logic. CEUR Workshop Proceedings, vol. 1195, pp. 256–271. CEUR-WS.org (2014)
18. Brewka, G., Eiter, T.: Equilibria in heterogeneous nonmonotonic multi-context systems. In: Proceedings of the 22nd AAAI Conference on Artificial Intelligence, pp. 385–390. AAAI Press (2007)
19. Brewka, G., Eiter, T., Fink, M.: Nonmonotonic multi-context systems: a flexible approach for integrating heterogeneous knowledge sources. In: Balduccini, M., Son, T.C. (eds.) Logic Programming, Knowledge Representation, and Nonmonotonic Reasoning. LNCS, vol. 6565, pp. 233–258. Springer, Heidelberg (2011)
20. Brewka, G., Ellmauthaler, S., Pührer, J.: Multi-context systems for reactive reasoning in dynamic environments. In: Schaub, T. (ed.) ECAI 2014, Proceedings of the 21st European Conference on Artificial Intelligence, IJCAI/AAAI (2014)
21. Brewka, G., Eiter, T., Fink, M., Weinzierl, A.: Managed multi-context systems. In: Walsh, T. (ed.) IJCAI 2011, Proceedings of the 22nd International Joint Conference on Artificial Intelligence, IJCAI/AAAI, pp. 786–791 (2011)
22. Costantini, S., Tocchio, A.: A logic programming language for multi-agent systems. In: Flesca, S., Greco, S., Leone, N., Ianni, G. (eds.) JELIA 2002. LNCS (LNAI), vol. 2424, p. 1. Springer, Heidelberg (2002)

23. Costantini, S., Tocchio, A.: The DALI logic programming agent-oriented language. In: Alferes, J.J., Leite, J. (eds.) JELIA 2004. LNCS (LNAI), vol. 3229, pp. 685–688. Springer, Heidelberg (2004)

24. Gelfond, M., Lifschitz, V.: The stable model semantics for logic programming. In: Kowalski, R., Bowen, K. (eds.) Proceedings of the 5th International Conference and Symposium on Logic Programming (ICLP/SLP 1988), pp. 1070–1080. The MIT Press (1988)

25. Baral, C.: Knowledge Representation, Reasoning and Declarative Problem Solving. Cambridge University Press, Cambridge (2003)

26. Gelfond, M.: Answer sets. In: Lifschitz, V., van Hermelen, F., Porter, B. (eds.) Handbook of Knowledge Representation. Elsevier, Amsterdam (2007)

27. Truszczyński, M.: Logic programming for knowledge representation. In: Dahl, V., Niemelä, I. (eds.) ICLP 2007. LNCS, vol. 4670, pp. 76–88. Springer, Heidelberg (2007)

28. Apt, K.R., Bol, R.: Logic programming and negation: a survey. J. Logic Program. **19–20**, 9–71 (1994)

29. Dao-Tran, M., Eiter, T., Fink, M., Krennwallner, T.: Distributed evaluation of nonmonotonic multi-context systems. JAIR, the Journal of Artificial Intelligence Research (2015) (to appear)

30. Bordini, R.H., Hübner, J.F.: BDI agent programming in agentspeak using *Jason* (tutorial paper). In: Toni, F., Torroni, P. (eds.) CLIMA 2005. LNCS (LNAI), vol. 3900, pp. 143–164. Springer, Heidelberg (2006)

31. Rao, A.S., Georgeff, M.P.: Modeling agents within a BDI-architecture. In: Fikes, R., Sandewall, E. (eds.) Proceedings of International Conference on Principles of Knowledge Representation and Reasoning (KR), Cambridge, Massachusetts, Morgan Kaufmann (1991)

32. Hindriks, K.V., van der Hoek, W., Meyer, J.-J.C.: GOAL agents instantiate intention logic. In: Artikis, A., Craven, R., Kesim Çiçekli, N., Sadighi, B., Stathis, K. (eds.) Sergot Festschrift 2012. LNCS, vol. 7360, pp. 196–219. Springer, Heidelberg (2012)

33. Dastani, M., van Riemsdijk, M.B., Meyer, J.C.: Programming multi-agent systems in 3APL. In: Bordini, R.H., Dastani, M., Dix, J., Fallah-Seghrouchni, A.E. (eds.) Multi-Agent Programming: Languages, Platforms and Applications. Multiagent Systems, Artificial Societies, and Simulated Organizations, vol. 15, pp. 39–67. Springer, New York (2005)

34. Fisher, M.: METATEM: The story so far. In: Bordini, R.H., Dastani, M., Dix, J., Fallah Seghrouchni, A. (eds.) PROMAS 2005. LNCS (LNAI), vol. 3862, pp. 3–22. Springer, Heidelberg (2006)

35. Bordini, R.H., Braubach, L., Dastani, M., Fallah-Seghrouchni, A.E., Gómez-Sanz, J.J., Leite, J., O'Hare, G.M.P., Pokahr, A., Ricci, A.: A survey of programming languages and platforms for multi-agent systems. Informatica (Slovenia) **30**(1), 33–44 (2006)

36. Bracciali, A., et al.: The KGP model of agency for global computing: computational model and prototype implementation. In: Priami, C., Quaglia, P. (eds.) GC 2004. LNCS, vol. 3267, pp. 340–367. Springer, Heidelberg (2005)

37. Gebser, M., Grote, T., Kaminski, R., Schaub, T.: Reactive answer set programming. In: Delgrande, J.P., Faber, W. (eds.) LPNMR 2011. LNCS, vol. 6645, pp. 54–66. Springer, Heidelberg (2011)

38. Brewka, G., Delgrande, J.P., Romero, J., Schaub, T.: asprin: customizing answer set preferences without a headache. In Bonet, B., Koenig, S. (eds.) Proceedings of the Twenty-Ninth AAAI Conference on Artificial Intelligence, pp. 1467–1474. AAAI Press (2015)

39. Bienvenu, M., Lang, J., Wilson, N.: From preference logics to preference languages, and back. In: Proceedings of the Twelfth International Conference on the Principles of Knowledge Represent and Reasoning (KR 2010), pp. 414–424 (2010)

40. Brewka, G., Niemelä, I., Truszczyński, M.: Preferences and nonmonotonic reasoning. AI Mag. 29(4), 69–78 (2008)

41. Delgrande, J., Schaub, T., Tompits, H., Wang, K.: A classification and survey of preference handling approaches in nonmonotonic reasoning. Comput. Intell. 20(12), 308–334 (2004)

42. Costantini, S., Formisano, A., Petturiti, D.: Extending and implementing RASP. Fundamenta Informaticae 105(1–2), 1–33 (2010)

43. Costantini, S., Formisano, A.: Modeling preferences and conditional preferences on resource consumption and production in ASP. J. Algorithms Cogn. Inform. Logic 64(1), 3–15 (2009)

44. Costantini, S., Tocchio, A.: About declarative semantics of logic-based agent languages. In: Baldoni, M., Endriss, U., Omicini, A., Torroni, P. (eds.) DALT 2005. LNCS (LNAI), vol. 3904, pp. 106–123. Springer, Heidelberg (2006)

45. Gelfond, M., Lifschitz, V.: Classical negation in logic programs and disjunctive databases. New Gener. Comput. 9, 365–385 (1991)

46. Niemelä, I.: Logic programs with stable model semantics as a constraint programming paradigm. Ann. Math. Artif. Intell. 25(3–4), 241–273 (1999)

47. Marek, V.W., Truszczyński, M.: Stable logic programming - an alternative logic programming paradigm. In: Apt, K.R., Marek, V.W., Truszczynski, M., Warren, D.S. (eds.) Logic Programming Paradigm, pp. 375–398. Springer, New York (1999)

48. Costantini, S., Formisano, A., Petturiti, D.: Extending and implementing RASP. Fundam. Inform. 105(1–2), 1–33 (2010)

49. Web-references: Some ASP solvers Clasp: potassco.sourceforge.net; Cmodels: www.cs.utexas.edu/users/tag/cmodels; DLV: www.dbai.tuwien.ac.at/proj/dlv; Smodels: www.tcs.hut.fi/Software/smodels

50. Calimeri, F., Ianni, G., Krennwallner, T., Ricca, F.: The answer set programming competition. AI Mag. 33(4), 114–118 (2012)

51. Dantsin, E., Eiter, T., Gottlob, G., Voronkov, A.: Complexity and expressive power of logic programming. ACM Comput. Surv. 33(3), 374–425 (2001)

52. Formisano, A., Petturiti, D.: Raspberry: an implementation of RASP (2010). http://www.dmi.unipg.it/~formis/raspberry/

53. Heintz, F., Kvarnström, J., Doherty, P.: Bridging the sense-reasoning gap: Dyknow - stream-based middleware for knowledge processing. Adv. Eng. Inform. 24(1), 14–26 (2010)

54. Costantini, S., De Gasperis, G.: Runtime self-checking via temporal (meta-)axioms for assurance of logical agent systems. In: Bulling, N., van der Hoek, W. (eds.) Proceedings of LAMAS 2014, 7th Workshop on Logical Aspects of Multi-Agent Systems, held at AAMAS 2014, pp. 241–255 (2014). Also in: Proceedings of the 29th Italian Conference on Computational Logic. CEUR Workshop Proceedings 1195

55. Costantini, S.: Knowledge acquisition via non-monotonic reasoning in distributed heterogeneous environments. In: Calimeri, F., Ianni, G., Truszczynski, M. (eds.) LPNMR 2015. LNCS, vol. 9345, pp. 228–241. Springer, Heidelberg (2015)

56. Costantini, S., Gasperis, G.D.: Exchanging data and ontological definitions in multi-agent-contexts systems. In: Paschke, A., Fodor, P., Giurca, A., Kliegr, T. (eds.) RuleMLChallenge track, Proceedings. CEUR Workshop Proceedings, CEUR-WS.org (2015)
57. Montali, M., Calvanese, D., De Giacomo, G.: Specification and verification of commitment-regulated data-aware multiagent systems. In: Proceedings of AAMAS 2014 (2014)

A Testbed for Agent Oriented Smart Grid Implementation

Jorge J. Gomez-Sanz[1]([⊠]), Nuria Cuartero-Soler[1],
and Sandra Garcia-Rodriguez[2]

[1] Universidad Complutense de Madrid, Madrid, Spain
{jjgomez,ncuarter}@ucm.es
[2] CEA Saclay, DRT/DM2I/LADIS, 91191 Gif-sur-Yvette Cedex, France
sandra.garciarodriguez@cea.fr

Abstract. The aim of this paper is to present a platform for helping agent researchers to become familiar with Smart Grids. Agent technology has been recognised as one of the enablers for Smart Grids. A Smart Grid intends to make an advanced use of available metering and generation capabilities in order to use more efficiently the electricity. Contributions of agent resealrchers to this domain are still reduced and this may be because of the highly specialised knowledge that is required to run current Smart Grid simulators and the cost of commercial ones. This paper aims to share the experience acquired during a project where distributed control approaches were devised using open source solutions. An important result is a simulator for Smart Grids that facilitates the research of how agents can operate such grids. This paper introduces an example case study and discusses how agents can be applied in these situations.

1 Introduction

In the last few years, power grids have gone through several changes to make them work as "Smart Grids". For instance, several elements have been added such as sensors and meters, network nodes with computation capabilities, switches or actuators, and so on. Together, they allow the grid setup to be highly configurable [8].

Traditionally, the term "electrical grid" is assigned to the interconnected energy transmission system. However, the concept "Smart Grid" has been more oriented to the entire electrical system including generation, transmission and distribution. Regarding distribution, several efforts target the increase of manageability and efficiency by dividing the smart distribution grid into sub-systems. Such sub-systems are called "Microgrids" and consist of energy consumers and producers at a small scale that are able to manage themselves [19]. Inside Microgrids, it is usual to find a number of Distributed Energy Resources (DERs), such as solar power plants or wind generators. Examples for Microgrids may be, for instance, villages, industry sites, or a university campus. Furthermore, a Microgrid can either be connected to the backbone grid, to other Microgrids, or it can run in island mode. Moreover, since the distribution system is considered as the largest and most complex part of the entire electrical system [10], most literature is focused on Smart Grids located at this level.

© Springer International Publishing Switzerland 2015
M. Baldoni et al. (Eds.): EMAS 2015, LNAI 9318, pp. 92–108, 2015.
DOI: 10.1007/978-3-319-26184-3_6

Conventional power grid control is usually done in an automated and centralised manner, perhaps with some human-in-the-loop operations. There are security concerns that are implemented right at the transformation centres before achieving the customers location. Power grids processing power is usually located into SCADA (Supervisory Control And Data Acquisition) systems, which are centralised ones gathering information from connected sensors and, sometimes, issuing orders. Besides, power grids are not flexible enough to support future demands from customers. A customer may install one day a photovoltaic panel to address new needs. Such operation is inexpensive from the customer's point of view but adds instability to the power grid. Therefore, all kW produced needs to be consumed by someone or something. Having a thousand customers doing something like this means trouble in a conventional power grid. Power which is not consumed by anyone has to be dissipated by some specialised and expensive equipment. If the operational parameters of those equipments are exceeded, surely the safety mechanisms may cut down parts of the grid to protect them from the extra surge. All this could be avoided if additional measurement and control elements were added, which is what Smart Grids intend.

Rather creating isolated control artifacts for groups of Microgrids, or DERs inside them, it is more convenient to consider the Microgrid as a collection of interested parties that perform control functions to accommodate some higher level goal. The benefit comes mainly from the scalability of the resulting system (it can grow to have more control/DER elements) and the fault tolerance (parts can fall into island/disconnected mode in a controlled way). In order to operate with a Smart Grid, an advanced metering infrastructure is needed. Metering is made through devices which are in fact ARM-based computers, and they may even run Linux distributions. Hence, there is an important amount of new hosting devices where new information processing capabilities are available.

An agent researcher will recognise this setup as one scenario where agent technology, inherently distributed and capable of decentralised control, may be a key one [9]. Among current studies, it is appropriate to cite the two made by the IEEE Power and Energy Society Multi-Agent Systems Working Group (MASWG). The MASWG issued two reports [11,12] using as main information sources FIPA standards and frequently cited development tools. They discuss how this technology could change the way of designing power grid control. Though helpful, these reports, and other existing ones, are not using the agent technology to its full extent. As defended in [9], one of the key features of agent technology is its capability to provide a decentralised control by means of a peer-to-peer coordination, which is opposite to the client-server paradigm currently applied through SCADA systems. Another analysis [17] identifies areas where agent-related research could be applied, such as self-healing networks or virtual power plants, and points out the need of simulation tools to show stakeholders the benefits of agent oriented solutions.

Agent researchers have an opportunity to contribute to this area more intensively. It is necessary to overcome the lack of tools for performing actual research without prior knowledge of how a power grid works. Authors usually devise their own simulators, most using MatLab or SimuLink, and find ways to feed that data to the agents [14]. Others implement custom solutions based on their knowledge of how grid works [3]. Both requires extensive knowledge to define and reproduce the Microgrid behaviour in a reliable way. If a simpler, yet correct, way of defining and running the Microgrid was possible, more agent researchers would be able to contribute to this problem domain.

Another issue is the nature of the simulation. Most existing Microgrid simulation tools are discrete event ones where weeks of data can be generated in a few real time minutes. To evaluate or experiment with an agent oriented control system for the Microgrid, it necessarily needs to be included into the simulation loop. This requirement is a major drawback to reuse existing technologies for agent development, such as JADE or Jack, which run their own control threads. Ideally, if the simulator could be conceived also as an emulator of the Microgrid, integration of both systems could be easier. A prototyping development would start by connecting an external process, implemented with those technologies, with the Microgrid simulator. The process would feed from data from the simulator and issue orders in real time. To achieve this, the simulator must be able to perform real time simulation, i.e., to run the simulation loop using real time units. Real time simulation is in fact useful when the situation requires a software-in-the-loop or a hardware-in-the-loop approach. Those situations have in common that there is an external element interacting with the simulation, being it hardware or software [4].

The contribution of this paper is a testbed, called *SGSimulator*, that reduces the agent researchers' effort in defining and experimenting with Microgrid control while using an industrial grade simulation tool. This work bases on GridLAB-D [6], which is wide spread and extensively tested power grid simulation tool. This tool cannot act as a Microgrid emulator, though. *SGSimulator* provides with this aditional service and enables a researcher connects agents to the Microgrid emulation. The analysis and design of the MAS solution for operating the Microgrid will be aided by the *SGSimulator* in several ways. Agent researchers can run fast or slow experiments, and visually check the effect of orders in the Microgrid. The Microgrid can still be simulated separatedly in a discrete event simulation manner. It also can become an emulation of the Microgrid that the agents can connect to anytime. The testbed was developed during the MIRED-CON project, which pursued an intelligent decentralised control for Microgrids.

The testbed is developed using plain Java and RMI as technology. Hence, it ought to be compatible with different agent solutions as long as they allow referring to external Java Objects. The proof of concept is made with INGE-NIAS methodology [15] and JADE based agents. It shows how to define agents and connect them to the simulation platform. The testbed comes with a few pre-defined Microgrids, but the notation is friendly enough to ensure that new ones can be created. The case of study introduced in this paper defines a simple MAS that is connected to controllable elements in a Microgrid. The case study identifies some coordination problems and control issues and suggests how to deal with them. In particular, it shows how bad control coding can lead to undesirable cycles in the operation of Microgrid storage elements; and the necessity of coordinating the micro-generation of electricity so as not to inject current in the substation, which may lead to instability of the main grid. Links to the software are provided so that other researchers can download the framework and work out possible solutions to the scenarios.

The paper is organised as follows. First, Sect. 2 introduces the Smart and Micro-grids and how agents are supposed to operate within it. Section 3 explains the test-bed elements and how agents are expected to interact with them. Section 4 presents the case study with INGENIAS and shows some snapshots of the tool. The case study uses a simple Microgrid operated by agents that intend to reduce the billing costs and avoid producing more energy than required. Other similar frameworks are discussed into Sect. 5.

2   Agents in a Microgrid

This paper assumes a specific way of modeling the Microgrid and agents within. In a Microgrid, see Fig. 1, there are elements producing energy (Distributed Energy Resources or DER from now on), elements consuming this energy (loads from now on), power lines transporting the energy, transformation centres (TC from now on) isolating low voltage sections from medium/high voltage sections, and metering infrastructure or Smart Meters (SM from now on). There are also batteries, but they can act either as loads (while charging) or as DERs (while discharging). Microgrids can be connected to a main power line through a substation. When the energy generated inside the Microgrid is not enough to supply the consumption, the lack of energy is demanded from the power line through this substation. Readers should be aware that no one "demands" energy from the power line. There is no actual request. It just happens that energy is borrowed from the closer energy source.

Communication can be assumed to be widely available, though not always reliable. When there is no mobile networks, such as GPRS, Power Line Communication (PLC) can be an option. Hence, TCP/IP may be used just anywhere and be assumed to be sufficiently fast.

Agents can be hosted in any of the previous elements that is capable of having processing and has communication capabilities. Both conditions are met more easily in the SMs, which are expected to be deployed almost anywhere in a Smart Grid. If possible, a SM is needed per DER to measure how much power is consumed (a photovoltaic panel usually comes with a battery, so it consumes too) or produced; a SM per load (loads tend to be buildings); and one SM per TC. A TC may act as hub for the SMs underneath so that its SM may be more complex than others.

It can be assumed that, be it inside SM or be it inside some other processing capable element of the abovementioned elements, the agents can be hosted anywhere in the Microgrid and communicate with each other anytime. Despite this, disconnections are possible. Elements in the Microgrid may not provide measurements or react to orders because they maybe disconnected. A defect of the simulator in this version is that this disconnection does not affect inter-agent communication, though.

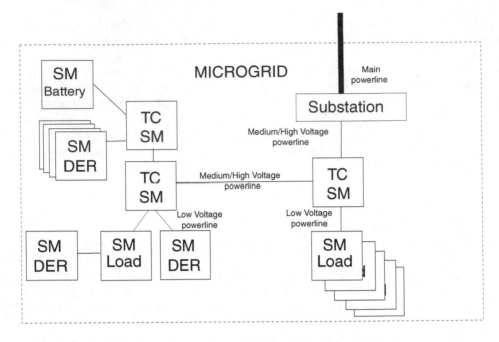

Fig. 1. Elements in a microgrid

What agents can do inside the Microgrid is a subject of further discussion. Reports from the MASWG [11,12] point out possible uses. Protection is not one of them. For instance, if it is not safe to operate a DER, the agent would not be in charge of forbidding its use, but a lower level hardware implemented mechanism. It seems that a main function of agents would be defining/choosing the strategy of the Microgrid and delivering orders accordingly. The term "strategy" has been chosen on purpose since agent actions have to fit into a medium/long term scenario. The electricity consumed everywhere comes from markets where energy production quotas are bought and sold. Selling the excess of energy production can be an alternative which requires scheduling in advance the operation of DERs. Sometimes, it may be cheaper to buy the energy than producing it, e.g. because the fuel used by a generator is more expensive. To add more complexity, energy production is subject of government regulations. For instance, in the case of Spanish regulations, a producer must be registered within a listing of producers and must ensure some operational parameters. When a Microgrid delivers energy when it is not supposed to, or delivers too much energy, a fine is issued. The reason is to harmonize the production with the consumption.

Agents can also take decisions about which DER ought to produce the required energy at a given moment. To satisfy the demand of a load, it is more efficient to increase the production of the closer DERs. The power line and TCs interconnecting the DER to the load are not one hundred percent efficient. There is some amount of energy which is lost during its distribution. The longer the distance, the higher the loss.

3   The Agent Testbed

The testbed is made by starting from a core that delivers the Microgrid simulation/emulation service. This service is based on GridLAB-D [6], an agent based Microgrid simulator that performs a static analysis of the grid. It focuses on the stable states a power grid achieves. It does not address problems with harmonics or the intermediate states that arise, for instance, when a new element starts producing energy. As a consequence, it is fast. GridLAB-D runs a discrete event agent based simulation to obtain, in a few minutes, weeks of simulation data.

In this contribution, and through some Java layers, the GridLAB-D was transformed into a real time simulation platform. This platform allows to run an emulated Microgrid together with the associated agents which will deliver orders and get results. Time can be accelerated, but unless agents are involved in the simulation cycle, the result may not be meaningful.

The interest of the real time version is the possibility of using the simulator as a Smart Grid emulator. With this transformation, the agent based simulator GridLAB-D can be used to experiment with agents working in real time with the system in a "software-in-the-loop" manner. Agents communicate with GridLAB-D through some interfaces that allow to send orders or to poll about the current state. Notification services are possible, but they are not implemented by default. In an event driven solution, however, agents would have to strictly stick to the simulation cycle and perform calculations just as the simulator progresses.

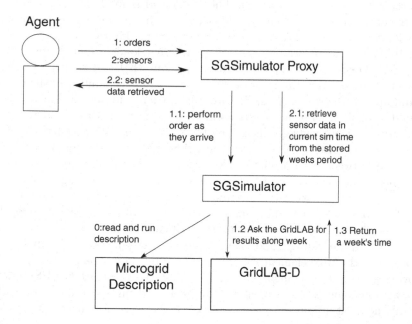

Fig. 2. Collaboration diagram showing how agents send orders and receive data from the simulator

This new system is called *Smart Grid Simulator* (SGSimulator from now on) whose behaviour is briefly described in Fig. 2. The agent sends orders to the simulator through a proxy which uses RMI to deliver orders to the simulator. The reason for this is to allow each agent to be hosted in a different machine and provide a suitable entry point so that this simulator can be used by other agent platforms. Integrating the proxy will be enough to start delivering orders and polling about the current status.

The orders are processed as they arrive to the emulator. There is a possible delay since the order is delivered until the order is processed, just as in real systems. GridLAB-D executes the orders as delivered by the SGSimulator and returns a sufficiently large set of measurements. This set becomes a buffer which is then used to deliver measurements in real time to the agent until the buffer is empty or a new order arrives or an event happens. Such cases require a new run of GridLAB-D to obtain the data for the new configuration.

In the MIRED-CON project, it was intended that the conditions met by the agents were as close as possible to the real Microgrid. From this perspective, it was necessary to simulate delays in the order processing, missing or ignored orders, and orders which do not produce the expected results in time.

4   Case Study with INGENIAS

Figure 3 introduces the case study Smart Grid. Power lines transport 3 phased AC electricity along the case study. The Microgrid is made of seven buildings. Each one of them consumes energy according to a predetermined pattern, which will be explained later on. All PV panels are the same kind with a max through-put of 10kW. Buildings are represented by different loads, ranging from 5000 W to 6000W. The single battery is a Lithium-ion one that can deliver as much as 30kW and store 60kWh. Inverters of the battery are not included in the description and are added by default in the produced Microgrid description.

Buildings and other elements are connected to transformers which are hosted into transformation centres. There are three transformation centres and one substation. The substation connects the Microgrid with the main power line. Connection between transformation centres is made through medium voltage power lines. Downstream the transformation centres, lower voltage is used. The existence of transformation centres matters because if one PV panel produces energy for a building situated into another different transformation centre, there will be energy transport loses due to the transformation process (from lower voltage, to medium voltage, and then to lower voltage) and the implicit power line loses. Controllable elements in the grid will be the battery, *battery 31*, and photovoltaic panels, e.g. *Solar 11* or *Solar 312*. If the Smart Grid Simulation is run without agents, no element will be switched on and only loads will be taken into account. Figure 4 presents this particular case, showing all controllable elements as powered off.

Load and DER performance is coded as a CSV file and can be understood as a scenario description. The scenario is shown in Table 1. Each building or

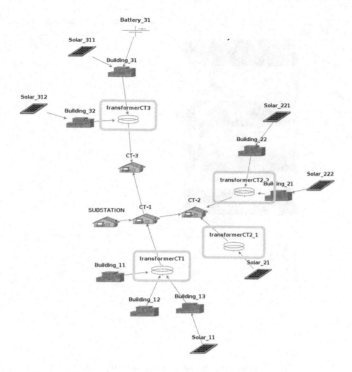

Fig. 3. Microgrid representation using SGSimulator grid rendering tool

DER generator is associated to a maximum consumption or generation output. The profile from Table 1 declares the amount of load or generation that will take part at the particular time of the day identified in the first column. As expected, maximum PV generation will take place starting at 12:00 and ending at 18:00. Wind generators will have maximum performance during the night, mainly. Load will be maximum during working hours.

The Microgrid definition as well as the generation scenario is processed by SGSimulator to generate a detailed GridLAB-D definition and to start running in emulation mode. Figure 3 shows the previous configuration in execution. At the left side, there is a depiction of the abovementioned Smart Grid. The status of each controllable element is shown in the middle of the screen. All of them are off in Fig. 4. Also, disconnect actions are available in the middle column. The weather is measured at the bottom right of the figure. Wind and sun are changing along the day according to a predefined profile. To simplify the problem, the chart represents which amount of the expected power is being generated. The information is taken from the profile introduced in Table 1. When the sun is at 25 %, it means photovoltaic panels (PV from now on) produce 25 % of their maximum throughput. The bottom right part of the figure shows a panel from which different parts of the Smart Grid can be disconnected. This feature is used to simulate the disconnection of elements. Finally, the top right of the figure shows a chart with the status of the Smart Grid. Meaningful data obtained from

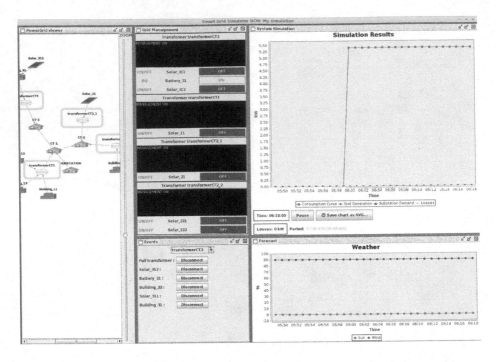

Fig. 4. Smart grid simulator dash control without agents

the system is the amount of consumed power in the grid (consumption curve), power generated within the grid (grid generation curve), the amount of power demanded from the main power line (substation demand), and losses due to the distribution of the energy (losses curve).

The default scenario runs with a simulation cycle at one minute per second. Each second in real time is equivalent to almost one minute in simulated time. This configuration was chosen to facilitate observing the effect of orders. Agents can get in and out anytime. As a proof of concept, the agents from Fig. 5 are instantiated. There are agents in charge of PV panels and agents responsible of batteries. They pursue the goal of reducing the total bill the Microgrid owner pays. Those agents are directly connected to specific controllable devices, but could be hosted as well in their corresponding transformation centres. Agents access to the controlled devices through a *SMClient* instance, which is automatically created and connected to the Smart Grid emulation. The *SMClient* is translated as set of Java classes accessible by agents playing the role *TCManager*. The role *TCManager*, or *Tranformation Centre Manager*, aims to reduce the power grid consumption and reduce the monthly expenses.

The instantiation of the agents is done in two different deployments, according to Fig. 6. The first deployment, named *sample case*, involves two agents: one of the PV panel *Solar 11* and another for *Battery 31*. The second deployment, named *full case*, launches one agent per PV panel and one agent per battery.

Table 1. Scenario description with per hour percentage over the maximum grid load and maximum PV/Wind throughput

#Time	Load	Sun	Wind
00:00:00	15	0	90
01:00:00	15	0	90
02:00:00	15	0	90
03:00:00	15	0	90
04:00:00	15	0	90
05:00:00	15	0	90
06:00:00	15	0	90
07:00:00	30	10	80
08:00:00	50	30	70
09:00:00	50	60	50
10:00:00	90	60	50
11:00:00	90	60	0
12:00:00	90	95	0
13:00:00	90	95	0
14:00:00	90	60	0
15:00:00	90	95	0
16:00:00	50	95	50
17:00:00	50	95	50
18:00:00	60	95	90
19:00:00	60	70	90
20:00:00	50	30	50
21:00:00	50	0	50
22:00:00	50	0	90
23:00:00	50	0	90

As a result, this second deployment launches seven agent instances, whereas the first launched only two. Each *PV controller* instance is initialized with a reference to the controlled device, which is defined in a separated diagram.

The battery controller agent runs a task to check the status of the battery and operate it. This task is executed repeatedly each 9 seconds, which are 6 min in simulated time approximately. Rather than having a fine grain decomposition of this task, for this paper it was decided to just put together the pieces into a single task. This task uses the *SMClient* to perform status queries to the Microgrid and to send orders to the battery. The orders in this case is to charge the battery until 10kWh are stored and then deliver them to the grid. Nothing prevents that this task sends orders to other elements or that the agent gains global knowledge of the whole simulator rather than its closest scope. Whether the simulation works

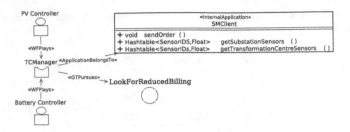

Fig. 5. Agents and roles in the system

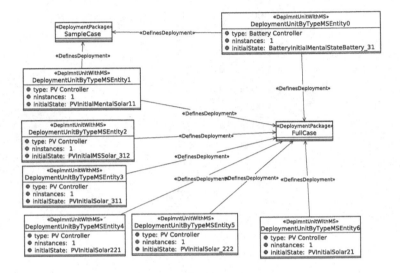

Fig. 6. Agents and roles in the system

with total or partial information, and total or partial controlling capabilities is a decision left to the developer.

Similarly, the PV control agent, see Fig. 8, checks the PV Panels and switch them on each 3 s in real time, which are approximately 2 min in simulated time. In the case of PV panels, an additional piece of information, *associated unit*, informs the task which is the ID of the controlled device. The entity *associated unit* is assigned a specific value during the deployment, as explained in the Fig. 6.

The result of the two defined deployments is introduced in Figs. 9 and 10. The naive definition of the behaviour of the agents points at the need of coordination between them and a better control of the battery. Both figures include timing information to tell the developer when, in simulated time, the order was received, the first part of the timestamp, and when it was executed, the second part of the timestamp. This information is also available in CSV form for careful inspection after each system run. Information is referred to the sensors hosted at the substation point. CSV information include the measured energy; the power

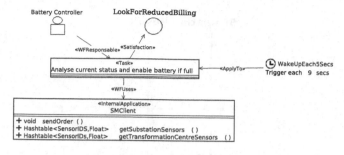

Fig. 7. Controlling the battery

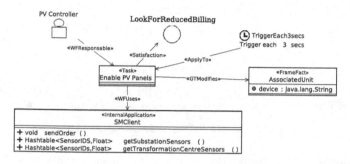

Fig. 8. Controlling the PV panels

demand; the voltage in phases A, B, and C; the current (real and imaginary) at phases A,B, and C; power peaks; reactive power; and orders issued at the inspected timestamp.

Figure 9 shows a cycle problem due to the definition of the battery charge cycle. The task is not taking into account the need of perform full charge/discharge cycles, if possible. Also, it is not looking for periods where the energy is more expensive. As a result, Fig. 9 starts demanding energy from the substation at 8:30AM, 8:41AM, and 8:54AM to charge the battery. The energy is used to reduce the load curve which is stable at 17.5kW. The grid generation capabilities oscillates too with the battery. When the battery is producing electricity, there is a huge reduction of the substation demand. The reason is that the battery is not demanding power and it is also returning the stored energy.

Figure 10 situation is worse from the billing perspective. Besides the cycle problem which already existed in the two agent simulation case, there is also an excess of production. In the deployment *full case*, all PV panels are activated. As a result, there is more electricity than it is consumed. The excess is injected into the main power line, up to 30kW. This adds instability to the main grid unless the transport operator is aware of the Microgrid production capability. The case illustrates well one of the technical issues with renewall energy where a big number of individuals decide to connect to the grid PV panels. Again, coordination between the *PV controller* agents would be needed to switch off from the grid PV panels when the generation does not match the demand.

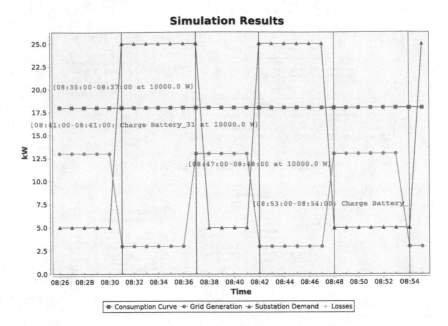

Fig. 9. Evolution of the microgrid with deployment *Sample case*. Right hand side of the text of each order is aligned with a vertical line showing when the order was executed.

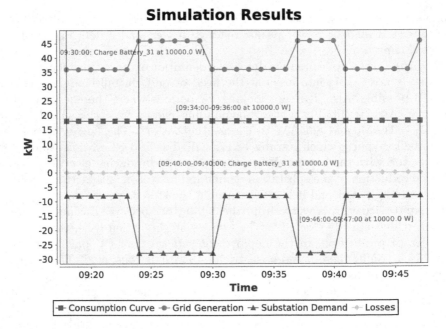

Fig. 10. Evolution of the microgrid with deployment *Full case*. Right hand side of the text of each order is aligned with a vertical line showing when the order was executed.

Also to coordinate with the *battery controller* agents when the demand from the buildings require the stored energy.

This case study stops here because it was not the purpose to find a solution, but to show the problems and the capability of the *SGSimulator* to capture them. At this point, agent research is needed to address the previous issues. Adding communications to the different agents ought to be a first step. According to Sect. 2, it can be assumed there are TCP/IP communications across the Microgrid. Possibilities include adding awareness to *PV controllers* agents so that they recognise each other in the Microgrid and find emergent patterns of interaction adequate to the problem. Interaction with battery agents is necessary too so as not to inject the excess of power at the substation. It could be the case that the researcher is interested in handling that excess and reselling it to others. The definition of markets is feasible from this point, as well as the coordination of electricity production across several Microgrids, as the Virtual Power Plant concept proposes.

Eventhough INGENIAS was used, all the interaction with *SGSimulator* was used with RMI clients. The software demoing SGSimulator launches the basic RMI server and includes the API for developing alternative clients. The demonstration is GPL v3 software and can be downloaded from GitHub in https://github.com/escalope/sgsim-ingenias. The real time simulator is published at http://sgsimulator.sf.net.

5   Related Work

The need of a testbed for agents in Smart Grids has not been strongly defended in the literature. Most published multi-Agent based systems have been produced without such testbeds.

For instance, Oyarzabal et al. [14] addresses a Microgrid management system built using a JADE based system. Agents in the experiments took data from real hardware and measurements were taken each 20 seconds. The contribution of this paper would have facilitated earlier experimentation in cases like this. Besides, it is cheaper to run a simulator than creating a real Microgrid. It is less reliable too. A working solution in the simulator may not work in a real setup. However, adapting a working solution surely will take less effort than developing everything from scratch in the real scenario. Other researchers created their own simulator, for instance, with MatLAB. This is the case of IDAPS [16].

The alternative for most agent researchers is reusing existing simulators. There are several works proposing powergrid simulators, such as GridLAB-D [6] which is the one used in this contribution. The two main open source ones are GridLAB-D and OpenDSS [7]. The later considers the transitory analysis, which may enable the developer to study the effect of switching on elements, like engines. There is the DSSIM-PC which is an initiative to make OpenDSS a non-deterministic real time simulator [13].

Literature cites other real time simulators, like eMEGAsim [5] and GridSim [1]. None of them could be found to deliver open source software and enable a similar experimentation as the one done in this contribution. The eMEGAsim uses

FPGAS and multiple CPUs to run Simulink instances and provide almost real time data of systems. Its goal is not to reproduce control elements but to address hardware-in-the-loop experiments. Simulated elements are run together with real ones. The control devices are then embedded inside the simulated elements rather than decoupled as in this contribution. GridSim [1] is a complete tool made of three parts: a framework for collecting data (GridStat), a framework for simulating the communication network (GridNet), a cloud extension (GridCloud), and the powergrid itself (GridSim). It considers too the transitory states of the system through a modified version of an commercial product and combining the generated output in a similar way as SGSimulator does. It is not evident from the documentation if distributed control is allowed. The paper cites explicitly a *control center* which is where all data from current SCADAS is stored. On the other hand, the GridSim site suggests that there is a power control software inside each substation in the simulated system. In any case, it is not considered control at the DER or transformation centre level, or event at a lower scale, as shown in the case study of this contribution. This may allow a higher capability of SGSimulator for a finer grain decentralisation.

Not all works remark what kind of simulation is used, though. The work [18] shows a project for a decentralized control system where consumer energy demands aligns with the actual production. The way the grid is simulated is not explained. The evaluation framework, from [2], points out at issues in Smart Grids and how MAS could deal with them. Several MAS related works in the literature are cited and evaluated according to this evaluation framework. The underlying simulation framework is not considered in most cases, focusing on the features each MAS implements. Only Matlab/Simulink is cited in the case of IDAPS work. Nevertheless, prospective works, like [17], remark the importance of having simulation systems that can accurately represent both the grid and the reaction of consumers.

6   Conclusions

The paper has introduced some basic concepts about the role of agents in the control of Microgrids. In particular, it has discussed where agents can be hosted and what they are expected to do. In this paper, agents are expected to hosted by Smart Meters which are essential elements in Smart Grids. The paper has also introduced the Smart Grid Simulator and how agents can be connected to it. As a proof of concept, INGENIAS methodology and JADE agents have been used to model and run the agents used in the simulation. Other agent platforms and methodologies could be applied provided they integrate with RMI technology. The case of study is a simple one whose purpose is twofold: to show there are control problems that could be solved using agent technology; and also provide software so that other researchers can experiment with it and compare the performance of proposed solutions. Disconnection issues were not studied, but they are very relevant to justify the use of agent technology. A distributed decentralized MAS will be less sensible to disconnection issues. Disconnected parts may still become stable islands where production of electricity still matches the demand.

Acknowledgement. This work has been co-funded by the project MIRED-CON IPT-2012-0611-120000, supported by Spanish Ministry for Economy and Competitiveness, and Fondo Europeo de Desarrollo Regional (FEDER). It also has been supported by the Programa de Creación y Consolidación de Grupos de Investigación UCM-Banco Santander, call GR3/14, for the group number 921354 (GRASIA group).

References

1. Anderson, D., Zhao, C., Hauser, C.H., Venkatasubramanian, V., Bakken, D.E., Bose, A.: Intelligent design real-time simulation for smart grid control and communications design. IEEE Power Energy Mag. **10**(1), 49–57 (2012)
2. Basso, G., Gaud, N., Gechter, F., Hilaire, V., Lauri, F.: A framework for qualifying and evaluating smart grids approaches: focus on multi-agent technologies. Smart Grid Renew. energy **4**(04), 333 (2013)
3. Basso, G., Hilaire, V., Lauri, F., Roche, R., Cossentino, M.: A MAS-based simulator for the prototyping of smart grids. In: 9th European Workshop on Multiagent Systems (EUMAS11), November 2011
4. Bélanger, J., Venne, P., Paquin, J.N.: The what, where and why of real-time simulation (2010). http://www.opal-rt.com/technical-document/what-where-and-why-real-time-simulation
5. Bélanger, J., Lapointe, V., Dufour, C., Schoen, L.: eMEGAsim: an open high-performance distributed real-time power grid simulator. architecture and specification. In: Proceedings of the International Conference on Power Systems (ICPS 2007), pp. 12–24 (2007)
6. Chassin, D.P., Fuller, J.C., Djilali, N.: Gridlab-d: An agent-based simulation framework for smart grids. J. Appl. Math. **2014**, 12 (2014). doi:10.1155/2014/492320
7. Dugan, R.: Opendss, introductory training, level 1. Electric Power Research Institute, Palo Alto, California (2009)
8. Farhangi, H.: The path of the smart grid. IEEE Power Energy Mag. **8**(1), 18–28 (2010)
9. Gomez-Sanz, J.J., Garcia-Rodriguez, S., Cuartero-Soler, N., Hernandez-Callejo, L.: Reviewing microgrids from a multi-agent systems perspective. Energies **7**(5), 3355–3382 (2014)
10. Hassan, R., Radman, G.: Survey on smart grid. In: Proceedings of the IEEE SoutheastCon 2010 (SoutheastCon), pp. 210–213. IEEE, March 2010
11. McArthur, S.D.J., Davidson, E.M., Catterson, V.M., Dimeas, A.L., Hatziargyriou, N.D., Ponci, F., Funabashi, T.: Multi-agent systems for power engineering applications - part i: concepts, approaches, and technical challenges. IEEE Trans. Power Syst. **22**(4), 1743–1752 (2007)
12. McArthur, S.D.J., Davidson, E.M., Catterson, V.M., Dimeas, A.L., Hatziargyriou, N.D., Ponci, F., Funabashi, T.: Multi-agent systems for power engineering applications - part ii: technologies, standards, and tools for building multi-agent systems. IEEE Trans. Power Syst. **22**(4), 1753–1759 (2007)
13. Montenegro, D., Hernandez, M., Ramos, G.A.: Real time opendss framework for distribution systems simulation and analysis. In: Transmission and Distribution: Latin America Conference and Exposition (T D-LA), 2012 Sixth IEEE/PES, pp. 1–5, September 2012

14. Oyarzabal, J., Jimeno, J., Ruela, J., Engler, A., Hardt, C.: Agent based micro grid management system. In: 2005 International Conference on Future Power Systems, p. 6, November 2005
15. Pavón, J., Gómez-Sanz, J.J.: Agent oriented software engineering with INGENIAS. In: Mařík, V., Müller, J.P., Pěchouček, M. (eds.) CEEMAS 2003. LNCS (LNAI), vol. 2691, pp. 394–403. Springer, Heidelberg (2003)
16. Pipattanasomporn, M., Feroze, H., Rahman. S.: Multi-agent systems in a distributed smart grid: Design and implementation. In: Power Systems Conference and Exposition. PSCE '09. IEEE/PES, pp. 1–8 (2009)
17. Ramchurn, S.D., Vytelingum, P., Rogers, A., Jennings, N.R.: Putting the 'smarts' into the smart grid: a grand challenge for artificial intelligence. Commun. ACM **55**(4), 86–97 (2012)
18. Ramchurn, S.D., Vytelingum, P., Rogers, A., Jennings, N.: Agent-based control for decentralised demand side management in the smart grid. In: The 10th International Conference on Autonomous Agents and Multiagent Systems, AAMAS '11, vol. 1, pp. 5–12, Richland, SC. International Foundation for Autonomous Agents and Multiagent Systems (2011)
19. Sobe, A., Elmenreich, W.: Smart microgrids: Overview and outlook. CoRR, abs/1304.3944 (2013)

Quantitative Analysis of Multiagent Systems Through Statistical Model Checking

Benjamin Herd[(✉)], Simon Miles, Peter McBurney, and Michael Luck

Department of Informatics, King's College London, London, UK
{benjamin.c.herd,simon.miles,peter.mcburney,michael.luck}@kcl.ac.uk

Abstract. Due to their immense complexity, large-scale multiagent systems are often unamenable to exhaustive formal verification. Statistical approaches that focus on the verification of individual traces can provide an interesting alternative. However, due to its focus on finite execution paths, trace-based verification is inherently limited to certain types of correctness properties. We show how, by combining sampling with the idea of trace fragmentation, statistical model checking can be used to answer interesting quantitative correctness properties about multiagent systems on different observational levels. We illustrate the idea with a simple case study from the area of swarm robotics.

Keywords: Verification · Statistical model checking · Multiagent systems · Quantitative analysis

1 Introduction

Due to their distributed nature and their capability to exhibit emergent behaviour, multiagent systems can be hard to engineer and to understand. Similar to other software systems, however, questions of correctness arise and verification plays an important role. Formal verification aims to answer correctness questions in a rigorous and unambiguous way. Temporal logic model checking, for example, aims to find an accurate solution to a given correctness property by exhaustively searching the state space underlying the system under consideration (the *model*) and thus exploring all possible execution paths [1]. This is only possible if the state space of the model is of manageable size. In the presence of non-determinism which may, for example, arise from the different possible interleavings of individual agent actions or from uncertainty w.r.t. the representation of individual agent behaviours, the state space may grow exponentially which renders formal exhaustive verification infeasible for non-trivial systems. This exponential blow-up in the number of states is a well-known problem and commonly referred to as 'state space explosion'. In order to address this issue, a wide range of techniques has been developed. For example, if one can assume that agents are homogeneous, then the symmetry within the system can be exploited to reduce the complexity of verification significantly [5,14–16,26]. Unfortunately, such simplifying assumptions are not always possible.

M. Baldoni et al. (Eds.): EMAS 2015, LNAI 9318, pp. 109–130, 2015.
DOI: 10.1007/978-3-319-26184-3_7

Another interesting alternative way to circumvent combinatorial explosion that works for probabilistic systems is to use a *sampling approach* and employ statistical techniques to obtain approximate verification results. In this case, n finite execution paths or *traces* are sampled from the underlying state space and a property ϕ is checked on each of them. By increasing the number of traces that ϕ is checked on, the probability of ϕ can be estimated to the desired level of precision. Techniques for statistical inference, e.g. *hypothesis testing*, can then be used to determine the significance of the results. Approaches of this kind are summarised under the umbrella of *statistical model checking* [21]. Due to its approximate nature, statistical model checking allows for the verification of large-scale (or even infinite) systems in a timely manner. Traces are typically obtained through *simulation*, either by repeatedly executing an existing real-world system, or by 'unrolling' a formal state transition representation of a system for a certain number of time steps (as in the case of statistical model checking).

Consider, for example, a robot swarm whose efficiency is defined by its emergent collective behaviour. Due to the high level of interconnectivity and the global focus, it is not sufficient to verify individual robots in isolation. On the other hand, aspects such as a heterogeneity, complex environments, or simply an interest in the individual behaviours may also render the application of pure macro-level verification insufficient. In this case, statistical verification represents an interesting alternative. However, because of its focus on finite execution paths, trace-based verification is inherently limited to linear time properties and lacks some of the quantitative capabilities of its non-statistical counterpart [18]. For example, due to the lack of branching information, properties about the transition behaviour are not verifiable in a trace-based context. Furthermore, existing statistical model checking approaches generally ignore the internal structure of the traces which limits their use for the verification of complex multiagent systems.

On the other hand, the statistical approach provides interesting opportunities. In this paper, we present our research efforts with respect to the aforementioned problems by showing how trace-based verification in combination with statistical analysis can be used to answer interesting quantitative correctness properties about multiagent systems. The contributions of this paper can be summarised as follows.

1. In Sect. 5, we introduce a simple specification language for the formulation of properties about multiagent system traces. The language supports the formulation of statements on *different observational levels* as well as the formulation of statements about the *average behaviour* of agents.
2. In Sect. 6, we show that simulation traces of multiagent systems represent *sets of sets of samples* obtained from *different sample spaces*, the choice of which depends on the question to be answered. We formally introduce the notion of *trace fragments* and describe how they correspond with fine-grained correctness properties. We also introduce the idea of *in-trace sampling*.

3. In Sect. 7, we show how a combination of trace fragmentation and statistical verification can be used to estimate *residence probabilities* and *transition probabilities*, and to detect *correlations* between different types of events.

The usefulness of quantitative analysis is illustrated with a small case study from the area of swarm robotics which is introduced in Sect. 4 and further elaborated upon in Sect. 8. We start with some theoretical background in Sect. 2, followed by an overview of related work in Sect. 3.

2   Background

Model checking [6] is a popular verification technique which uses a formal representation $\mathcal{M}$ of the system under consideration (usually a finite state model) together with a specification of the system's desired properties p, typically given in temporal logic. The verification of a system's correctness is then done by checking whether $\mathcal{M}$ satisfies p (formally $\mathcal{M} \models p$) in all possible execution paths. In the case of violation, the model checker can provide a counterexample. In order to deal with inherently random systems, probabilistic extensions to model checking have been developed [19]. Despite impressive advances, exponential growth of the underlying finite-state model (the so-called *state space explosion*) remains a central problem which makes the verification of non-trivial real-world systems difficult or even impossible. In order to tackle this problem, a number of reduction, abstraction, compositional verification, and approximation techniques have been developed.

Whilst the classical, non-probabilistic approach to model checking produces a clear yes/no answer to a given correctness property, quantitative analysis aims to use verification techniques to produce numeric insights into the system under consideration, e.g. *transition probabilities*, *costs* or *rewards*. It is thus not surprising that quantitative analysis forms an important part of probabilistic approaches to model checking. PRISM [20], for example, the most widely used probabilistic model checker, allows for the verification of a wide range of quantitative properties, among them best-case, worst-case, and average-case system characteristics [18]. PRISM uses BDD-based symbolic model checking and allows for the verification of properties formulated in a variety of different logics — among them probabilistic versions of Computation Tree Logic (CTL) and Linear Temporal Logic (LTL), as well as Continuous Stochastic Logic (CSL) — on different types of models, e.g. Discrete-Time (DTMC) and Continuous-Time Markov Chains (CTMC) and Markov Decision Processes (MDP). It is, for example, possible to integrate costs and rewards into the verification process which allows for the formulation of properties about *expected* quantities, e.g. the 'expected time', or the 'expected number of lost messages'. Due to its exhaustive nature, PRISM generally suffers from the same combinatorial issues as other non-probabilistic model checkers. In order to circumvent this problem, it also allows for simulation-based (i.e. trace-based) verification using different statistical model checking approaches [25]. In this context, both conventional probabilistic linear time properties, i.e. $P_{=?}(\phi)$, and reward-based properties, i.e. $R_{=?}(\phi)$, can be answered.

At the current stage, PRISM views traces as monolithic entities and does not exploit their internal structure. This limits its usefulness for the verification of complex multiagent systems, i.e. systems in which there are many, possibly heterogeneous, components acting and interacting with each other.

3   Related Work

Model Checking Multiagent Systems: Since its beginnings around 30 years ago, model checking has gained huge significance in computer science and software engineering in particular and has been successfully applied to many real-world problems. Model checking has also gained increasing importance in the multiagent community and numerous approaches have been presented in literature [8]. In alignment with the classical problems studied in the community, multiagent verification typically focusses on qualitative properties involving notions such as time, knowledge, strategic abilities, permissions, obligations, etc. In order to allow for the verification of larger agent populations, model checking algorithms for temporal-epistemic properties have also been combined successfully with ideas such as bounded model checking [24], partial order reduction [23] and parallelisation [17]. Despite impressive advances, however, verification still remains limited to relatively small populations. A particularly promising approach is based on *parametrised interleaved interpreted systems (PIIS)* [15]. A PIIS models a *template agent* from which all agents in the population are derived (i.e. agents are required to be identical) together with a parameter that denotes the number of agents. Lomuscio and Kouvaros showed that, within a restricted class of PIIS, populations with an unbounded number of agents are verifiable. A related approach based on strong homogeneity assumptions has been presented by Pedersen and Dyrkolbotn [26].

In recent years, probabilistic approaches to model checking and quantitative analysis have also gained increasing importance in the multiagent community. Examples include the verification of systems with uncertainty w.r.t. communication channels and actions [7], qualitative and quantitative analysis of agent populations with uncertain knowledge [28], verification of probabilistic swarm models [14], or automated game analysis [2]. Similar to their non-probabilistic counterparts, these approaches also suffer from the state space explosion and are thus either limited to relatively small systems or dependent upon strong homogeneity or symmetry assumptions which increase their scalability but also limit the range of systems that they are applicable to.

Quantitative Analysis and Trace-Based Verification: Apart from the general work on simulation-based verification using PRISM, quantitative analysis in the context of trace-based verification has been largely neglected to date. An interesting idea has been presented by Sammapun *et al.* [27]. The authors propose a trace decomposition based on the idea of *repetitive behaviour*. The decomposition is performed by means of conditional probabilities. This is then extended with hypothesis testing in order to determine the confidence in the estimation.

As opposed to our approach which assumes the presence of a (possibly large) number of individual sample traces (e.g. obtained through simulation), the work of Sammapun *et al.* is focussed on a pure runtime verification setting in which only one consistently growing trace is available. The decomposition is used to obtain from the runtime trace a number of individual sample traces which are then used to answer conventional probabilistic linear-time properties such as done by PRISM. A related approach has been presented by Finkbeiner *et al.* [9]. They propose an extension of LTL which allows for the formulation of additional statistics over traces, e.g. the *"average number of X"* or *"how often does X happen"*. Similar to the work of Sammapun *et al.*, they focus on a single trace obtained by observing a running system.

4   Motivational Example: Swarm Foraging

In order to motivate the usefulness of quantitative analysis in the context of trace-based verification, we use a small example from the area of swarm robotics. The choice is motivated by the fact that, albeit often conceptually startlingly simple, swarm models exhibit a significant level of complexity which typically prevents them from being amenable to conventional formal verification. On the other hand, they may require a high level of provable correctness. We show how, through statistical model checking in combination with quantitative analysis as described above, interesting properties that reach beyond pure reachability and safety checking can be answered efficiently and with a good level of precision. We focus here on *foraging*, a problem which has been widely discussed in the literature on *cooperative robotics* [4]. Foraging describes the process of a group of robots searching for food items, each of which delivers energy. Individual robots strive to minimise their energy consumption whilst searching in order to maximise the overall energy intake. The study of foraging is important because it represents a general metaphor for a broad range of (often critical) collaborative tasks such as *waste retrieval, harvesting* or *search-and-rescue*.

The model described in this section is based on the work of Liu *et al.* [22]. A certain number of food items are scattered across a two-dimensional space. Robots move through the space and search for food items. Once an item has been detected within the robot's field of vision, it is brought back to the nest and deposited which delivers a certain amount of energy to the robot. Each action that the robot performs also consumes a certain amount of energy. The model is deliberately kept simple. Each robot can be in one of five states: *searching* for food in the space, *grabbing* a food item that has been found, *homing* in order to bring a food item back to the nest, *depositing* a food item in the nest, and *resting* in order to save energy. Transitions between states are probabilistic and either fixed or (which is clearly more realistic) dependent upon the state of the other agents. The overall swarm energy is the sum of the individual energy levels.

Instead of viewing a population of robots as an abstract entity in which agents have a certain probability of finding food (as, for example, done in [14]), we focus here on an agent-based representation of the scenario in which the world that robots inhabit is represented *explicitly*. As opposed to an idealised representation in which, for example, robots are assumed to be entirely symmetric, this allows us to take into account the heterogeneity that arises from the agents' situatedness in a environment in which food is randomly distributed. It is common to model the environment as a two-dimensional grid, in our case a grid of 100×100 cells. Each grid cell can be inhabited by an arbitrary number of agents. Food items are distributed uniformly across the grid. In the current version of the model, there are 1,000 food items distributed across 10,000 grid cells, which amounts to a food density of 10 %. Agents of make 0 are able to detect all food items within a radius of 1, agents of make 1 are able to detect all food items within a radius of 4. The behavioural protocol that each agent follows is shown below.

- If *searching*: look for food. If food has been found, move to the cell and start *grabbing*; otherwise remain *searching*. If no food can be found within T_s time steps, start *homing*.
- If *grabbing*: if the food is still there after T_g time steps, grab it and start *depositing*; otherwise start *homing*.
- If *depositing*: start *resting* after T_d time steps.
- If *homing*: start *resting* after T_h time steps.
- If *resting*: start *searching* after T_r time steps.

It is important to stress that our goal is not to construct an overly realistic model here; the main focus is on illustration and the model is thus kept deliberately simple. Despite its conceptual simplicity, however, the model already exhibits a significant level of complexity which prevents it from being amenable to conventional exhaustive verification. Due to the use of floating point variables for the agents' energy levels, the state space is effectively infinite. Even if the energy level is limited to a comparatively small value (e.g. 1,000), the number of possible states would be beyond what is currently verifiable formally. In order to make things even more interesting, we assume that there are initially two different types or *makes* of agent which only differ in terms of their field of vision.

An important aspect when assessing the correctness of the swarm is its energy consumption. A basic requirement could, for example, be formulated as the following safety property: "the swarm must never run out of energy" (formally: $\neg \mathbf{F}(energy \leq 0)$). Although useful, a pure macro-level criterion like this is rarely sufficient since, despite the whole swarm always having enough energy, individual agents may still run out. If we can access the energy levels of the individual agents at any point in time, then we could formulate a more fine-grained criterion using quantification. Rather than stating that the swarm as a whole must never run out of energy, we may, for example, stipulate that "no individual agent must ever run out of energy" (formally: $\forall a \bullet \neg \mathbf{F}(energy_a \leq 0)$). Checking this criterion would catch those cases in which individual agents run out of energy, but we would still not know (i) *how many* of them do, and (ii) *why* this is the case. Quantitative analysis may help to shed further light on the dynamics of the system. In addition to the two safety criteria above, it may, for example, be useful to collect the following measurements.

- *Average/minimum/maximum probability* of an agent running out of energy.
- *Fraction of time* spent homing, resting, etc.
- *Fraction of time* spent transitioning, e.g. from depositing to resting (= overall probability of recharging).
- *Probability* of transitioning
  - from searching to grabbing (= probability of finding food)
  - from grabbing to depositing (= probability of losing out on food)
- *Correlation* between agent type and probabilities.

It is clear that neither transition probabilities or times spent in a certain state nor any other quantitative criteria are generally sufficient to prove the correctness of a complex system; but they can, if collected in good combination and to a sufficient extent, provide insights into the dynamics which a human user can then use to make its own judgement.

As described in Sect. 3, probabilistic model checkers such as PRISM are capable of performing such quantitative analyses, yet they suffer from state space explosion just like any other purely qualitative model checker [18,20]. In the following sections, we describe our efforts to circumvent this problem by determining quantitative measures such as those mentioned above through a combination of statistical model checking and trace analysis. We start by introducing a simple property specification language in Sect. 5, followed by some theoretical background and necessary algorithms in Sects. 6 and 7. In Sect. 8, we return to the swarm robot scenario and give a detailed description of its quantitative verification.

5   Formulating Multiagent Correctness Properties

In order to be able to better explain the ideas described in the following sections and formulate properties about multiagent simulation traces, we need an appropriate specification language. We start with a formal representation of the type of multiagent system that we are interested in. We are not concerned with advanced modalities like knowledge or strategies here, so we assume that the state of an individual agent is defined as a simple set of attributes and their values. The state space of the multiagent system can then be described as a simple state transition system. Let S_i denote the set of states of agent i. For n agents, $S = S_1 \times S_2 \times ...S_n$ then denotes the set of global states[1].

We assume that the multiagent system is probabilistic in nature, i.e. in the presence of multiple successor states, a probabilistic choice about which state the system transitions into will be made. Let therefore $P : S \times S \to [0, 1]$ be a *probabilistic transition function* such that $\forall s : S \bullet \sum_{s' \in S} P(s, s') = 1$. The multiagent system can then be described formally as a *probabilistic transition system* $\mathcal{M} = (S, P, s_0)$ where $s_0 \in S$ is the initial state. We denote each possible finite path $\omega = \langle s_0, s_1, ..., s_k \rangle$ through $\mathcal{M}$ as a *simulation trace*. In the presence of individual agents, simulation traces have an internal structure. Given n agents,

---

[1] For simplicity, we omit the environment in our formal description.

a simulation trace can be subdivided into n *agent traces*. We denote with ω^i the i−th agent trace within ω. We further denote with $\omega[t]$ (or $\omega^i[t]$, resp.) the t−th state of trace ω (or ω^i, resp.).

Since each trace comprises a sequence of states, it is natural to assume linear temporal flow and thus linear temporal logic (LTL) as the basis for a specification language. In the context of multiagent systems, it is useful to formulate properties both about *individual agents* as well as about *arbitrary groups of agents*. Conventional LTL is not expressive enough in that case. We thus present here $\mathcal{L}$, a simple LTL-based specification language which satisfies those requirements. $\mathcal{L}$ is a simplified version of simLTL [11], the specification language used in the verification tool MC²MABS [10].

The syntax of $\mathcal{L}$ is subdivided into two separate layers, an *agent layer* and a *population layer*, which allows for a distinction between *agent properties* ϕ_a and *population properties* ϕ_p. The syntax of agent and population formulae is defined as follows.

$$\phi_a ::= \mathbf{true} \mid p \mid \neg\, \phi_a \mid \phi_a \wedge \phi_a \mid \phi_a \vee \phi_a \mid \mathbf{X}\phi_a \mid \phi_a\, \mathbf{U}\, \phi_a \mid att \bowtie val$$
$$\phi_p ::= \mathbf{true} \mid p \mid \neg\, \phi_p \mid \phi_p \wedge \phi_p \mid \phi_p \vee \phi_p \mid \mathbf{X}\phi_p \mid \phi_p\, \mathbf{U}\, \phi_p \mid att \bowtie val$$

ϕ_a describes the syntax of an *agent property*, i.e. a property formulated about the behaviour of an individual agent; ϕ_p describes the syntax of a *population property*, i.e. a property formulated about the behaviour of the entire population. The basic building blocks are atomic propositions p, the Boolean connectives $\wedge$ ('and'), $\vee$ ('or') and $\neg$ ('not') and the temporal connectives $\mathbf{X}$ ('next') and $\mathbf{U}$ ('until'). The formulae of $\mathcal{L}$ are evaluated over finite simulation traces (and, of course, the agent traces contained in them). In general, for formula ϕ and (agent or simulation) trace ω, ϕ holds in ω (formally $\omega \models \phi$) iff ϕ holds in the first state of ω. For any state s, $\mathbf{true}$ always holds, p holds iff p is true in s, $\phi_1 \wedge \phi_2$ holds iff ϕ_1 holds and ϕ_2 holds in s, $\phi_1 \vee \phi_2$ holds iff either ϕ_1 or ϕ_2 holds in s, $\neg\, \phi$ holds iff ϕ does not hold in s, and $\mathbf{X}\phi$ holds iff s has a direct successor state s' (i.e. s is not the final state of the trace) and ϕ holds in s'.[2] For formulae ϕ_1 and ϕ_2, $\phi_1\, \mathbf{U}\, \phi_2$ holds iff ϕ_1 holds in s and ϕ_2 holds at some future point s' along the finite trace. Other logical connectives such as '$\Rightarrow$' or '$\Leftrightarrow$' can be derived in the usual manner: $\phi_1 \Rightarrow \phi_2 \equiv \neg\, \phi_1 \vee \phi_2$ and $\phi_1 \Leftrightarrow \phi_2 \equiv (\phi_1 \Rightarrow \phi_2) \wedge (\phi_2 \Rightarrow \phi_1)$. Additional temporal operators such as $\mathbf{F}$ ('eventually'), $\mathbf{G}$ ('always') and $\mathbf{W}$ ('weak until') can be derived as follows: $\mathbf{F}\phi \equiv \mathbf{true}\, \mathbf{U}\phi$ (ϕ *holds eventually*), $\mathbf{G}\phi \equiv \neg\, \mathbf{F}(\neg\, \phi)$ (ϕ *holds always*) and $\phi_1\mathbf{W}\phi_2 \equiv (\phi_1\, \mathbf{U}\, \phi_2) \vee \mathbf{G}\phi_1$ (ϕ_1 *may be succeeded by* ϕ_2). Although not formalised explicitly above, the state of both individual agents and groups of agents is defined by the values of their *attributes*. In the case of individual agents, attributes are either basic (e.g. 'age') or aggregate in nature (e.g. 'total income from all jobs'); in the case of groups of agents, attributes are typically only aggregate in nature (e.g. 'total income of all agents'). In order to include those attributes into the verification process, $\mathcal{L}$ also

---

[2] For simplicity, we ignore some of the intricate semantic issues of LTL in the presence of finite traces. For more information, please refer to the literature [3].

allows for the specification of attribute–value relations. $att : Name$ denotes an (agent or group) attribute name and $val : Value$ denotes an attribute value, and $\bowtie \in \{=, \neq, <, \leq, >, \geq\}$ is a comparison operator. This allows us to formulate properties such as $\mathbf{F}(age > 20)$.

Building upon the notion of agent and population properties, the syntax of any $\mathcal{L}$ full formula ϕ is then defined as follows:

$$\phi ::= \langle\!\langle \phi_a \rangle\!\rangle \phi_p \mid [i] \phi_a$$

$\langle\!\langle \phi_a \rangle\!\rangle \phi_p$ describes a *selective population property*; it is true iff ϕ_p is true for the group of all agents that satisfy property ϕ_a, formally $\omega \models \langle\!\langle \phi_a \rangle\!\rangle \phi_p \Leftrightarrow \{\omega^i \in \omega \mid \omega^i \models \phi_a\} \models \phi_p$. $[i]\phi_a$ describes an *indexed agent property*; $i : \mathbb{N}$ denotes an identifier that specifies which agent trace within the current simulation trace formula ϕ_a is to be evaluated upon[3], formally $\omega \models [i]\phi_a \Leftrightarrow \omega^i \in \omega \wedge \omega^i \models \phi_a$.

The ability to formulate properties about groups of agents as well as about individual agents is important, yet there is more to be done. In a multiagent context, we often have to deal with large populations of agents. In this case, in addition to the probability of a property about a *particular* agent, it is also interesting to obtain the probability of a property about the *average* agent. For example, instead of asking for the probability of the income of agent 1 falling below x, we may be interested in the probability of an agent's income falling below x *on average*. This can be achieved through *in-trace sampling*, i.e. the repeated evaluation of an agent property on randomly selected agent traces as described in Sect. 6 further below. In order to integrate this mechanism into $\mathcal{L}$, we simply assume that, if the agent identifier is omitted from an indexed agent property, then the property is checked on a *uniformly randomly chosen agent trace*.

6   Events, Properties, and Their Probability

Up until now, we used the term 'events' loosely when speaking about the formulation of properties. The purpose of this section is to give a formal definition for the notion of events and their association with formulable correctness properties.

6.1   Structure and Probability of Simulation Traces

The purpose of this section is to formally associate the set of traces of a multiagent system obtained through simulation with a *probability space*. This allows us to talk about *events* and their *probability*. We show that, by varying the set of outcomes that one focusses on, events of different granularity become detectable.

In the presence of transition probabilities (as described in Sect. 5), it is intuitively clear that each simulation trace ω occurs with a certain probability, denoted $Pr(\omega)$, which is the product of all individual transition probabilities:

---

[3] We assume that agents are numbered from 1 to n and that the number of agents is fixed.

$$Pr(\omega) = P(s_0, s_1) \cdot P(s_1, s_2) \cdot \ldots \cdot P(s_{n-1}, s_n) = \prod_{0 \le i < n} P(s_i, s_{i+1}) \qquad (1)$$

In the presence of long simulation runs, restricting the focus of attention to the probability of full traces may be too coarse-grained. Traces represent (possibly long) sequences of system states which themselves also have a complex internal structure; in the course of a simulation run, numerous *events* take place which constitute themselves as changes to the state of the system. A trace represents all the states of the underlying run and can thus be seen as a rich source of analysis. In addition to the probability of the trace itself, it is therefore useful to also determine the probability of all individual events represented by it. However, in order to talk about events and their probability, we first need to make sets of traces *measurable*. To this end, we associate a *probability space* with the set of simulation traces. A probability space is a triple (Ω, Σ, Pr) where Ω is the *sample space*, $\Sigma \subseteq \mathbb{P}\Omega$ is a σ-algebra and $Pr : \Sigma \to [0, 1]$ is a probability measure. The sample space Ω can be seen as the set representing all possible *outcomes* of an experiment. Imagine, for example, throwing a die. In this case, the sample space is $\Omega = \{1, 2, 3, 4, 5, 6\}$. We can now start to define possible events within the set of outcomes. A single event represents a set of outcomes which all satisfy a common criterion. For example, getting an even number when throwing a die is represented by the set $\{2, 4, 6\}$. Formally, the set of events forms a σ-*algebra* $\Sigma \subseteq \mathbb{P}\Omega$ on Ω, where Σ is a subset of the power set of Ω. A σ-algebra Σ also needs to satisfy the following requirements: (i) Σ contains the empty set $\varnothing$, (ii) Σ is closed under complements: if A is in Σ then so is its complement $\overline{A} = (\Omega \backslash A)$, and (iii) Σ is closed under countable unions: if $A_1, A_2, \ldots$ are in Σ then so is their union $A = \bigcup A_n$. Furthermore, in order to assign a probability with an event, we need a *probability measure* $Pr : \Sigma \to [0, 1]$ which is a function that assigns to each event $E \in \Sigma$ a number between 0 and 1. Pr also needs to satisfy the following requirements: (i) Pr is countably additive: for all countable collections $A = \{A_1, A_2, \ldots, A_n\} \in \Sigma$, $Pr(\bigcup A_i) = \sum(Pr(A_i))$, and (ii) $Pr(\varnothing) = 0$ and $Pr(\Omega) = 1$. A probability space is then defined as a triple (Ω, Σ, Pr) comprising the sample space Ω, σ-algebra Σ and probability measure Pr. In the context of probability theory, the events $\omega \in \Sigma$ are said to be *measurable* [1].

6.2   Simulation and Sampling: Trace Fragmentation

In order to talk about events in the context of simulation runs, the set Tr_s of simulation traces which a simulation can produce needs to be made measurable by associating it with a probability space. We start with the sample space. A trace obtained through a single simulation run (if properly randomised, which we assume here) can be seen as a single sample drawn from the *set of finite traces* as defined by the logic within the model. However, at the same time, a single trace of length k also represents a set of k samples drawn from the *set of states* defined by the model. Furthermore, it also represents a set of $\binom{k}{2}$ samples drawn from the *set of state tuples*, a set of $\binom{k}{3}$ samples drawn from the *set of state triples*, and so on. Even more, given n agents, each simulation trace also represents n samples drawn from the *set of agent traces*, each of which itself represents a set of k samples from the *set of agent states*, etc.

In general, the description of a probabilistic state-based model yields a large range of different sets of outcomes that one can draw from: a set of agent or group states (one for each possible group of agents), of agent or group state pairs, of agent or group state triples, etc. Each individual simulation run represents one or many samples from each of those sets. As described above, each set of outcomes corresponds with a different probability space and thus allows for the detection of different events. Just by interpreting the same outcome in different ways, different types of events become detectable.

Let us now briefly look at the types of outcomes that one is *typically* interested in. We can assume that, in a simulation context, we are mostly interested in events defined over *coherent trace fragments*, rather than over arbitrary tuples of states. Informally, a coherent trace fragment is any sequence of states which exists in the underlying state space. Fragments of length 1 represent individual states, fragments of length 2 represent states and their direct successors, fragments of length 3 represent states and their two subsequent states, etc. Formally, the set $\mathcal{F}_k$ of coherent trace fragments of length k is defined as the set of sub-sequences of states, i.e. sub-traces, of length k:

$$\mathcal{F}_k == \bigcup_{\omega \in Tr_s} \{p \text{ in } \omega \mid \#p = k\} \tag{2}$$

Each fragment size represents a certain level of *granularity* with respect to the simulation outcome. Before defining the sample space of a simulation, it is therefore important to clarify the granularity necessary to answer a given question. For example, some questions are formulated over entire simulation traces, i.e. members of the set $\mathcal{F}_t$. Typical representatives of this group are temporal questions that involve statements like, for example, *eventually* or *always*. In this case, the set from which samples need to be drawn is the set of all full traces, i.e. $\Omega = Tr_s$. The σ-algebra Σ (the set of possible events defined as a subset of $\mathbb{P}\Omega$) thus represents the set of all possible sets of traces.

For other questions, a finer level of granularity is needed. Consider, for example, a question about the existence of a particular state transition. On a full simulation trace, the state transition of interest may occur several times. In order to detect all occurrences (and thus measure the event's probability), it is not sufficient to look at complete traces. Instead, we need to look at *trace fragments* of length 2, i.e. at tuples of immediately succeeding states drawn from the set $\mathcal{F}_2$. This is necessary since any state transition is described by its start and end state. If questions about the probability of a single agent attribute valuation are to be answered, i.e. questions about a particular property of an individual state, then the set that samples need to be drawn from is the set of trace fragments of length 1, i.e. the set of individual states.

We can generalise that, in order to answer any question, we need trace fragments of length k where $0 < k \leq t$ and t is the maximum number of time steps in the simulation. The sample space is then defined as the set of all fragments of length k, i.e. we have $\Omega = \mathcal{F}_k$. The σ-algebra Σ is a subset of the power set of Ω and thus represents the set of all possible sets of trace fragments of length k, i.e. $\Sigma \subseteq \mathbb{PF}_k$.

In order to define a probability measure for any event in Σ, we first need to define the probability of a certain trace fragment. The probability of fragment $f = \langle s_j, s_{j+1}, ..., s_k \rangle$ of trace $t = \langle s_0, s_1, ..., s_n \rangle$ where $0 \le j \le n$ and $j \le k \le n$ is the probability of trace t divided by the number of coherent fragments of t of size $(k - j)$:

$$Pr(\langle s_j, ...s_k \rangle) = \frac{\prod_{0 \le i < n} P(s_i, s_{i+1})}{n - (k - j) + 1} \tag{3}$$

The probability measure for any event $\sigma \in \Sigma$ (which represents a set of trace fragments) can then be defined as the sum of the probabilities of each trace fragment $\omega \in \sigma$:

$$Pr(\sigma) = \sum_{\omega \in \sigma} Pr(\omega) \tag{4}$$

The association of a probability space with a simulation transition system makes it possible to talk about events and their probability. Events are described by *properties*. A property refers to a set of possible outcomes of a simulation. Consider, for example, a property φ which states that the system will *eventually* reach a given state s. This clearly needs to be answered on *full simulation traces*, i.e. the set of outcomes is defined as the set of all trace fragments of length t where t is the maximum trace length. $\Sigma = \{\sigma \in \mathcal{F}_t \mid \sigma \models \varphi\}$ is then defined as the set of those trace fragments σ that satisfy this condition (denoted $\sigma \models \varphi$) and thus eventually end up in state s. On the other hand, let ψ denote a property that states that the population transitions from state x to state y. This represents a statement about the full population, yet, due to its focus on transitions, it requires trace fragments of length 2 in order to be answered correctly, i.e. we have $\Sigma = \{\sigma \in \mathcal{F}_2 \mid \sigma \models \psi\}$. As a final example, let ψ denote a property which states that *a single agent* transitions from state x to state y. Similar to the previous property, it describes a state transition and thus requires trace fragments of length 2. However, it is also of individual nature, i.e. the set of outcomes that it refers to is the set of all fragments of length 2 *of individual agent traces*. By formulating the properties in the appropriate way, we can answer quantitative properties about the behaviour of the full population, about the behaviour of groups within the population or about the behaviour of individual agents. By evaluating an individual property on independent and randomly chosen agent traces, we can even answer questions about the *average behaviour* of individual agents. We refer to this process as *in-trace sampling*.

Since, as described above, the traces of a simulation are measurable, the probability of any property ϕ is defined as the sum of the probabilities of all trace fragments of length k in the associated σ-algebra $\Sigma = \{\sigma \in \mathcal{F}_k \mid \sigma \models \phi\}$:

$$Pr(\phi) = \sum_{\sigma \in \Sigma} Pr(\sigma) \tag{5}$$

In order to make clear what fragment size a property is being verified upon (and thus, which interpretation of the sample space is being chosen), we add the sample size as a subscript variable to Pr. For example, we refer to the probability of a property ϕ that is to be evaluated upon trace fragments of size 2 as $Pr_2(\phi)$. We omit the subscript if (i) the formula is to be evaluated upon sets of *full* traces, or, (ii) if the fragment size does not matter for the purpose of description.

Let us briefly summarise the ideas described above. Essentially, a simulation trace, i.e. the output of a single simulation run, can be seen as a single sample from the set of finite traces defined by the underlying model. Following this interpretation, the set of outcomes, i.e. the set that events and thus also properties are being formulated upon, is fixed as the set of finite traces. However, a single simulation trace can also be interpreted as a set of sample states drawn from the set of states, as a set of sample state tuples drawn from the set of state tuples, as a set of sample state triples drawn from the set of state triples, and so forth. Furthermore, sampling can be performed on the macro, meso and micro level and thus refer to the behaviour of the population, of groups of agents or of individual agents. Depending on how the set of possible outcomes is interpreted, different events can be defined which, ultimately, allows for the expression of richer properties. Given a property ϕ, its meaning and, of course, also its probability may vary depending on which set of outcomes it is interpreted on. It is therefore important to make the fragment size a central parameter of the verification algorithm.

6.3   Complexity

It is obvious that trace fragmentation has an impact on the complexity of property evaluation. Rather than once for each state in the trace in worst case, fragmentation requires each property ϕ to be evaluated once for each state *for each fragment*. Since fragments are, in most cases, overlapping, most states are evaluated twice.

We start the complexity analysis by assuming that ϕ is a conventional LTL formula, i.e. does not allow for quantification. This assumption is relaxed further below.

Lemma 1. *Let ϕ be a propositional (i.e. non-temporal) formula. The complexity of checking ϕ on a system state s is $O(|\phi|)$.*

We prove by induction on the structure of propositional formulae. Evaluating an atomic proposition p requires a constant number c of steps; evaluating a negated formula $\neg \phi$ requires $|\phi|$ steps; evaluating $\phi_1 \wedge \phi_2$ requires $|\phi_1| + |\phi_2|$ steps, as does $\phi_1 \vee \phi_2$. In general, every subformula of ϕ needs to be evaluated once. The complexity of evaluating any propositional formula ϕ on a state is thus in $O(|\phi|)$. $\qquad\qquad\square$

Lemma 2. *Let ϕ be a conventional LTL formula. The complexity of checking ϕ on a trace of length t is $O(t \cdot |\phi|)$.*

In order to check a temporal formula ϕ on a trace of length t, we can use a recursive labelling procedure (see, e.g. [10] for details). Here, each state s of the trace is labelled with those subformulae of ϕ that hold in s. As a consequence, the whole trace needs to be iterated over $|\phi|$ times. The complexity of evaluating ϕ is thus in $O(t \cdot |\phi|)$.   □

Theorem 1. *The complexity of checking an LTL formula ϕ on a trace of length t and subdivided into coherent fragments of length k s.t. $0 < k \leq t$ is in $O\left(t^2 \cdot |\phi|\right)$.*

Proof. Each trace of length t contains $t - k + 1$ coherent fragments of length k. ϕ needs to be evaluated once for each fragment. In worst case, $t/2$ fragments need to be examined, each of which requires $t/2 \cdot |\phi|$ steps (see Lemma 2). The evaluation of ϕ on a trace of length t, subdivided into coherent fragments of length k is thus in $O(t^2 \cdot |\phi|)$.   □

For Lemma 1 we assumed ϕ to be a conventional LTL formula which does not contain quantifiers. If the property specification language allows for nested quantifiers (as, for example, described in Sect. 5), then the complexity of checking a property on an individual state needs to be adapted accordingly.

The following theorem makes a more general statement about the complexity of evaluating a property ϕ formulated in an arbitrary language $\mathcal{L}$.

Theorem 2. *Given a property ϕ of language $\mathcal{L}$, let $\mathcal{C}$ denote the complexity of evaluating ϕ on a given trace of length t. Then the complexity of evaluating ϕ on a trace of length t which is subdivided into fragments of length k is in $O\left(t^2 \cdot \mathcal{C}\right)$.*

Proof. The proof follows from Lemmas 1 and 2, and Theorem 1. Fragmentation thus adds a factor that is, in worst case, quadratic in the length of the trace to the overall complexity of verification.   □

7   Quantitative Trace-Based Analysis

The purpose of this section is to illustrate the usefulness of trace fragmentation in combination with sampling for the purpose of quantitative analysis. In Sect. 6, the probability of a property has been defined as the sum of the probabilities of all traces (or, more precisely, trace fragments) in the associated σ-algebra. Or, in other words, the probability of ϕ being true in a set of traces Tr denotes the ratio between those traces $tr \in Tr$ for which ϕ holds (denoted $tr \models \phi$) and those traces $tr' \in Tr$ for which ϕ does not hold (denoted $tr' \not\models \phi$). It remains to discuss, *how* this probability can be computed practically. Clearly, if a complete set of traces is available, then the exact probability can be obtained in a straightforward way, by simply counting those traces for which ϕ holds and dividing their number by the overall number of traces. In general, however, complete sets of traces cannot be assumed to be available. Given the vast size of real-world state spaces, the number of possible traces will be too large and we can only expect to have access to a small subset. In this case, statistical analysis is used to *esimate* the actual probability of a property [21]. In the remainder of this paper, when we refer to a probability $Pr(\phi)$, we thus always mean the estimated probability.

7.1 Analysis Types

Up until now, we have completely ignored the fact that properties correspond with trace *fragments* rather than with full traces, as described in Sect. 6. In this section, we bring together the two ideas of (i) *probability estimation* and (ii) *trace fragmentation* in order to describe advanced types of quantitative analysis. In the following paragraphs, we are mostly interested in the relationship between *states* of a system. States correspond with trace fragments of length 1 which, in turn, correspond with atemporal properties (i.e. properties that do not contain a temporal operator). To that end, we denote with $\mathcal{L}^a$ the *atemporal subset* of $\mathcal{L}$. Furthermore, we abbreviate $(\phi_1 \wedge \mathbf{X}\phi_2)$ with $\phi_1 \rightarrow \phi_2$.

State Residency: We start with the notion of a *state residency probability*, i.e. the probability of *being* in a certain state. Informally, of all the time spent in any state, the residency probability of state s describes the fraction of time that is spent in s. Properties about individual states are inherently atemporal in nature and thus correspond with trace fragments of length 1. Given an atemporal property ϕ, the probability of an agent (or any groups of agents) being in a state that satisfies ϕ can then be obtained by simply calculating the probability of ϕ on trace fragments of length 1, i.e. $Pr_1(\phi)$. The *state residency probability* srp can thus be formally defined as follows:

$$srp : \mathcal{L}^a \rightarrow \mathbb{R}$$
$$\forall\, \phi : \mathcal{L}^a \bullet srp(\phi) = Pr_1(\phi)$$

Transition Residency: In addition to the probability of being in a certain state, it is crucial to ask properties about the *transitions* between states. Similar to the residency w.r.t. states defined above, we may, for example, be interested in how much of its time a given agent spends in a particular transition. This can be calculated by simply obtaining the probability of a temporal succession property describing on trace fragments of size 2 (because of the 'next' operator). For example, if we are interested in the transition from ϕ_1 to ϕ_2 (where both ϕ_1 and ϕ_2 are atemporal), then the transition residency probability can be obtained by calculating $Pr_2(\phi_1 \rightarrow \phi_2)$. This leads to the following formal description of the transition residency probability trp:

$$trp : \mathcal{L}^a \times \mathcal{L}^a \rightarrow \mathbb{R}$$
$$\forall\, \phi_1, \phi_2 : \mathcal{L}^a \bullet trp(\phi_1, \phi_2) = Pr_2(\phi_1 \rightarrow \phi_2)$$

Transition Probability: The purpose of the next type of quantitative analysis is to determine a particular transition probability, i.e. the probability of transitioning into a particular successor state in which ϕ_2 holds, given that we are currently in state in which ϕ_1 holds. The transition probability is obtained by dividing the probability of transitioning from ϕ_1 to ϕ_2 by the residency probability of ϕ_1, i.e. $trp(\phi_1, \phi_2)/Pr_2(\phi_1)$. It is important to note that both probabilities need to be obtained on trace fragments of size 2 (even the second, atemporal one!). A formal definition of the transition probability tp can now be given as follows:

$$tp : \mathcal{L}^a \times \mathcal{L}^a \to \mathbb{R}$$
$$\forall\, \phi_1, \phi_2 : \mathcal{L}^a \bullet tp(\phi_1, \phi_2) = trp(\phi_1, \phi_2)/Pr_2(\phi_1)$$

Correlation Analysis: Probabilistic analysis can be used conveniently to determine *probabilistic dependence* or *correlation*. Correlation analysis represents an important building block in the quality assurance process. It can give insights into the system's dynamics by revealing behaviours that are coupled, i.e. whose occurrence is (entirely or to some extent) synchronised. Furthermore, the analysis of correlations may indicate *causal relationships* and can thus be used to detect symptoms that can motivate further, more tailored experiments. For example, if A and B are positively correlated, one can be sure that one of the following three facts is definitely true: (i) A is a cause of B, (ii) B is a cause of A or, (iii) there is a common cause for A and B. Positive correlation can be defined formally as follows[4]:

$$posCorr : \mathcal{L} \times \mathcal{L} \to \{\mathbf{true}, \mathbf{false}\}$$
$$\forall\, \phi_1, \phi_2 : \mathcal{L} \bullet posCorr(\phi_1, \phi_2) \Leftrightarrow Pr(\phi_1 \wedge \phi_2) > Pr(\phi_1) \cdot Pr(\phi_2)$$

This concludes the description of our analyses. As illustrated in the case study in the next section, quantitative analysis becomes most powerful if it is performed on different observational levels.

8   Example: Quantitative Analysis of a Robot Swarm

Following the description of our approach to quantitative analysis, we now return to the motivational example from swarm robotics described in Sect. 4 and describe its verification. As described above, our goal is to determine whether the model is reasonably robust, i.e. whether agents have enough energy during the simulated timespan[5]. We start with the following (largely arbitrary) parametrisation:

---

[4] The definition of functions for negative correlation and non-correlation, i.e. statistical independence, are omitted; they can be given accordingly.

[5] All experiments were conducted on a Viglen Genie Desktop PC with four Intel® Core™ i5 CPUs (3.2 GHz each), 3.7 GB of memory and Gentoo Linux (kernel version 3.10.25) as operating system, using the verification tool MC²MABS [10]. Results are based on experiments involving 100 replications of the given model.

Table 1. Transition probabilities for all agents, agents of make 0 and agents of make 1

| | All agents | | Make 0 | | Make 1 | |
Transition	Total time	Probability	Total time	Probability	Total time	Probability
$S \rightarrow G$	1 m 52 s	0.1701	2 m 40 s	0.0363	2 m 50 s	0.6223
$G \rightarrow D$	2 m 01 s	0.1735	2 m 40 s	0.1945	2 m 40 s	0.1678
$G \rightarrow H$	2 m 09 s	0.0076	2 m 46 s	0.0034	2 m 42 s	0.0090
$D \rightarrow R$	2 m 02 s	0.1868	2 m 50 s	0.1912	2 m 42 s	0.2111
$R \rightarrow S$	2 m 03 s	0.1913	2 m 55 s	0.1950	2 m 47 s	0.1833

- 100 agents, 1,000 ticks
- Time spent in each state: $T_s = T_g = T_r = T_h = T_d = 5$
- Energy consumed in each state: $E_s = 12, E_g = 12, E_h = 6, E_r = 2, E_d = 62$
- Initial level of energy per agent: 40

In order to check if this parametrisation already satisfies the given requirements, we first define the following population-level property stating that the swarm as a whole will never run out of energy (note the use of '$\langle\!\langle \textbf{true} \rangle\!\rangle$' to refer to the whole population):

$$\phi_1 = \mathbf{G}(\langle\!\langle \textbf{true} \rangle\!\rangle (swarm\_energy \geq 0))$$

Despite every robot having 40 units of initial energy, the verification of Property ϕ_1 returns a probability of 0 which shows that the parametrisation given above is not suitable for this version of the model. In order to gain a deeper understanding of why this may be the case, it is useful to study how frequently robots switch from one state into another by determining their *average transition probabilities*. Following the description in Sect. 7, this requires the comparison of different probabilities, each of which has been obtained on trace fragments of length 2. We illustrate the formulation for the transition probability from searching to grabbing. In order to verify this property, we need the following two subformulae: $\phi_G = grabbing$ and $\phi_S = searching$. The overall transition probability for an individual agent is then calculated as follows:

$$Pr(S \rightarrow G) = tp(\phi_S, \phi_G) \tag{6}$$

The results for 100 replications are shown in the first section of Table 1[6]. We can see that robots have an equal probability of finding and grabbing food ($\approx 17\%$). We can also see that agents have a very low probability of transitioning into the homing state, which is positive since homing is always caused by a timeout and is thus undesirable.

However, when calculating the transition probabilities, we need to take into account that we have two different makes of agent, each of which can be expected

---

[6] For clarity, we abbreviate states with their capitalised first letters in all subsequent tables.

Table 2. Expected individual transition prob. and prob. of constant positive swarm energy

Vision	$Pr(S \to G)$	$Pr(G \to D)$	$Pr_t(\phi_1)$	$trp(depositing, resting)$
1	0.3416	0.1889	0.0	0.0108
2	0.1344	0.1853	0.0	0.0300
3	0.3735	0.1711	0.0	0.0438
4	0.6571	0.1631	0.0	0.0460
5	0.8364	0.1630	0.0	0.0470

to have different probabilities. In order assess whether this is really the case, we could, for example, check whether being of make 0 is *positively correlated* (or being of make 1 is negative correlated, respectively) with finding food. We will instead 'zoom in' and assess robots of different makes separately. This can be achieved by using a selection operator $\langle\!\langle\rangle\!\rangle$ as described in Sect. 5. For example, for robots of make 0 (for which we assume that proposition $make0$ is always true), the properties necessary for calculating the transition probability $Pr(S \to G)$ from searching to grabbing can be formulated as follows: $\psi_S = \langle\!\langle make0 \rangle\!\rangle searching$ and $\psi_G = \langle\!\langle make0 \rangle\!\rangle grabbing$. The overall transition probability can then be calculated similar to the previous property, i.e. $Pr(S \to G) = tp(\psi_S, \psi_G)$. The results for all checks are shown in Table 1. It is obvious that robots of make 1 have a significantly higher probability of finding food which, given their larger field of vision, is intuitively correct. What is also interesting, however, is that a robot's make seems to have a small but obvious impact on its probability of grabbing food; this is indicated by the lower probability of transitioning from grabbing to depositing for robots of make 1. One possible explanation is that, due to their larger field of vision and their consequently higher probability of finding food, robots of make 1 may block each other by 'stealing' food that is already aimed for by a different robot. This explanation may also be underpinned by the slightly higher probability of robots of make 1 moving from grabbing to homing than robots of make 0: the only reason for performing this transition is that a food item aimed for is lost to a different agent. Given the small sample size, however, care needs to be taken when interpreting the numbers — especially when differences are very small, as in this case.

The numbers seem to suggest that the size of the field of vision has a positive impact on the food finding probability and a slightly negative impact on the food grabbing probability. This hypothesis can be investigated further by performing a range of experiments in which the vision parameter is constantly increased. The results are shown in Table 2. The numbers in the second column indicate that, in fact, the size of the field of vision has a significant positive impact on the probability of finding food (as expected). This shows that there is a *causal dependence* between an agent's field of vision and its probability of finding food. The numbers in the third column indicate that there is a slightly negative correlation between the field of vision and the probability of grabbing food. The fourth column of the table shows the probability of Property ϕ_1 which is 0 in

Table 3. Expected individual state distribution

Vision	srp(searching)	srp(grabbing)	srp(homing)	srp(resting)	srp(depositing)
1	0.2952	0.0563	0.2694	0.3234	0.0555
2	0.2147	0.1553	0.1668	0.3122	0.1505
3	0.1251	0.2486	0.0810	0.3119	0.2337
4	0.0873	0.2896	0.0470	0.3083	0.2647
5	0.0691	0.3087	0.0330	0.3109	0.2763

Table 4. Expected state distribution and energy development for $T_r = 1$ and $T_g = 1$

Vision	Scenario	srp(S)	srp(G)	srp(H)	srp(R)	srp(D)	$Pr_t(\phi_1)$	$Pr_t(\Box(energy > 0))$
5	$T_r = 1$	0.0925	0.4095	0.0466	0.0828	0.3691	0.0	0.0
5	$T_g = 1$	0.0923	0.0816	0.0262	0.4135	0.3893	1.0	0.78

all cases; varying the field of vision alone is thus not sufficient for sustaining a positive energy level (at least not in the current scenario).

The numbers suggest that, despite the slight loss in grabbing probability, the swarm designer is best off by giving all robots a high field of vision. In order to confirm this assumption, we can formulate another property which denotes the *overall probability of an agent gaining energy*. Remember that energy is always gained in the final time step of the depositing state, i.e. before the agent starts resting. In order to determine the overall probability of an agent gaining energy, we can formulate the following property:

$$trp(depositing, resting) = Pr_2(depositing \rightarrow resting) \tag{7}$$

Since this is a property whose truth needs to be ascertained on state transitions, it needs to be checked on trace fragments of size 2. It is also important to note that, since it is not conditional upon the agent's being depositing (i.e. it does not use logical implication), this property does *not* describe a transition probability in its strict sense. Instead, it describes the *overall* probability of performing this particular transition and can thus be used to determine the overall probability of an agent gaining energy. For simplicity, we assume that 5 is the maximum level of vision that can be realised technically. The verification results are shown in the last column of Table 2. They strengthen the assumption that the scenario with the largest field of vision is the most efficient one since, in this case, agents are most likely to gain energy.

The numbers so far give a strong indication that the probability of grabbing food should be increased. In order to choose the right strategy for achieving this goal, it is essential to *explain* its current level first, i.e. to understand *why* it is so low. The intuitive assumption is that an increased field of vision also increases competition among robots which itself increases the probability of agents missing out when trying to grab food. This assumption can be checked by determining the *expected state distribution*, i.e. the *amount of time a robot is expected to spend in each of the states.* The properties are formulated with the help of the state residency probability *srp* described in Sect. 7.1. The expected state distribution can be obtained by checking all properties above on trace fragments of size 1, i.e. on individual states. This is important since the properties are state properties and, in order to determine their probability, we need to sample from the distribution of states. The verification results are shown in Table 3. It becomes apparent that in case of lower vision, a significantly higher proportion of robots spend their time searching and homing (due to timeouts) than in case of higher vision. However, it also becomes apparent, that in case of higher vision, a significantly higher proportion of agents spend their time grabbing. This suggests that grabbing becomes a bottleneck which impedes foraging. Apart from grabbing, in all scenarios, a significant number of agents spend their time resting.

We now have two possible directions to improve the overall efficiency of the swarm: we can either try to decrease the time individuals spend for resting or we can try to decrease the time spent for grabbing food items. In order to compare the effect of both changes, we determine again the expected state distribution for each of the two cases. The results are shown in Table 4[7]. Reducing the resting time to 1 has the effect of forcing more robots into searching, grabbing and depositing. Likewise, reducing the grabbing time to 1 forces more robots into searching, resting and depositing. Both scenarios only differ with respect to the number of agents grabbing or resting. Taking into account the energy consumption of each agent intuitively suggests that scenario 2 (reduced grabbing time) must be significantly more effective since, in this case, more agents are resting which consumes significantly less energy than depositing. This assumption can be strengthened by looking at the overall probability of Property ϕ_1 (shown in Column 7) of Table 4. In the case of reduced resting time, the probability of the swarm always having positive energy is 0; in the case of reduced grabbing time, the probability is 1.0. In terms of individual energy levels, individual robots have an *average probability* of always having positive energy of $\approx 78\%$, as shown by the unindexed individual agent property in Column 8 of Table 4.

We have now reached a situation in which the overall swarm energy level as well as the majority of all individual energy levels are always positive. This concludes our small case study. In fact, there is still a significant number of individual robots ($\approx 22\%$) running out of energy. Their calibration, however, is not further discussed here.

9   Conclusions and Future Work

Statistical model checking can provide a powerful alternative for the verification of systems that are unamenable to conventional formal verification. Because of its focus on finite traces, statistical verification is typically focussed on comparatively simple properties. This critically limits the verifiability of large-scale multiagent systems with their complex, internal structure. In this paper, we

---

[7] For space limitation, the states are abbreviated with lower-case letters, e.g. *s* for *searching*.

showed how, by combining statistical verification with an advanced type of sampling and trace fragmentation, interesting quantitative analyses on different observational levels can be performed. Using a simple case study from the area of swarm robotics, we showed that, albeit approximate in nature, those types of analyses can be helpful to shed light on the dynamics of complex systems and uncover some of their internal mechanisms.

In this paper, we restricted our attention to a small number of quantitative analyses. Combining the expressiveness of temporal logics with statistical verification, a much wider range of analyses is possible. For example, in statistical time series analysis, correlation can be generalised to the temporal case by measuring the *autocorrelation* of a time series. The same idea could be applied in a trace-based verification scenario. Furthermore, probabilistic analysis provides an interesting basis for the analysis of *causal* relationships, either in a statistical sense (e.g. *Granger causality*) or by utilising probabilistic theories of causation [12]. In a verification context, causal analysis is a powerful tool for the *explanation* of phenomena. We plan to further investigate this idea, with a particular focus on the work of Kleinberg and Mishra [13].

References

1. Baier, C., Katoen, J.-P.: Principles of Model Checking. The MIT Press, Cambridge (2008)
2. Ballarini, P., Fisher, M., Wooldridge, M.: Uncertain agent verification through probabilistic model-checking. In: Barley, M., Mouratidis, H., Unruh, A., Spears, D., Scerri, P., Massacci, F. (eds.) SASEMAS 2004-2006. LNCS, vol. 4324, pp. 162–174. Springer, Heidelberg (2009)
3. Bauer, A., Leucker, M., Schallhart, C.: Comparing LTL semantics for runtime verification. J. Logic Comput. **20**(3), 651–674 (2010)
4. Cao, Y.U., Fukunaga, A.S., Kahng, A.: Cooperative mobile robotics: antecedents and directions. Auton. Robots **4**(1), 7–27 (1997)
5. Clarke, E., Emerson, E., Jha, S., Sistla, A.: Symmetry reductions in model checking. In: Vardi, M.Y. (ed.) CAV 1998. LNCS, vol. 1427, pp. 147–158. Springer, Heidelberg (1998)
6. Clarke, E., Grumberg, O., Peled, D.A.: Model Checking. MIT Press, Cambridge (1999)
7. Dekhtyar, M.I., Dikovsky, A.J., Valiev, M.K.: Temporal verification of probabilistic multi-agent systems. In: Avron, A., Dershowitz, N., Rabinovich, A. (eds.) Pillars of Computer Science. LNCS, vol. 4800, pp. 256–265. Springer, Heidelberg (2008)
8. Dix, J., Fisher, M.: Specification and verification of multi-agent systems. In: Multiagent Systems. MIT Press, Cambridge (2013)
9. Finkbeiner, B., Sankaranarayanan, S., Sipma, H.B.: Collecting statistics over runtime executions. Formal Methods Syst. Des. **27**(3), 253–274 (2005)
10. Herd, B.: Statistical runtime verification of agent-based simulations. Ph.D. thesis, King's College London (2015)
11. Herd, B., Miles, S., McBurney, P., Luck, M.: An LTL-based property specification language for agent-based simulation traces. Technical Report 14–02, King's College London, October 2014

12. Hitchcock, C.: Probabilistic causation. In: Zalta, E.N. (ed.) The Stanford Encyclopedia of Philosophy. Winter 201 edn. (2012)
13. Kleinberg, S., Mishra, B.: The temporal logic of causal structures. In: Proceedings of the 25th Conference on Uncertainty in Artificial Intelligence, pp. 303–312. AUAI Press (2009)
14. Konur, S., Dixon, C., Fisher, M.: Formal verification of probabilistic swarm behaviours. In: Dorigo, M., et al. (eds.) ANTS 2010. LNCS, vol. 6234, pp. 440–447. Springer, Heidelberg (2010)
15. Kouvaros, P., Lomuscio, A.: Automatic verification of parameterised multi-agent systems. In: Proceedings of the 12th International Conference on Autonomous Agents and Multi-agent Systems, Richland, SC, pp. 861–868 (2013)
16. Kouvaros, P., Lomuscio, A.: A cutoff technique for the verification of parameterised interpreted systems with parameterised environments. In: Proceedings of the 23rd International Joint Conference on Artificial Intelligence, pp. 2013–2019. AAAI Press (2013)
17. Kwiatkowska, M., Lomuscio, A., Qu, H.: Parallel model checking for temporal epistemic logic. In: Proceedings of the 19th European Conference on Artificial Intelligence, pp. 543–548. IOS Press, Amsterdam (2010)
18. Kwiatkowska, M., Norman, G., Parker, D.: Quantitative analysis with the probabilistic model checker PRISM. Electron. Notes Theor. Comput. Sci. 153(2), 5–31 (2006). Proc. 3rd Workshop on Quantitative Aspects of Programming Languages
19. Kwiatkowska, M., Norman, G., Parker, D.: Stochastic model checking. In: Bernardo, M., Hillston, J. (eds.) SFM 2007. LNCS, vol. 4486, pp. 220–270. Springer, Heidelberg (2007)
20. Kwiatkowska, M., Norman, G., Parker, D.: PRISM 4.0: verification of probabilistic real-time systems. In: Qadeer, S., Gopalakrishnan, G. (eds.) CAV 2011. LNCS, vol. 6806, pp. 585–591. Springer, Heidelberg (2011)
21. Legay, A., Delahaye, B., Bensalem, S.: Statistical model checking: an overview. In: Barringer, H., et al. (eds.) RV 2010. LNCS, vol. 6418, pp. 122–135. Springer, Heidelberg (2010)
22. Liu, W., Winfield, A., Sa, J.: Modelling swarm robotic systems: a case study in collective foraging. In: Towards Autonomous Robotic Systems, pp. 25–32 (2007)
23. Lomuscio, A., Penczek, W., Qu, H.: Partial order reductions for model checking temporal-epistemic logics over interleaved multi-agent systems. Fundamenta Informaticae 101(1–2), 71–90 (2010)
24. Lomuscio, A., Penczek, W., Woźna, B.: Bounded model checking for knowledge and real time. Artif. Intell. 171(16–17), 1011–1038 (2007)
25. Nimal, V.: Statistical approaches for probabilistic model checking. MSc Mini-project Dissertation, Oxford University Computing Laboratory (2010)
26. Pedersen, T., Dyrkolbotn, S.K.: Agents homogeneous: a procedurally anonymous semantics characterizing the homogeneous fragment of ATL. In: Boella, G., Elkind, E., Savarimuthu, B.T.R., Dignum, F., Purvis, M.K. (eds.) PRIMA 2013. LNCS, vol. 8291, pp. 245–259. Springer, Heidelberg (2013)
27. Sammapun, U., Lee, I., Sokolsky, O., Regehr, J.: Statistical runtime checking of probabilistic properties. In: Sokolsky, O., Taşıran, S. (eds.) RV 2007. LNCS, vol. 4839, pp. 164–175. Springer, Heidelberg (2007)
28. Wan, W., Bentahar, J., Ben Hamza, A.: Model checking epistemic and probabilistic properties of multi-agent systems. In: Mehrotra, K.G., Mohan, C.K., Oh, J.C., Varshney, P.K., Ali, M. (eds.) IEA/AIE 2011, Part II. LNCS, vol. 6704, pp. 68–78. Springer, Heidelberg (2011)

Semantic Mutation Testing
for Multi-agent Systems

Zhan Huang$^{(\boxtimes)}$ and Rob Alexander

Department of Computer Science, University of York, York, UK
{zhan.huang,robert.alexander}@cs.york.ac.uk

Abstract. This paper introduces semantic mutation testing (SMT) into multi-agent systems. SMT is a test assessment technique that makes changes to the interpretation of a program and then examines whether a given test set has the ability to detect each change to the original interpretation. These changes represent possible misunderstandings of how the program is interpreted. SMT can also be used to assess robustness to and reliability of semantic changes. This paper applies SMT to three rule-based agent programming languages, namely Jason, GOAL and 2APL, provides several contexts in which SMT for these languages is useful, and proposes three sets of semantic mutation operators (i.e., rules to make semantic changes) for these languages respectively, and a systematic approach to derivation of semantic mutation operators for rule-based agent languages. This paper then shows, through preliminary evaluation of our semantic mutation operators for Jason, that SMT has some potential to assess tests, robustness to and reliability of semantic changes.

Keywords: Semantic mutation testing · Agent programming languages · Cognitive agents

1 Introduction

Testing multi-agent systems (MASs) is difficult because MASs may have some properties such as autonomy and non-determinism, and they may be based on models such as BDI which are quite different to ordinary imperative programming. There are many test techniques for MASs, most of which attempt to address these difficulties by adapting existing test techniques to the properties and models of MASs [9, 15]. For instance, SUnit is a unit-testing framework for MASs that extends JUnit [19].

Some test techniques for MASs introduce traditional mutation testing, which is a powerful technique for assessing the adequacy of test sets. In a nutshell, traditional mutation testing makes small changes to a program and then examines whether a given test set has the ability to detect each change to the original program. These changes represent potential small slips. Work on traditional mutation testing for MASs includes [1, 10, 16–18].

In this paper, we apply an alternative approach to mutation testing, namely semantic mutation testing (SMT) [5], to MASs. Rather than changing the program, SMT changes the semantics of the language in which the program is written. In other words, it makes changes to the interpretation of the program. These changes represent

© Springer International Publishing Switzerland 2015
M. Baldoni et al. (Eds.): EMAS 2015, LNAI 9318, pp. 131–152, 2015.
DOI: 10.1007/978-3-319-26184-3_8

possible misunderstandings of how the program is interpreted. Therefore, SMT assesses a test set by examining whether it has the ability to detect each change to the original interpretation of the program.

SMT can be used not only to assess tests, but also to assess robustness to and reliability of semantic changes: Given a program, if a change to its interpretation cannot be detected by a trusted test set, the program is considered to be robust to this change, in other words, this change is considered to be reliable for the program. It is possible for SMT to further explore whether some reliable change leads to better performance.

This paper makes several contributions. First, it applies SMT to three rule-based agent programming languages, namely Jason, GOAL and 2APL. Second, it provides several contexts (scenarios) in which SMT for these languages is useful. Third, it proposes sets of semantic mutation operators (i.e., rules to make semantic changes) for these languages respectively, and a systematic approach to derivation of semantic mutation operators for rule-based agent languages. Finally, it presents a preliminary evaluation of the semantic mutation operators for Jason, which shows some potential of SMT to assess tests, robustness to and reliability of semantic changes.

The remainder of this paper is structured as follows: Sect. 2 describes two types of mutation testing, namely traditional mutation testing and semantic mutation testing. Section 3 describes SMT for Jason, GOAL and 2APL by showing several contexts in which it is useful and the source of semantic changes required to apply SMT in each context. Section 4 proposes sets of semantic mutation operators for these languages and an approach to derivation of semantic mutation operators for rule-based agent languages. Section 5 evaluates the semantic mutation operators for Jason. Section 6 compares our approach to related work, summarizes our work and suggests where this work could go in the future.

2   Mutation Testing

2.1   Traditional Mutation Testing

Traditional mutation testing is a test assessment technique that generates modified versions of a program and then examines whether a given test set has the ability to detect the modifications to the original program. Each modified program is called a *mutant*, which represents a potential small slip. Mutant generation is guided by a set of rules called *mutation operators*. For instance, Fig. 1(a) shows a piece of a program and Fig. 1(b)–(f) show five mutants generated as the result of the application of a single mutation operator called *Relational Operator Replacement*, which replaces one of the relational operators ($<, \leq, >, \geq, =, \neq$) by one of the others.

After mutant generation, the original program and each mutant are executed against all tests in the test set. For a mutant, if its resultant behaviour differs from the behaviour of the original program on some test, the mutant will be marked as *killed*, which indicates that the corresponding modification can be detected by the test set. Therefore, the fault detection ability of the test set can be assessed by the *mutant kill rate*– the ratio of the killed mutants to all generated mutants: the higher the ratio is, the more adequate the test set is. In the example shown in Fig. 1, a test set consisting of a single test in

which the input is *x = 3, y = 5* cannot kill the mutants shown in Fig. 1(b) and
(f) because on that test these two *live* mutants result in the same behaviour as the
original program (i.e., *return a*). Therefore, the mutant kill rate is 3/5. According to this
result we can enhance the test set by adding a test in which the input is *x = 4, y = 4* and
another test in which the input is *x = 4, y = 3* in order to kill these two live mutants
respectively and get a higher mutant kill rate (the highest kill rate is 1, as this example
shows).

```
if(x<y) {                if(x<=y) {                if(x>y) {
    return a;                return a;                 return a;
} else {                 } else {                  } else {
    return b;                return b;                 return b;
}                        }                         }

      (a)                      (b)                       (c)


if(x>=y) {               if(x==y) {                if(x!=y) {
    return a;                return a;                 return a;
} else {                 } else {                  } else {
    return b;                return b;                 return b;
}                        }                         }

      (d)                      (e)                       (f)
```

Fig. 1. An example of traditional mutation testing

Many studies provide evidence that traditional mutation testing is a very rigorous
test assessment technique, so it is often used to assess other test techniques [2, 14].
However, the mutation operators used to guide mutant generation may lead to a large
number of mutants because a single mutation operator has to be applied to each
relevant point in the program and a single mutant only contains a modification to a
single relevant point (as shown in Fig. 1). This makes comparing the behaviour of the
original program with that of each mutant on each test is computationally expensive.

Another problem is that traditional mutation testing unpredictably produces
equivalent mutants– alternatives to the original program that are not representative of
faulty versions, in that their behaviour is no different from the original in any way that
matters for the correctness of the program. Thus, no reasonable test set can detect the
modifications they contain. Equivalent mutants must therefore be excluded from test
assessment (i.e., the calculation of the mutant kill rate). The exclusion of equivalent
mutants requires much manual work although this process may be partially automated.

2.2   Semantic Mutation Testing

Clark et al. [5] propose semantic mutation testing (SMT) and extend the definition of
mutation testing as follows: suppose N represents a program and L represents the
semantics of the language in which the program is written (so L determines how N is
interpreted), the pair (N, L) determines the program's behaviour. Traditional mutation

testing generates modified versions of the program namely N → (N$_1$, N$_2$, ..., N$_k$) while SMT generates different interpretations of the same program namely L → (L$_1$, L$_2$, ..., L$_k$). For SMT, L$_1$, L$_2$, ..., L$_k$ represent *semantic mutants*, their generation is guided by a set of rules called *semantic mutation operators*. For instance, Fig. 2 shows a piece of a program, a semantic mutant (i.e., a different interpretation of this program) is generated by the application of a single semantic mutation operator that causes the *if* keyword to be used for mutual exclusion (i.e., when an *if* is directly followed by another *if*, the second *if* statement is interpreted the same as an *else-if* statement).

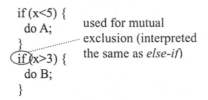

Fig. 2. An example of semantic mutation testing

SMT assesses a test set in a similar way as traditional mutation testing– comparing the behaviour under each semantic mutant with that under the original interpretation, in order to detect the killed mutants. In the example shown in Fig. 2, a test set consisting of a single test in which the input is *x* = 2 cannot kill the semantic mutant because on that test the mutant results in the same behavior as the original interpretation (i.e., only *do A*). Therefore, the mutant kill rate is 0/1 = 0. We can enhance this test set by adding another test in which the input is *x* = 4 in order to kill the live mutant.

Compared with traditional mutation testing, SMT aims to simulate a different class of faults, namely possible misunderstandings of how the program is interpreted. Although many semantic misunderstandings can also be simulated by mutation of the program, a single semantic change may require multiple changes to the program rather than a single, small change made by traditional mutation testing. In addition, some semantic misunderstandings may lead to complex faults that simple program changes are hard to represent, and these complex faults may be harder to detect than small slips, e.g., [5] shows that SMT has potential to capture some faults that cannot be captured by traditional mutation testing.

SMT has another difference to traditional mutation testing: it generates far fewer mutants because a single semantic mutation operator only leads to a single semantic mutant[1], namely a different interpretation of the same program (as shown in Fig. 2), while a single traditional mutation operator may lead to many mutants each of which contains a modification to a single relevant point in the program (as shown in Fig. 1). This makes SMT much less computationally costly.

---

[1] This rule can be relaxed, namely mutating the semantics of only parts of the program instead of mutating the semantics of the whole program. This is useful, e.g., when the program is developed by several people.

SMT can be used not only to assess tests, but also to assess robustness to and reliability of semantic changes. Given a semantic mutant, if it cannot be killed by a trusted test set[2], it will be considered to be "equivalent"[3], which indicates that the program is robust to the corresponding semantic change or the semantic change is reliable for the program, otherwise the program may need to be improved to resist this change, or this change has to be discarded. In the example shown in Fig. 2, if the program is required to be robust to the semantic change, it can be modified to ensure that at most one branch is executed in any case.

We know that SMT makes semantic changes for assessing tests, robustness to and reliability of semantic changes. For a particular language, which semantic changes should be made by SMT are context-dependent. For instance, to assess tests for a program written by a novice programmer, semantic changes to be made can be derived from common novices' misunderstandings of the semantics. To assess the portability of a program between different versions of the interpreter, semantic changes to be made can be derived from semantic differences between these versions.

3 Semantic Mutation Testing for Jason, GOAL and 2APL

We investigate semantic mutation testing for MASs by applying it to three rule-based programming languages for cognitive agents, namely Jason, GOAL and 2APL. These languages have generally similar semantics – an agent deliberates in a cyclic process in which it selects and executes rules according to and affecting its mental states. They also have similar constructs to implement such agents such as beliefs, goals and rules. The details of these languages can be found in [4, 6, 8] and are not provided here.

From Sect. 2.2 we know that for a particular language, the semantic changes that can most usefully be made by SMT is context-dependent. In the remainder of this section we provide several contexts in which SMT for the chosen agent languages is useful – use of a new language, evolution of languages, common misunderstandings, ambiguity of informal semantics and customization of the interpreter. We also show the source of semantic changes required to apply SMT in each context.

3.1 Use of a New Language

When a programmer starts to write a program in a new (to him or her) language, he or she may have misunderstandings that come from the semantic differences between the new language and the old one(s) he or she has ever used. Therefore, in order for SMT to simulate such misunderstandings, we should first find out their source, namely the semantic differences, by comparison between the new and the old languages. We use

---

[2] A trusted test set is the one that is considered to be "good enough" for the requirement. It doesn't need to be the full test set that is usually impractical; instead it can choose not to cover some aspects or to tolerate some errors.

[3] Here the term "equivalent" is different to the one used in the context of test assessment, in which a mutant is equivalent only if there exist no tests that can kill the mutant. In the context of robustness/reliability assessment, a mutant is equivalent if only the trusted test set cannot kill it.

Jason, GOAL and 2APL as an example: a programmer who has ever used one of these languages may start to use one of the others. Since these languages each have large semantic size and distinctive features, we use the following strategies to guide the derivation of the semantic differences between them.

- Dividing the semantics of each of these languages into five aspects, as shown in Table 1. We do this because first of all, it provides a focus on examining four aspects of the semantics, namely *deliberation step order*, *rule selection*, *rule execution*, and *mental state query and update*, all of which are important and common to rule-based agent languages, while including *other* aspects that will be generally examined in order for completeness. Second, it is reasonable that common aspects of the semantics are more likely to cause misunderstandings than distinctive aspects in the context of using a new language, because distinctive aspects are usually supported by distinctive constructs that a programmer would normally take time to learn.
- Focusing on semantic differences between similar constructs. As [5] suggests, such differences easily cause misunderstandings because when writing a program in a new language a programmer may copy the same or similar old constructs without careful examination of their semantics given by the new language.
- Examining both formal and informal semantics of these languages. We start with examining the formal semantics because they can be directly compared. We also verify those that are informally defined through coding and reviewing the interpreter source code.
- Focusing on the default interpreter configuration. The interpreters of these languages are customizable, for instance, the Jason agent architecture can be customized by inheritance of the Java class that implements the default agent architecture; the GOAL rule selection order can be customized in the GOAL agent description. We think the default interpreter configuration is more likely to cause misunderstandings in the context of using a new language because if a programmer customizes an element it suggests he or she is familiar with its semantics.

Table 1. The aspects of the semantics of Jason, GOAL and 2APL (those marked with an asterisk are the ones we focus on)

ID	Aspect	Description
1	Deliberation step order*	Each deliberation cycle consists of a sequence of steps, e.g., rule selection → rule execution is a two-step sub-sequence
2	Rule selection*	Rule selection is an important deliberation step in which one or several rules are chosen to be new execution candidates
3	Rule execution*	Rule execution is an important deliberation step in which one or several execution candidates are chosen to execute
4	Mental state query and update*	Mental states (i.e., beliefs and goals) can be queried in some deliberation steps such as rule selection and updated by execution of rules
5	Other	Other aspects of the semantics not listed above

Table 2 shows the semantic differences we found between Jason, GOAL and 2APL. These form the source of semantic changes required to apply SMT in the context of starting to use one of Jason, GOAL and 2APL from one of the others.

Table 2. Semantic differences between Jason, GOAL and 2APL

ID	Source	Jason	GOAL	2APL
1	The order of rule selection and rule execution	select a rule → execute a rule	(select and execute event rules → select and execute an action rule) x Number_of_Modules	select action rules → execute rules → select an external event rule → select an internal event rules → select a message event rule
2	Rule selection	• applicable • linear	• enabled • linear (action rules) and linearall (event rules)	• applicable • linear (event rules) and linearall (action rules)
3	Rule execution	• one rule/cycle	• one rule/cycle (action rules) and all rules/cycle (event rules)	• all rules/cycle
		• one action/rule	• all actions/rule	• one action/rule
4	Belief query	linear	random	linear
5	Belief addition	start	end	end
6	Goal query	$E \rightarrow I$; linear	random	linear
7	Goal addition	end of E	end	start or end
8	Goal deletion	delete the event and intention that relates to the goal φ	delete all super-goals of the goal φ	delete only the goal φ, all sub-goals of φ or all super-goals of φ
9	Goal type	procedural	declarative	declarative
10	Goal commitment strategy	no	blind	blind

Difference 1 comes from the order of two important deliberation steps, namely rule selection and rule execution. A Jason agent first selects a rule to be a new execution candidate and then chooses to execute an execution candidate. A GOAL agent processes its *modules* one by one, in each module it first selects and executes event rules and then selects and executes an action rule (both event and action rules are defined in the module being processed). A 2APL agent first selects action rules to be new execution candidates, and then executes all execution candidates, next selects an external event rule, an internal event rule and a message event rule to be new execution candidates.

Difference 2 comes from the rule selection deliberation step. Jason, GOAL and 2APL differ in two aspects of this step, namely the rule selection condition and the default rule selection order. For the rule selection condition, a Jason or 2APL rule can be selected to be a new execution candidate if both its trigger condition and guard condition get satisfied ("applicable"), while a GOAL rule can be selected if it is applicable and the pre-condition of its first action gets satisfied ("enabled"). For the default rule selection order, Jason rules are selected in linear order (i.e., rules are examined in the order they appear in the agent description, and the first applicable rule is selected), GOAL action rules are selected in linear order while GOAL event rules are selected in "linearall" order (i.e., rules are examined in the order they appear in the agent description, and all enabled rules are selected), 2APL action rules are selected in "linearall" order while 2APL event rules of each type (external, internal, message) are selected in linear order.

Difference 3 comes from the rule execution deliberation step. In this step a Jason agent chooses a single execution candidate and then executes a single action in this candidate, a GOAL agent executes all actions in each selected event rule and each selected action rule[4], a 2APL agent executes a single action in each execution candidate.

Difference 4 comes from the belief query. In a Jason or 2APL agent, beliefs are queried in linear order (i.e., beliefs are examined in the order they are stored in the belief base, and the first matched belief is returned). In a GOAL agent, beliefs are queried in random order (i.e., beliefs are randomly accessed, and the first matched belief is returned).

Difference 5 comes from the belief addition. In a Jason agent, a new belief is added to the start of the belief base. In a GOAL or 2APL agent a new belief is added to the end of the belief base.

Difference 6 comes from the goal query. In a Jason agent, since goals exist in related events and intentions, the agent queries a goal by first examining its event base then its intention set following linear query order. In a GOAL agent, goals are queried in random order. In a 2APL agent, goals are queried in linear order.

Difference 7 comes from the goal addition. In a Jason or GOAL agent, a new goal is added to the end of the event or goal base. In a 2APL agent, a new goal is added to the start or the end of the goal base according to the relevant agent description (i.e., *adopta* or *adoptz*).

Difference 8 comes from the goal deletion. Given a goal φ to be deleted, a Jason agent deletes the event and intention that relates to φ, a GOAL agent deletes all goals that have φ as a logical sub-goal, a 2APL agent deletes only φ, all goals that are a logical sub-goal of φ, or all goals that have φ as a logical sub-goal according to the relevant agent description (i.e., *dropgoal*, *dropsubgoal* or *dropsupergoal*).

Difference 9 comes from the goal type. Jason adopts procedural goals– goals that only serve as triggers of procedures although it supports declarative goal patterns. GOAL and 2APL adopt declarative goals– goals that also represent states of affairs to achieve.

---

[4] Unlike Jason and 2APL, a GOAL agent has no intention set or similar structure, so a GOAL rule is immediately attempted to execute to completion once selected.

Difference 10 comes from the goal commitment strategy. Jason doesn't adopt any goal commitment strategy (i.e., a goal is just dropped once its associated intention is removed as the result of completion or failure) although it supports various commitment strategy patterns. GOAL and 2APL adopt blind goal commitment strategy, which requires a goal is pursued until it is achieved or declaratively dropped.

3.2 Evolution of Languages

When a programmer moves a program from a language to its successor (either a different language or a newer version of the same language), he or she may have misunderstandings that come from the semantic evolution, or may want to examine whether a program is robust to the semantic evolution or whether the semantic evolution is reliable. To derive semantic changes required to apply SMT in these cases, we should first find out their source, namely the semantic differences between the language and its successor. We take 2APL and its predecessor 3APL [7], and different versions of Jason as examples: Table 3 shows some semantic differences between 2APL and 3APL; Table 4 shows some semantic differences between different versions of Jason, which are derived from the Jason changelog [11]. We explain these differences as follows.

Semantic Differences Between 2APL and 3APL. Difference 1 comes from the PR-rules. In 2APL, the abbreviation "PR" means "plan repair", a PR-rule (i.e. an internal event rule) is selected if a relevant plan fails. In 3APL, "PR" means "plan revision", a PR-rule is selected if it matches some plan.

Difference 2 comes from the order of rule selection and rule execution deliberation steps. The order adopted by a 2APL agent has been described in Sect. 3.1. In contrast, a 3APL agent selects an action rule then a PR-rule to be new execution candidates, then chooses to execute an execution candidate.

Difference 3 comes from the action rule selection order. As described in Sect. 3.1, 2APL action rules are selected in "linearall" order. In contrast, 3APL action rules are selected in linear order.

Difference 4 comes from the rule execution deliberation step. As described in Sect. 3.1, a 2APL agent executes all execution candidates in a deliberation cycle. In contrast, a 3APL agent chooses to execute a single execution candidate.

Table 3. Some semantics differences between 2APL and 3APL

ID	Source	2APL	3APL
1	PR-rules	plan repair	plan revision
2	The order of rule selection and rule execution	see Table 2	select an action rule → select a PR-rule → execute a rule
3	Action rule selection	linearall	linear
4	Rule execution	all rules/cycle	one rule/cycle

Semantic Differences Between Different Versions of Jason. Difference 1 comes from the belief deletion action. Since Jason v0.95 the belief deletion action-*b* deletes *b* if *b* is a mental note (i.e. *b* has the annotation *source(self)*), while this action deletes *b* wherever it originates from before that version of Jason.

Difference 2 comes from the drop desire action. Since Jason v0.96 the drop desire action *.drop_desire(d)* removes the event and intention that is related to *d*, while this action removes only the related event before that version of Jason.

Table 4. Some semantic differences between different versions of Jason

ID	Source	Before some version	Since that version
1	Belief deletion action	-*b* deletes *b* wherever it originates from	-*b* deletes *b* if *b* has the annotation *source(self)*
2	Drop desire action	Remove only the related event	Remove the related event and intention

3.3 Common Misunderstandings

A programmer may have semantic misunderstandings that are common to a particular group of people he or she belongs to. Such misunderstandings can be identified by analysis of these people's common mistakes or faults. We take GOAL as an example: Table 5 shows some possible misunderstandings of the GOAL's semantics, which are derived from some common faults made by GOAL novice programmers [20]. We explain these misunderstandings as follows.

Possible misunderstanding 1 comes from the fault of the wrong rule order. If a programmer makes this fault in the GOAL agent description, he or she may have the misunderstanding that rules are selected in another available order[5] by default, e.g., action rules are selected in "linearall" order rather than linear order.

Possible misunderstanding 2 comes from the fault of a single rule including two user-defined actions. If a programmer makes this fault, he or she may have the misunderstanding that this is allowed like other agent languages.

Possible misunderstanding 3 comes from the fault of using "if then" instead of "forall do". If a programmer makes this fault, he or she may have the misunderstanding that "if then" is interpreted the same as "forall do".

Table 5. Some possible novice programmers' misunderstandings of GOAL

ID	Fault	Possible misunderstanding
1	Wrong rule order	By default rules are selected in another available order
2	A single rule including two user-defined actions	A rule can have more than one user-defined action
3	Using "if then" instead of "forall do"	"if then" is interpreted the same as "forall do"

---

[5] GOAL supports four available rule evaluation orders: linear, linearall, random and randomall.

3.4   Ambiguity of Informal Semantics

A programmer may have misunderstandings of the semantics that are imprecisely or informally defined. For instance, [3] gives two examples of such misunderstandings of Jason as shown in Table 6. We explain these misunderstandings as follows.

Possible misunderstanding 1 comes from the goal deletion event. A goal deletion event (-!e or -?e) is generated if an intention that has the corresponding goal addition triggering event (+!e or +?e) fails. A programmer may have the misunderstanding that this event is generated if this intention is removed as the result of completion or failure.

Possible misunderstanding 2 comes from the test action. A test action (?e) generates a test goal addition event if it fails. A programmer may have the misunderstanding that a test action generates a test goal addition event if it is executed, which is similar to an achievement goal action (!e).

Table 6. Some possible misunderstanding of the Jason's informal semantics

ID	Source	Possible misunderstanding
1	Goal deletion event	"if an intention fails" → "if an intention is removed"
2	Test action	Generate a test goal addition event if the action fails → Generate a test goal addition event if the action is executed

3.5   Customization of the Interpreter

The interpreters of Jason, GOAL and 2APL can be customized through modifying/overriding the functions of the interpreter or choosing between the provided options that can change the interpreter behaviour. Given an agent description, a programmer may want to know whether a custom interpreter provides an alternative to the original interpretation of the description. (The programmer may further examine whether the alternative interpretation leads to better performance, e.g., higher execution efficiency.) SMT can be applied in this context to represent potential customizations of the interpreter. We take Jason as an example: Table 7 shows some Jason interpreter configuration options, which are derived from the Jason changelog [11].

Table 7. Some Jason interpreter configuration options

ID	Option description
1	Enable/disable tail recursion optimization for sub-goals
2	Enable/disable cache for queries in the same cycle
3	Choose whether the event generated by the belief revision action will be treated as internal or external

3.6   Discussion

SMT is interesting to Jason, GOAL and 2APL in the contexts discussed above considering:

- These languages are declarative languages. They provide a focus on describing capabilities and responsibilities of an agent in terms of beliefs, goals, plans, etc., while encapsulating in the interpreter how an agent goes about fulfilling the responsibilities using the available capabilities. As a result, programmers are likely to pay insufficient attention to how an agent works, and therefore have relevant misunderstandings.

- These languages have customizable semantics. Since the semantics affects the agent behaviour and performance as well as the agent program, it is useful to explore different customizations of the semantics.

4 Semantic Mutation Operators for Jason, GOAL and 2APL

According to our derived sources of semantic changes required to apply SMT in different contexts, we derive three respective sets of semantic mutation operators for Jason, GOAL and 2APL as shown in Tables 8, 9 and 10. Due to space limitations we don't explain each semantic mutation operator in details.

It is worth noting that each operator set does not cover each context discussed in Sect. 3, e.g., the operator set for Jason has no operators that are derived from common misunderstandings of Jason. Therefore, we will improve each set when we acquire more sources of potential semantic changes to the corresponding language. In Table 8 each operator is labeled with its context(s) from which it is derived, e.g., the rule selection order change (RSO) operator for Jason is labeled with UNL (use of a new language), which indicates that this operator is derived from and can be used in (but is not limited to) the context of use of a new language discussed in Sect. 3.1.

Another noteworthy thing is that not every possible semantic change derived from Tables 2, 3, 4, 5, 6, and 7 develops into a (or part of a) semantic mutation operator because some of them are considered to be unrealistic. Therefore, these unrealistic changes are adapted or simply discarded. A semantic change is considered to be unrealistic if it satisfies one of the following.

- It requires a significant change in the interpreter. We think that a programmer is not very likely to misunderstand the semantics a lot or to make such semantic change.
- It leads to the significantly different behaviour of each of our selected agent programs written in the corresponding language (i.e., 6 Jason programs, 6 GOAL programs or 4 2APL programs). We think that this semantic change is very easy to detect.

After analysis of these semantic mutation operators we find that most of them concern three kinds of the interpreter behaviour, namely *select*, *query* and *update*[6]. The elements to be selected include deliberation steps, rules, intentions, actions, etc; those to be queried or updated include beliefs, goals, events, etc. We also find that most

---

[6] We ever considered two more kinds of the interpreter behaviour, namely *transit* (between deliberation steps) and *execute* (a rule or action). However, we find that these two kinds can be classified as *select*, namely select between deliberation steps and select a rule or action to execute. This simplifies our classification.

operators change certain aspects of the interpreter behaviour, i.e., *order*, *quantity*, *position* and *condition*[7]. Tables 11(a) and (b) list the kinds of the interpreter behaviour and the changeable aspects respectively (*other* kinds and aspects not mentioned above are included in order for completeness). Therefore, we propose a systematic approach to derivation of semantic mutation operators for rule-based agent languages, namely application of a changeable aspect into a kind of the interpreter behaviour. In Table 8 each semantic mutation operator is labeled with the kind of the interpreter behaviour it concerns and the aspect it changes, both of which are identified by their IDs shown in Table 11 (i.e., KID and AID respectively).

Abbreviations for the contexts discussed in Section 3

Use of a New Language: UNL   Evolution of Languages: EL
Common Misunderstandings: CM   Ambiguity of Informal Semantics: AIS
Customization of Interpreter: CI

Table 8. Semantic mutation operators for Jason

ID	Semantic mutation operator	Description	Context	KID	AID
1	Rule selection order change(RSO)	linear → linearall	UNL	1	1
2	Intention selection order change (ISO)	one intention/cycle → all intentions/cycle	UNL	1	1
3	Intention selection order change 2 (ISO2)	interleaved selection of intentions → non-interleaved selection of intentions	UNL	1	1
4	Belief query order change (BQO)	linear → random	UNL	2	1
5	Belief addition position change (BAP)	start → end	UNL	3	3
6	Belief revision action semantics change (BRAS)	generate internal events → generate external events[a]	CI	3	3
7	Belief deletion action semantics change (BDAS)	-b deletes b if b has the annotation source(self) → -b deletes b	EL	3	4
8	Goal addition position change (GAP)	end → start	UNL	3	3

(*Continued*)

[7] These changeable aspects may have overlaps, e.g., the change "select one rule → select all rules" can be a change to the order or the quantity.

Table 8. (*Continued*)

ID	Semantic mutation operator	Description	Context	KID	AID
9	Drop desire action semantics change (DDAS)	remove the related event and intention → remove only the related event	EL	3	2
10	Test goal action semantics change (TGAS)	generate a test goal addition event if the action fails → generate a test goal addition event if the action is executed	AIS	3	4
11	TRO enable/disable (TRO)	enable/disable tail recursion optimization for sub-goals	CI	3	5
12	Query cache enable/disable (QC)	enable/disable cache for queries in the same cycle	CI	2	5

[a]The plan chosen for an internal event will be pushed on top of the intention from which the event is generated; the plan chosen for an external event will become a new intention

Table 9. Semantic mutation operators for GOAL

ID	Semantic mutation operator	Description	Context	KID	AID
1	Rule selection and execution order change (RSEO)	select and execute event rules then an action rule → select and execute an action rule then event rules	UNL	1	1
2	Rule selection condition change (RSC)	enabled → applicable	UNL	1	4
3	Rule selection order change (RSO)	change between linear, linearall, random and randomall	UNL, CM	1	1
4	Belief query order change (BQO)	random → linear	UNL	2	1
5	Belief addition position change (BAP)	end → start	UNL	3	3
6	Goal query order change (GQO)	random → linear	UNL	2	1
7	Goal addition position change (GAP)	end → start	UNL	3	3
8		"delete φ' if it is a super-goal of φ" → "delete φ' if it is φ"	UNL	3	4

(*Continued*)

Table 9. (*Continued*)

ID	Semantic mutation operator	Description	Context	KID	AID
	Goal deletion semantics change (GDS)	or "delete φ' if it is a sub-goal of φ"			
9	The maximum number of user-defined actions change (MNUA)	1 → more than 1	CM	4	2
10	"if then" semantics change (ITS)	make "if then" interpreted the same as "forall do"	CM	2	2

Table 10. Semantic mutation operators for 2APL

ID	Semantic mutation operator	Description	Context	KID	AID
1	Rule selection and rule execution order change (RSREO)	change the original order "select action rules → execute rules → select event rules" to "select action rules → select event rules → execute rules" or "select event rules → select action rules → execute rules"	UNL, EL	1	1
2	Rule selection condition change (RSC)	applicable → enabled	UNL	1	4
3	Rule selection order change (RSO)	change between linear and linearall	UNL, EL	1	1
4	Plan selection order change (PSO)	all plans/cycle → one plan/cycle	UNL, EL	1	1
5	Belief query order change (BQO)	linear → random	UNL	2	1
6	Belief addition position change (BAP)	end → start	UNL	3	3
7	Goal query order change (GQO)	linear → random	UNL	2	1
8	PR-rule selection condition change (PRSC)	select a PR-rule if the relevant plan fails → select a PR-rule if it matches some plan	EL	1	4

Table 11. (a) Kinds of the interpreter behaviour (b) Changeable aspects of the interpreter behaviour

(a)

KID	Kind
1	Select
2	Query
3	Update
4	Other

(b)

AID	Aspect
1	Order
2	Quantity
3	Position
4	Condition
5	Other

5   Evaluation of Semantic Mutation Operators for Jason

In order to assess the potential of SMT to assess tests, robustness to and reliability of semantic changes, we develop a semantic mutation system for Jason called *smsJason*. *smsJason* has three components, namely *tests*, *semantic mutation operators*, and *controller*, which are explained as follows.

- *tests* contains the following two custom parts for a particular Jason project:
  - A collection of tests. Each test is an array of values that can be used to instantiate the parameterized agent/environment description. A random test generator is employed to generate random tests given the constraints of each parameter. In addition, each test will be assigned a lifetime at runtime. This lifetime equals to the time taken by the Jason project under the original interpretation to pass this test plus a specified generous tolerance value for this test[8]. The Jason project under any mutant on this test will terminate anyhow when reaching this lifetime, if the project does not terminate as the result of passing this test yet.
  - Test pass criteria. The test pass criteria will be constantly examined at runtime in order to judge whether the Jason project has passed the current test. If the Jason project under the original interpretation is found to pass the current test, it will terminate and the lifetime of the test will be derived; if the project under any mutant is found to pass the current test before the lifetime of the test, it will terminate and the mutant will be marked as "live", otherwise it will terminate when reaching this lifetime and the mutant will be marked as "killed".
- *semantic mutation operators* implements our derived semantic mutation operators for Jason as shown in Table 8. Each operator leads to a modified version of the Jason interpreter (v1.4.1) which is pointed by a branch in Git [12] and can therefore be switched to another at runtime via Git API.
- *controller* implements the process of semantic mutation testing as shown in the following pseudo-code. *JRebel* [13], a powerful class reload technique, is employed to deploy each test (namely each instance of the parameterized agent/environment description) at runtime quickly.

---

[8] The tolerance value is added because the exact time taken by the Jason project varies over a limited range in different runs. It is generous because the execution efficiency is not considered as part of the test pass criteria.

```
1:   On each test:
2:       Run the Jason project under the original
             interpreter until it passes the test
3:       Derive the lifetime of the test

4:   Under each generated mutant:
5:       On each test:
6:           Run the Jason project until it passes the test
                 or reaches the lifetime of the test
7:           Mark the mutant as "live" or "killed"
8:           Update the number of tests that killed the
                 mutant if the test killed the mutant

9:   Display the SMT result
```

We apply *smsJason* into two Jason projects released with the Jason interpreter, namely *Domestic Robot* (DR) and *Blocks World* (BW). In DR, a robot constantly gets beer from the fridge and then serves its owner the beer until the owner exceeds a certain limit of drinking. The robot will ask the supermarket to deliver beer when the fridge is found empty. In BW, an agent restacks the blocks as required, by a series of actions of carrying or putting down a single block. We specify tests and test pass criteria for DR and BW as summarized in Tables 12 and 13, after which we start the semantic mutation testing for each project. We analyze the SMT results displayed by *smsJason* and present the final results in Table 14.

Table 12. The tests and test pass criteria for the *Domestic Robot*

Parameter	Constraints	Test Pass Criteria
Drinking limit (*Dl*)	$Dl \in [0, 16]$	*All* of the following must be satisfied.
Map size (*S* x *S*)	$S \in [1, 16]$	1. The robot is not carrying beer; 2. The robot has advised the owner about
Initial beer in the fridge (*Ib*)	$Ib \in [0, 16]$	having exceeded the drinking limit;
Initial position of the robot (*Pr*)	*Pr*, *Pf* and *Po*	3. The robot has checked the current time as requested by the owner;
Initial position of the fridge (*Pf*)	take the form of (*X, Y*), where *X*,	4. $Dl + 1 = Ib + Db - Rb$, where *Db* is the beer delivered by the supermarket and *Rb* is the remaining beer in the fridge.
Initial position of the owner (*Po*)	$Y \in [0, S - 1]$	
Total number of tests: 160		

smsJason identifies the killed mutants (K), and we further classify those live mutants. First, by static analysis of the agent program we find that some live mutants are inapplicable (N/A) because the program has no constructs concerning the mutated semantics. For instance, the BW agent program has no actions of belief revision, belief deletion, drop desire and test goal, hence BRAS, BDAS, DDAS and TGAS are inapplicable to BW. Second, we attempt to identify equivalent mutants (E) among the

Table 13. The tests and test pass criteria for the *Blocks World*

Parameter	Constraints	Test pass criteria
Original Stacks of Blocks (*OS*)	*OS* or *ES* is a set of lists and a partition of the set {"a", "b", "c", "d", "e", "f", "g"} representing all blocks; 1	*OS* = *ES*
Expected Stacks of Blocks (*ES*)	$\leq |OS|, |ES| \leq 3$	

Total number of tests: 80

Table 14. Results of semantic mutation testing

SMOP	Domestic robot		Blocks world	
	Percentage of tests that kill the mutant	Mutant type	Percentage of tests that kill the mutant	Mutant type
RSO	0	NE	0	E
ISO	0	E	0	E
ISO2	100%	K	0	E
BQO	0	E	0	NE
BAP	0	E	37.5%	K
BRAS	0	N/A	0	N/A
BDAS	0	E	0	N/A
GAP	0	E	0	E
DDAS	0	N/A	0	N/A
TGAS	91.88%	K	0	N/A
TRO	0	E	0	E
QC	0	E	0	E

applicable mutants by static and dynamic analysis of the agent program. For instance, we find that the DR or BW agent program has no constructs that cause the order of goal related events to matter; we also verify this through observing in Jason's mind inspector the relevant changes in agents' mental attitudes on all tests. Therefore, we conclude that GAP probably leads to the equivalent mutant. If we find a mutant likely to be not equivalent we will attempt to improve the tests or test pass criteria in order to kill it and classify it as non-equivalent (NE).

5.1   Assessment of Tests

The non-equivalent mutants (NE) indicate the weaknesses in the tests or test pass criteria. In order to kill such a mutant that RSO leads to, we need to capture the differences in the resultant agent behaviour between selecting all applicable plans and selecting only the first applicable plan. These plans must have the same triggering event, the contexts that are not mutually exclusive and the ability to affect the agent behaviour. In the DR agent program, the only two such plans are the robot's plan to get beer when the fridge is empty (*p1*) and the robot's plan to get beer when the owner exceeds the limit of drinking (*p2*). Therefore, we need a test on which the owner just exceeds the limit of drinking when there is no beer in the fridge. This test will cause *p2* to execute twice under the mutant so that the robot will advise the owner twice about having exceeded the drinking limit. We also need to improve the test pass criteria to capture the number of advices given by the robot.

In order to kill the non-equivalent mutant that BQO leads to, we need to capture the differences in the resultant agent behaviour between querying beliefs in linear order and in random order. In the BW agent program, there is only one place that causes the belief order or belief query order to matter, namely the context of the plan (*p*) which is to remove a block from the top of a stack in order to further move a block (*b*) in the same stack. It is worth noting that *b* can belong to more than one stack held by the belief base, for instance, there are two stacks, namely *S(b1, b2, b)* and *S(b2, b)*, where the former contains the latter. In order to move *b*, *b1* has to be removed first.

Under the original interpretation where beliefs are queried in linear order, the context of *p* always first returns *S(b1, b2, b)* so that *b1* can be removed first. This is because the larger the stack is, the more recently it is added to the start of the belief base, as the result of the application of the belief revision rule to derive stacks. In contrast, under the mutant that BQO leads to, the context of *p* is likely to first return *S (b2, b)*, which causes *p* to retry until *S(b1, b2, b)* is returned because *b2* cannot be removed before *b1*. Therefore, we need to improve the tests or test pass criteria in order to capture the retrying of *p*, e.g., we can design a test on which there exists a large stack *S(b1, b2, b3, b4, b5, b6, b)* while the target block to be moved is *b*. This test will probably cause *p* to retry many times so that the number of the slots, each of which is assigned by an execution of *p* to place a block, will exceed the table capacity.

5.2   Assessment of Robustness to Semantic Changes

The equivalent mutants (E) indicate that the agent program is robust to the corresponding semantic changes, while the killed or non-equivalent mutants (K or NE) indicate the weaknesses in robustness. In order for the DR agent program to be robust to the semantic change caused by RSO, we can improve the program by ensuring that there is only one applicable non-empty plan at most in every deliberation cycle. As mentioned in Sect. 5.1, there are only two non-empty plans (*p1* and *p2*) which are likely to become applicable simultaneously in the same cycle, therefore, we can make their contexts mutually exclusive, e.g., by strengthening the context of *p2*.

In order for the BW agent program to be robust to the semantic changes caused by BQO and BAP, we need to make the program's behaviour independent of the order of beliefs or querying beliefs. As mentioned in Sect. 5.1, there is only one place that causes these orders to matter, namely the context of *p*. Therefore, we can strengthen this context to ensure that it always first returns the largest stack.

As for the semantic changes caused by ISO2 and TGAS, we find it very expensive hence inappropriate to make the agent program be robust to these changes.

5.3   Assessment of Reliability of Semantic Changes

We have improved the DR agent program to resist the semantic change caused by RSO and the BW agent program to resist the semantic changes caused by BQO and BAP, as suggested in Sect. 5.2. Therefore, RSO, BQO and BAP lead to reliable alternative interpretations of the corresponding agent program as well as the equivalent mutants as shown in Table 14. To further assess the execution efficiency that these reliable alternative interpretations lead to, we make *smsJason* be able to compare the test execution time under the original interpretation and under each reliable alternative interpretation. We present the results of execution efficiency assessment in Table 15.

Table 15. Results of execution efficiency assessment

SMOP	Domestic robot		Blocks world	
	Percentage of avg saved time	Percentage of tests that saved time	Percentage of avg saved time	Percentage of tests that saved time
RSO	−0.06%	45.63%	−0.33%	41.25%
ISO	7.5%	100%	28.42%	100%
ISO2	N/A		−0.72%	37.5%
BQO	0.49%	53.75%	0.16%	63.75%
BAP	−0.34%	38.75%	−0.15%	41.25%
BRAS	N/A		N/A	
BDAS	−0.01%	43.75%	N/A	
GAP	0.23%	50.63%	0.19%	51.25%
DDAS	N/A		N/A	
TGAS	N/A		N/A	
TRO	0.33%	45.63%	0.08%	50%
QC	0.13%	43.13%	0.27%	46.25%

In Table 15, the inapplicable or unreliable mutants are marked as "N/A". Among the reliable mutants, the one caused by ISO is interesting because it significantly reduces the average execution time of DR and BW by 7.5 and 28.42 percent respectively, and it leads to efficiency improvement on all tests.

The changes in efficiency that are caused by other reliable mutants are not significant hence may be mainly caused by normal floating of execution time.

6   Related Work and Conclusions

In Sect. 2 we compared SMT to traditional mutation testing. Here we compare them in terms of multi-agent systems, by two examples showing that the semantic mutation operators for GOAL as shown in Table 9 can simulate some faults that cannot be captured by the traditional mutation operators for GOAL which are derived by Savarimuthu and Winikoff [18].

The RSO semantic mutation operator for GOAL can change the action rule selection order from "linear" to "linearall", which is similar to the change from *else-if* to *if*. We examine the traditional mutation operators for GOAL and find no operators that can simulate this semantic change. For instance, one traditional mutation operator can *drop* a single rule and another can *swap* two rules, however, they cannot simulate this semantic change.

The BQO semantic mutation operator changes the belief query order from "random" to "linear". Again we cannot find any traditional mutation operator for GOAL that can simulate this semantic change.

In this paper, we applied SMT to Jason, GOAL and 2APL. We showed that SMT for these languages is useful in several contexts, namely use of a new language, evolution of languages, common misunderstandings, ambiguity of informal semantics and customization of the interpreter. We derived sets of semantic mutation operators for these languages, and proposed a systematic approach to derivation of semantic mutation operators for rule-based agent languages. Finally, we used two Jason projects in a preliminary evaluation of the semantic mutation operators for Jason. The results suggest that SMT has some potential to assess tests, robustness to and reliability of semantic changes.

Our future work will focus on further evaluation of the semantic mutation operators for Jason. To further evaluate the ability of these operators to assess tests, we will examine their *representativeness* by comparing to realistic semantic misunderstandings and their *power* by looking for more hard-to-kill mutants (as we have done in this paper), as suggested by [10]. To further evaluate the ability of these operators to assess robustness to and reliability of semantic changes, we will apply them to more Jason projects so as to provide more suggestions on improving program robustness and optimizing interpreter.

References

1. Adra, S.F., McMinn, P.: Mutation operators for agent-based models. In: Proceedings of 5th International Workshop on Mutation Analysis. IEEE Computer Society (2010)
2. Ammann, P., Offutt, J.: Introduction to Software Testing. Cambridge University Press, New York (2008)
3. Bordini, R.H., Hübner, J.F.: Semantics for the Jason variant of AgentSpeak (plan failure and some internal actions). In: Proceedings of ECAI 2010, pp. 635–640 (2010)
4. Bordini, R.H., Hübner, J.F., Wooldridge, M.: Programming Multi-Agent Systems in AgentSpeak using Jason. Wiley, Hoboken (2007)
5. Clark, J.A., Dan, H., Hierons, R.M.: Semantic Mutation Testing. Science of Computer Programming (2011)
6. Dastani, M.: 2APL: a practical agent programming language. Auton. Agent. Multi-Agent Syst. **16**(3), 214–248 (2008)
7. Dastani, M., van Riemsdijk, M.B., Meyer, J.J.C.: Programming multi-agent systems in 3APL. In: Bordini, R.H., Dastani, M., Dix, J., El Fallah Seghrouchni, A. (eds.) Multi-Agent Programming. Languages, Platforms and Applications, pp. 39–67. Springer, Heidelberg (2005)

8. Hindriks, K.V.: Programming rational agents in GOAL. In: Bordini, R.H., Dastani, M., Dix, J., El Fallah Seghrouchni, A. (eds.) Multi-agent programming. Languages, platforms and applications, vol. 2, pp. 3–37. Springer, Heidelberg (2009)
9. Houhamdi, Z.: Multi-agent system testing: a survey. Int. J. Adv. Comput. Sci. Appl. (IJACSA) 2(6), 135–141 (2011)
10. Huang, Z., Alexander, R., Clark, J.: Mutation testing for Jason agents. In: Dalpiaz, F., Dix, J., van Riemsdijk, M. (eds.) EMAS 2014. LNCS, vol. 8758, pp. 309–327. Springer, Heidelberg (2014)
11. Jason changelog. http://sourceforge.net/p/jason/svn/HEAD/tree/trunk/release-notes.txt
12. JGit documentation. https://eclipse.org/jgit/documentation/
13. JRebel documentation. http://zeroturnaround.com/software/jrebel/learn/
14. Mathur, A.P.: Foundations of Software Testing. Pearson, New Delhi (2008)
15. Nguyen, C.D., Perini, A., Bernon, C., Pavón, J., Thangarajah, J.: Testing in multi-agent systems. In: Gomez-Sanz, J.J. (ed.) AOSE 2009. LNCS, vol. 6038, pp. 180–190. Springer, Heidelberg (2011)
16. Saifan, A.A., Wahsheh, H.A.: Mutation operators for JADE mobile agent systems. In: Proceedings of the 3rd International Conference on Information and Communication Systems, ICICS (2012)
17. Savarimuthu, S., Winikoff, M.: Mutation operators for cognitive agent programs. In: Proceedings of the 2013 International Conference on Autonomous Agents and Multi-Agent Systems (AAMAS 2013), pp. 1137–1138 (2013)
18. Savarimuthu, S., Winikoff, M.: Mutation operators for the GOAL agent language. In: Winikoff, M. (ed.) EMAS 2013. LNCS, vol. 8245, pp. 255–273. Springer, Heidelberg (2013)
19. Tiryaki, A.M., Öztuna, S., Dikenelli, O., Erdur, R.C.: SUNIT: a unit testing framework for test driven development of multi-agent systems. In: Padgham, L., Zambonelli, F. (eds.) AOSE VII/AOSE 2006. LNCS, vol. 4405, pp. 156–173. Springer, Heidelberg (2007)
20. Winikoff, M.: Novice programmers' faults & failures in GOAL programs. In: Proceedings of the 2014 International Conference on Autonomous Agents and Multi-Agent Systems (AAMAS 2014), pp. 301–308 (2014)

A Formal Description of a Mapping from Business Processes to Agents

Tobias Küster[(✉)], Marco Lützenberger, and Sahin Albayrak

DAI-Labor, Technische Universität Berlin,
Ernst-Reuter-Platz 7, 10587 Berlin, Germany
tobias.kuester@dai-labor.de

Abstract. Having many notions in common with multi-agent systems, business processes are well suited for modelling agents and their interrelations. However, often vague semantics and structural differences make a mapping from business processes to multi-agent systems difficult. In this paper, we formally describe a mapping from business process models to multi-agent systems that can be applied to different agent frameworks and languages. Using the same mapping, we created three semantically equivalent and interoperable implementations suiting different areas of application.

Keywords: Technological · Methodological

1 Introduction

Business process modelling has many notions in common with agents-oriented programming: It serves as a high-level abstraction for distributed systems composed of many cooperative or competing actors, communicating via messages and services, and reacting to events. Thus, it is not surprising that process modelling has been adopted for the modelling of multi-agent systems in a number of works (cf. [4–6], and others).

One common problem with translating processes to agents (or, in fact, most other programming systems) is the mapping of free-form process graphs to block structured programming languages. Also, the mapping is often informal and ambiguous, or it covers just a part of the notation, particularly for more expressive (and thus interesting) notations like BPMN [18].

In this paper, we describe a mapping from BPMN processes to multi-agent systems. The mapping covers diverse aspects of processes and agents, such as actors/roles, reaction rules, behaviours, events, services, and message-based communication [13], and can be applied to different agent programming languages and frameworks. It also includes a formal description of how individual process structures can be mapped to equivalent structures in block-oriented languages.

The mapping has been implemented in three different fashions for the JIAC V agent framework [16]. While each implementation has individual strength and weaknesses, making it suited for different applications, they behave the same

© Springer International Publishing Switzerland 2015
M. Baldoni et al. (Eds.): EMAS 2015, LNAI 9318, pp. 153–170, 2015.
DOI: 10.1007/978-3-319-26184-3_9

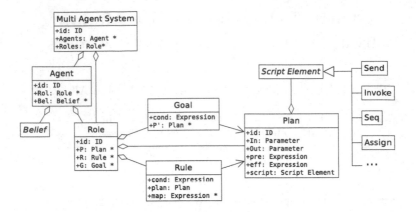

Fig. 1. Class diagram of agent meta model, slightly simplified

and are all interoperable with each other, such that different parts of the same process can be mapped to different implementation styles.

The remainder of this paper is structured as follows: In Sect. 2 we describe the models used for agents and processes. In Sect. 3, we use those models to define a mapping between them. Then, in Sect. 4, we present three different implementations of the mapping. Finally, we present related work in Sect. 5 and conclude in Sect. 6.

2   Agent and Process Model

In this section, we describe the meta models used for modelling the agent systems and processes. While some models can be found in the literature [3], we decided to provide our own definitions in order to have a uniform representation and to focus on those parts most relevant to the mapping.

2.1   Agent Meta Model

A common problem when dealing with agent systems is that the notion of an agent is not very clearly defined (see [8] for a number of possible definitions). Thus, in the following we provide a semi-formal definition of what constitutes an agent, and what those agents have to provide for the mapping to be applicable. Note that we are not pursuing to provide a general and exhaustive definition for agents, but to have a meta model streamlined for the task at hand: as a foundation for the mapping from processes to agents (Fig. 1).

The field of agents is immensely broad, and not only is it near impossible to define an agent meta model that suits all the different aspects of agents, but neither could a process modelling notation like BPMN be used to model all of those aspects. Thus, our goal is to keep this model as simple and as abstract as possible, so that the mapping is applicable to many different agent frameworks, even though it may not cover all of their specialities.

Agent Architecture. A multi-agent system $mas = (id, Agents, Roles)$ consists of several defined roles, and a number of concrete agents implementing those roles. Each agent $agent = (id, Rol, Bel)$ is primarily defined by the roles $Rol \subseteq Roles$ it implements. It may also have a number of beliefs Bel, both initial and those added at runtime. How those beliefs are represented is not of importance for this mapping. Roles define the behaviour of the agent. Each role $role = (id, Plans, Rules, Goals)$ consists of a number of plans, rules, and optionally goals. While the plans hold the actual actions to be taken, rules and goals specify when those actions should be executed.

Each plan $plan = (id, In, Out, pre, eff, script)$ describes one behaviour, which is detailed in an agent script. Plans have inputs and output lists, holding the names and types of the parameters and return values, as well as a semantic description in the form of preconditions and effects (IOPE). Rules $rule = (cond, plan, map)$ link an execution condition, matched against the agent's current beliefs, to a plan, and provide a mapping of values and variables from the condition to input parameters of the plan. Goals $goal = (cond, P')$ are defined by a condition, or world state to be achieved, and a number of plans from the agent's set of plans $P' \subseteq Plans$ available for fulfilling that goal.[1]

Agent Behaviour. The agent's plans are made up of script elements. How these scripts are implemented in an actual agent framework is irrelevant for the mapping, as long as the following atomic behaviours are supported:

- $send(m)$: Send message $m = (snd, rec, cnt)$ with given content cnt from sender snd to recipient rec.
- $receive(m)$: Receive message matching template $m = (snd, rec, cnt)$.
- $invoke(p, i, o)$: Call plan p with input i and store output in o.
- $ass(x, y)$: Evaluate expression y and assign result to variable x.
- $achieve(g)$: Add goal condition g to agent's goals and wait for completion.
- nop: No Operation.

Further, the following control-flow structures are required, including simple conditions and loops, but also basic threading for parallel execution:

- $seq(s_1, \ldots, s_n)$: Execute scripts $s_1, \ldots, s_n$ sequentially.
- $par(s_1, \ldots, s_n)$: Execute scripts $s_1, \ldots, s_n$ in parallel.
- $cond(c, x, y)$: Execute x, if condition c is true, else y.
- $while(c, s)$: Execute script s, while condition c is true.
- $fork(id, x)$: Execute script x in thread with ID id.
- $join(id)$: Wait for thread with ID id to finish.
- $stop(id)$: Interrupt Thread with ID id.
- $wait(t)$: Suspend execution for time t.

---

[1] We are only regarding *achieve* goals here. While there are several types of goals [21], *achieve* goals and *maintain* goals are clearly the most interesting of those. Further, *maintain* goals can easily be emulated with achieve goals and rules, by having a rule set a new achieve goal whenever the condition to be maintained is violated.

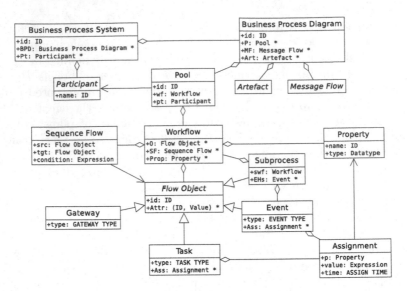

Fig. 2. Class diagram of process meta model, slightly simplified

While statements such as as *fork* and *join*, may not be present in some high-level agent languages, they could be emulated with different language elements, e.g., additional reaction rules. Otherwise, some features of the mapping, particularly the mapping of event handlers, can not be applied.

2.2 Process Meta Model

We decided to use BPMN (Business Process Model and Notation) [18] for modelling multi-agent systems. BPMN is a standardised notation that is widely used in practice [20]. It allows for modelling with a high level of abstraction while being detailed enough to generate readily executable systems. Also, it exhibits several language features that make it particularly useful for modelling distributed and autonomous systems, such as communication, interaction, and event handling.

While the BPMN specification focuses on the notational aspects of the language, there are several other works detailing its formal semantics (see, e.g., [7]). Still, we will define our own BPMN-based process meta model (see Fig. 2), being streamlined for describing the mapping proposed in this paper.

Process, Pool, Participant. At the top level, each business process system $bps = (id, BPD, Pt)$ consists of business process diagrams BPD and a set of participant names Pt. Process diagrams correspond to *use cases* and participants to *actors* having a role in those use cases. Each business process diagram $bpd = (id, Pl, MF, Art)$ (a BPMN diagram), with $bpd \in BPD$, contains one or more pools Pl, message flows MF, and optionally artefacts Art, such as text annotations.[2]

Each pool $pool = (id, wf, pt)$ is defined by a workflow $wf = (O, SF, Prop)$ and the name of the participant $pt \in Pt$ that is responsible for carrying out this workflow. A possible subdivision of pools into lanes is not regarded. The workflow consists of a set of flow objects O that are connected by (conditional) sequence flows $SF \subset O \times O \times (expressions \cup \{\varepsilon\})$. It can also declare a number of properties $Prop \subset name \times type$, i.e. variables.

Workflow Elements. The pool's workflows are made up of activities (*task* or *subprocess*), *events*, and *gateways*. Tasks, events and gateways are subdivided into different types, each with type-specific attributes $At \subset key \times value$. Further, tasks and events can have an arbitrary number of assignments $As \subset property \times expression \times \{\text{BEFORE}, \text{AFTER}\}$ that can be executed either before or after the element itself.

A task $task = (id, type_t, As, At_t)$ is an atomic' activity. The most important types of tasks ($type_t \in \{\text{SERVICE}, \text{SEND}, \text{RECEIVE}, \text{SCRIPT}, \dots \}$) for this mapping are for sending or receiving messages, invoking other services, or carrying out a given script.

Events $event = (id, type_e, As, At_e)$ of different types ($type_e \in \{\text{MESSAGE}, \text{TIMER}, \text{RULE}, \dots \}$) can be used for 'passive' behaviours like waiting for a message to arrive, for a specific time, or until some condition is satisfied. Events can be used in the normal flow of control, or in special situations like as event handlers to a subprocess or after an event-based gateway.

Gateways $gateway = (id, type_g, At_g)$ mark the boundaries of loops and conditional blocks. Their type ($type_g \in \{\text{XOR}, \text{OR}, \text{AND}, \text{EVENT}, \text{COMPLEX}\}$) can be *exclusive-* or *inclusive-or*, *parallel*, *event-based*, or *complex*. However, we are not considering the complex type, as its semantics are very vague.

Finally, subprocesses $subp = (id, swf, EH, succ_{EH}, At)$ can be used to aggregate several other activities and events into a sub-workflow $swf = (O', SF', Prop')$, i.e. a nested set of flow objects, sequence flows and properties defined in that subprocess.[3] Besides providing structure to the process, subprocesses also define an individual variable scope and can be endowed with event handlers EH that will interrupt the entire sub-workflow in case one of the events is triggered. The successor-relation of those event handlers is given by $succ_{EH} \subset EH \times O$.

2.3   Expressions, Data, Communication

In both models we are making use of *expressions*, e.g., for assignments and conditions. We are not specifying any particular language to be used for those

---

[2] Both artefacts and message flows are purely documentary; the actual messages are defined in the respective tasks and events sending and receiving those messages.

[3] Subprocesses could also be defined recursively, containing a *Call* activity invoking the parent (sub-)process, but this is not discussed here.

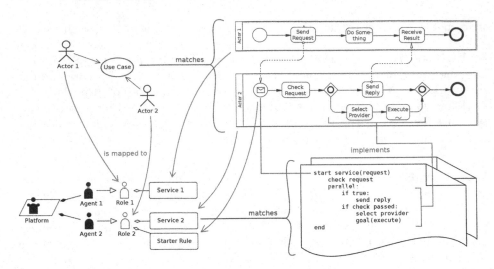

Fig. 3. Overview: Participants to roles, processes to plans, events to rules [14].

expressions; it should provide the usual mathematical and logical operations and grant access to the agent's beliefs and the properties of the process.

Another important aspect of both, multi-agent systems and business processes, are messages, which are defined by their sender, receiver, and content: *message* = (*sender, receiver, content*). Those attributes can also be used in expressions, e.g., for memorizing the sender of a message and later sending a reply to that same receiver. Here, sender and receiver can be individual agents/participants or multicast-addresses. The content is not restricted: It could be a FIPA message or any kind of serializable object.

Complementary to messages, services describe a particular action to be invoked: *service* = (*id, provider, Input, Output*). They are defined by a service ID, their respective provider, and input and output lists. In a multi-agent system, each plan could be considered as a service, although in practice only a subset of them will be, as some might be private. In BPMN, each pool that has a SERVICE start event will be exposed as a service.

3 Mapping Processes to Agents

In this section, we describe and formalize the mapping from BPMN processes to multi-agent systems according to the meta models defined in the previous section. In a nutshell, participants in the process are mapped to agent roles, their pools to plans, and the pools' start events to various mechanisms and rules for executing those plans (see Fig. 3). For a more in-depth discussion of the mapping, please refer to [14].

We are using the notation $x \implies z$ to denote that the process-element x is mapped to agent-element z. Analogously, we are using $(x, y) \implies z$ to indicate that the region of the process graph between x and y (i.e. a self-contained sub-graph with source x and sink y) is mapped to the (possibly complex) element z. We use ε for the empty, or *null* element.

3.1 Mapping of Agent Architecture

The business process system $bps = (id,\ BPD,\ Pt)$ is mapped to a multi-agent system, whereas only roles can be created; agents have to be specified later.[4]

$$bps \Longrightarrow mas = (id,\ Agents,\ Roles),\ \text{with}$$
$$Agents = \varnothing$$
$$Roles = \{role \mid \exists p \in Pt : p \Longrightarrow role\}$$

A participant name $pt \in Pt$ is mapped to a role, defined by plans and rules, with that name as its ID. The initial configuration knows neither goals nor beliefs, but both can be added at runtime. For each pool, one plan is created, as well as one rule for each start event in those pools.

$$pt \Longrightarrow role = (pt,\ P,\ R,\ G),\ \text{with}$$
$$P = \{plan \mid \exists p = (id',\ wf',\ pt) : p \Longrightarrow plan\}$$
$$R = \{rule \mid \exists e_s \in O_{wf'} : e_s \Longrightarrow rule\}$$
$$G = \varnothing$$

Let $bpd = (id_1,\ Pl,\ Art)$ be a BPD, and $pool = (id_2,\ wf,\ pt)$ a Pool, such that $pool \in Pl$ and $wf = (O,\ SF,\ Prop)$. For each pair of start- and end-events $e_s,\ e_e \in O$, with Z being an agent script element, such that $(e_s,\ e_e) \Longrightarrow Z$, a plan is created. The plan's IOPE remain undefined at first.

$$pool \Longrightarrow plan = (id_1 id_2,\ In,\ Out,\ pre,\ eff,\ Z),\ \text{with}$$
$$In = Out = \varnothing$$
$$pre = eff = \varepsilon$$

The start event $e_s = (id,\ type_e,\ As,\ At_e)$ is mapped to a reaction rule, triggering the same plan. The condition is a rule expression depending on $type_e$, and variables from that condition that are used in assignments are mapped to inputs of the plan of the same name.

$$e_s \Longrightarrow rule = (cond,\ plan,\ map),\ \text{with}$$
$$cond = [\ \text{rule expression, depending on type}\ ]$$
$$plan = p\ ,\ \text{such that}\ pool \Longrightarrow p$$
$$map = \{(x,\ x) \mid ass(x,\ y) \in As\}$$
$$In_{plan} \leftarrow In_{plan} \cup \{y \mid (x,\ y) \in map\}$$

---

[4] Different roles (participants) might get aggregated to one agent, or another role might be implemented in several agents. Neither of this is described in the process diagram and thus has to be added in a later stage.

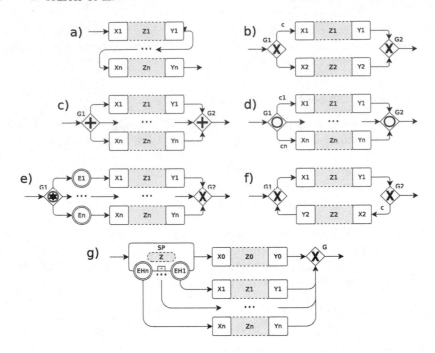

Fig. 4. Mapping of structures: (a) Sequence, (b) Condition, (c) Parallel, (d) Parallel-conditional, (e) Event-based condition, (f) While-Loop, (g) Subprocess with event-handler. Shaded regions correspond to previously matched structures.

3.2   Mapping of Agent Behaviours

In the following, we describe the mapping of the actual processes to different agent behaviours, i.e. plans. At first, we will take a look at different process structures, before considering individual elements.

Mapping of Structures. The transformation of process graphs to structured programs is a complicated task [10]. We are following a bottom-up "structure identification" approach [17], using different rules to match different structures (see Fig. 4). Those rules are applied to the elements of a pool $p = (id,\ wf,\ pt)$ or subprocess $sp = (id,\ wf,\ EH,\ succ_{EH},\ At)$ with $wf = (O,\ SF,\ Prop)$.

The simplest and yet most important structure is the *sequence*, connecting a number of flow objects $x_i,\ y_i \in O\ (i \le n)$, such that $\forall i < n :\ (y_i,\ x_{i+1},\ \varepsilon) \in SF$ and $\forall i \le n : \exists z_i : (x_i,\ y_i) \Longrightarrow z_i$.

$$(x_1,\ y_n) \Longrightarrow seq(z_1,\ \ldots,\ z_n)$$

Different structures, such as conditions and loops, are delimited by pairs of gateways, $g_1 = (id_1,\ type_1,\ At_1)$ and $g_2 = (id_2,\ type_2,\ At_2)$.

If $type_1 = type_2 = \text{XOR}$, they correspond to an *if/else*-style *condition*. Given $x_1,\ y_1,\ x_2,\ y_2 \in O$, and $(g_1,\ x_1,\ c),\ (g_1,\ x_2,\ \varepsilon),\ (y_1,\ g_2,\ \varepsilon),\ (y_2,\ g_2,\ \varepsilon) \in SF$, with $z_1,\ z_2$ script elements, such that $(x_1,\ y_1) \Longrightarrow z_1$ and $(x_2,\ y_2) \Longrightarrow z_2$.

$$(g_1, g_2) \Longrightarrow cond(c, z_1, z_2)$$

If $type_1 = type_2 = $ AND, they are mapped to *parallel* execution. In this case, all sequence flows are unconditional, i.e. $c = \varepsilon$. Also, instead of just two, an arbitrary number of branches (and corresponding script elements $z_1, \ldots, z_n$) is allowed in between the gateways.

$$(g_1, g_2) \Longrightarrow par(z_1, \ldots, z_n)$$

An inclusive-or gateway, i.e. $type_1 = $ OR, is mapped to a combination of *parallel and conditional* execution. In this case, each of the sequence flows going out of g_1 requires a condition $c_i \neq \varepsilon$.

$$(g_1, g_2) \Longrightarrow par(cond(c_1, z_1, nop), \ldots, cond(c_n, z_n, nop))$$

For an event-based gateway ($type_1 = $ EVENT), the first element of each branch has to be an event, i.e. for the ith branch, $e_i, x_i, y_i \in O$, e_i being an event, with $(g_1, e_i, \varepsilon), (e_i, x_i, \varepsilon), (y_i, g_2, \varepsilon) \in SF$, such that $e_i \Longrightarrow X_i$ and $(x_i, y_i) \Longrightarrow z_i$. The events are checked in separate threads, and the course of the process depends on the event triggered first.

$$(g_1, g_2) \Longrightarrow seq(A, [B_{1..n}], join(id_{g_1}), [stop(id_{eh1..n})], [C_{1..n}])$$
$$A = fork(id_{g_1}, while(\top, nop))$$
$$B_i = fork(id_{eh_i}, seq(X_i, ass(t_i, \top), stop(id_{g1})))$$
$$C_i = cond(t_i, z_i, nop)$$

If $type_1 = type_2 = $ XOR, and if the second branch is reversed, i.e. (g_1, x_1, ε), $(y_1, g_2, \varepsilon), (g_2, x_2, c), (y_2, g_1, \varepsilon) \in SF$, the structure is mapped to a loop.

$$(g_1, g_2) \Longrightarrow seq(z_1, while(c, seq(z_2, z_1)))$$

The mapping of a subprocess $sp = (id_s, swf, \varnothing, \varnothing, \varnothing)$ without event handlers corresponds to the mapping of its workflow.[5] Let $swf = (O_{sp}, SF_{sp}, Prop_{sp})$, and $e_s, e_e \in O_{sp}$ unique start- and end events, such that $(e_s, e_e) \Longrightarrow Z$.

$$sp \Longrightarrow Z$$

An *ad-hoc* subprocess $sp = (id_s, swf, \varnothing, \varnothing, At)$ with completion condition cc, i.e. ('comp-cond', cc) $\in At$, corresponds to the creation of a goal with the same condition. For this, the sub-workflow has to contain only *service* tasks, their respective plans being available for execution towards the goal, i.e. $swf = (\{t_1, \ldots, t_n\}, \varnothing, \varnothing)$, with $t_i = (id_i, $ SERVICE, $\varnothing, \{('impl', (P_i, \varepsilon, \varepsilon))\})$.

$$sp \Longrightarrow achieve((cc, \{P_1, \ldots, P_n\}))$$

---

[5] Depending on the implementation, the workflow might be wrapped into a separate method, service, or class.

A subprocess $sp = (id_s,\ swf,\ EH,\ succ_{EH},\ \varnothing)$ with event handlers behaves similar to an event-based gateway, even though instead of just waiting for the first event to occur, the subprocess is executed. If one of the events is triggered, the execution of the subprocess together with any remaining event handlers is aborted and the process continues after that event. Also, this adds another branch in case none of the events is triggered. Be $x_0,\ y_0,\ g \in O$, with $(sp,\ x_0,\ \varepsilon),\ (y_i,\ g,\ \varepsilon) \in SF,\ (i \leq n)$ and $e_i \in EH$ with $(e_i,\ x_i) \in succ_{EH}$ $(1 \leq i \leq n)$. Let Z be a script-element such that $sp \implies Z$.

$$(sp,\ g) \implies seq(A,\ [B_{1..n}],\ join(id_{sp}),\ [stop(id_{eh_{1..n}})],\ C)$$
$$A = fork(id_{sp},\ Z)$$
$$B_i = fork(eh_i,\ seq(X_i,\ ass(t_i,\ \top),\ stop(id_{sp})))$$
$$C = seq(ass(n,\ \top),\ [D_{1..n}],\ cond(n,\ z_0,\ nop))$$
$$D_i = cond(t_i,\ seq(ass(n,\ \bot),\ z_i),\ nop)$$

With those rules, the most important process structures can be mapped to equivalent agent script elements. Still, there are types of process graphs that can not be structured in any way [15]. However, this does not pose a significant limitation, as those graphs tend to contain structural errors leading to deadlocks and similar undesirable behaviour.

Mapping of Elements. At the bottom level, the above structures are made up of individual flow objects, i.e. tasks and events (subprocesses and gateways are part of the structures).

Both tasks and events can contain assignments, that, depending on their assign time, are to be executed either *before* or *after* the actual task or event, e.g., for handling the input and output of services. Thus, each flow object of the form $fo = (id,\ type,\ Ass,\ At)$ is mapped to a sequence of assignments together with the mapping of the task or event itself, Z, which depends only on its type and attributes, i.e. $(type,\ At) \implies Z$.

$$fo \implies seq(a_1^b,\ \dots,\ a_n^b,\ Z,\ a_1^a,\ \dots,\ a_n^a),\ \text{with}$$
$$a_i^b \in \{ass(prop,\ expr) \mid (prop,\ expr,\ \text{BEFORE}) \in As\}$$
$$a_i^a \in \{ass(prop,\ expr) \mid (prop,\ expr,\ \text{AFTER}) \in As\}$$

Depending on its respective type and attributes, a task $task = (id,\ type_t,\ As,\ At_t)$ can be mapped to different script elements, e.g., sending a message, invoking a service, or executing some given script.

$$(type_t,\ At_t) \implies \begin{cases} send(m) & \text{if } type = \text{SEND},\ (\text{`msg'},\ m) \in At_t \\ receive(m) & \text{if } type = \text{REC},\ (\text{`msg'},\ m) \in At_t \\ invoke(p,\ i,\ o) & \text{if } type = \text{SERVICE},\ (\text{`impl'},\ (p,\ i,\ o)) \in At_t \\ script & \text{if } type = \text{SCRIPT},\ (\text{`script'},\ script) \in At_t \\ nop & \text{otherwise} \end{cases}$$

Similarly, an event $event = (id, \; type_e, \; As, \; At_e)$ can be mapped to, e.g., receiving a message, or waiting for a certain time or condition. The same mapping is used whether the event occurs in normal flow or as a subprocess event handler.

$$
(type_e, \; At_e) \Longrightarrow \begin{cases} wait(t) & \text{if } type = \text{TIMER, ('time', } t) \in At_e \\ receive(m) & \text{if } type = \text{MESSAGE, ('msg', } m) \in At_e \\ while(\neg c, \; nop) & \text{if } type = \text{RULE, ('rule', } c) \in At_e \\ nop & \text{otherwise} \end{cases}
$$

These are the most important types of tasks and events for creating a usable system. Other types, such as *error* events or *user* tasks, are not regarded in this mapping, but can still be used in some of its implementations.

4   Implementation

Currently, the mapping has been implemented in three different ways for the JIAC V multi-agent framework [16]: For creating services in the high-level agent-scripting language JADL++ [14], for generating Java-based agent beans implementing the respective behaviours [12], and in the form of a JIAC-based process interpreter [22]. These implementations are integrated into the BPMN modelling tool VSDT (Visual Service Design Tool) [11].

The VSDT is an extension to the Eclipse IDE. Besides the basic BPMN editor it also provides a powerful transformation system that is used for the translation of process graphs to block structures. This structuring stage has been implemented using graph transformation rules, while the subsequent mapping of process elements to agent elements is done using a top-down visitor. We decided against using graph transformation rules for this part, too, as there are many interdependencies that would have been difficult to express in such rules.

JIAC V (Java Intelligent Agent Componentware, version 5) is a multi-agent framework that heavily lends from the service-oriented architecture (SOA) para-digm to create transparently distributed multi-agent systems communicating via messages and services, with a particular focus on industrial applications [16]. Consequently, the business process metaphor lends itself well to it.

4.1   Generation of JADL Services

At first, the mapping was realised as a transformation to JADL services. Being a high-level, service-oriented scripting language [9], the adoption of the BPMN notation was natural. JADL scripts can be passed to an agent at runtime, allowing for dynamically changing or extending its behaviour.

Each process is mapped to one JADL service, with its input and output determined by the start events. Most structures, including event-based conditions, can be mapped directly onto corresponding control flow elements. Simple subprocesses are embedded into a nested variable scope within the service, but subprocesses with event-handlers are not supported in this implementation.

Tasks and events for sending and receiving messages and for invoking other services are mapped directly onto according high-level language elements, thus making the resulting code particularly easy to understand and to maintain.

The reaction rules derived from the start events are mapped onto a set of Drools[6] rules. JIAC agents can be equipped with a Drools rule engine, syncing with the agent's memory and triggering the respective services in case the start condition – e.g., a message being received, or a timer – is fulfilled, by inserting an according *intention* into the agent's memory. The mapping of participants to agent roles is reflected in the creation of according JIAC configuration files, holding the different agent roles, each equipped with a JADL interpreter and a rule engine and the respective services and rules.

4.2   Creation of JIAC Agent Beans

Complementary to this implementation, BPMN diagrams can also be mapped to JIAC agent beans [12]. Those are more versatile and provide better extensibility, making them the best choice for implementing the agent's core components. Here, each pool is mapped to one agent bean (i.e. a Java class), encapsulating the behaviour for that role in that use case. All of the activities are mapped to *activity methods* that are orchestrated in a *workflow method*, representing the workflow as a whole.

The workflow method is made up of standard Java constructs, such as conditions and loops, calling the activity methods accordingly. Subprocesses are mapped to similarly structured nested classes. Parallel execution is implemented via threads, as are event handlers, where the event is monitored in a thread, eventually interrupting the main workflow thread and re-routing the execution accordingly. The activity methods encapsulate both that activities assignments and the actual activity, e.g. sending a message, making the workflow code much more compact and easy to understand by humans Properties are mapped to Java variables in the appropriate scope.

Start events are implemented making use of different mechanisms of the agent beans. For an unspecified, or NONE start event, the workflow method is triggered once when the agent starts; a MESSAGE start event with a service implementation will expose the workflow method as an action; a MESSAGE start event with a message channel will create an according message observer; and a TIMER start event will regularly check the time (or time since last execution) and start the workflow method accordingly.

4.3   JIAC Process Interpreter Bean

Finally, the mapping has been implemented as a JIAC-based process interpreter agent bean [22]. This one fundamentally differs form the other two, as no source code is generated, but the BPMN diagram file itself is passed to the bean and interpreted. Thus, no structuring of the process is necessary.

---

[6] JBoss Drools: http://www.jboss.org/drools/.

The process interpreter agent provides an action, accepting a BPMN diagram and the name of the participant to play, creating a new interpreter runtime for that process diagram and participant, i.e. role. It also acts as the "link" between the interpreted process and the outside world.

The processes are not started immediately; instead, those interpreter runtimes are responsible for monitoring the start events of that role's processes, and will create new interpreter instances each time a start event is triggered, e.g., when some message arrives. They also determine what processes should be exposed as actions of the interpreter agent (for service start events).

At the lowest level, the interpreter instances keep track of the internal state of each process. In each iteration of the interpreter agent's execution cycle, each process instance performs one 'step' in its respective process, keeping track of the current state of the process, evaluating branching conditions and routing the flow of control accordingly, until the last active flow object has been executed.

4.4   Comparison and Application

Each implementation has its strengths and weaknesses (see Table 1).

- While providing for compact and readable code, the mapping to JADL suffers from the language's lack of expressiveness in some points. Still, it is useful for high-level behaviours and services, and has the additional advantage that JADL scripts can be deployed and undeployed at runtime, thus dynamically changing the agent's behaviour.
- The generated JIAC agent beans have the highest expressiveness: Not only can nearly the entire BPMN be mapped to an according Java code, but if needed the generated beans can also easily be extended with additional code, e.g., for interaction with a GUI or data base. Those changes are preserved even when the code is generated anew. On the negative side, the agent beans are relatively static and not as easy to add to an agent at runtime.
- Not depending on generated code, the interpreter is not limited to processes following a block-structure but can run arbitrarily structured processes. This comes at the cost that the business process has to strictly contain everything that is needed in order to run, as there is no generated code that could be extended or edited before execution. As with JADL, processes can be dynamically added to and removed from the interpreter agent at runtime. Both arguments make the interpreter best suited for very high-level behaviour and composite services. Finally, the interpreter could be linked with the process modelling tool, showing the current state of the execution (future work).

The three implementations differ in both, their exact coverage of the mapping (see Table 2, including the mapping from BPMN to BPEL [18] for comparison) and their strengths and weaknesses, but they are all compatible with each other, e.g., a message sent by a generated agent bean can be received by the interpreter or a JADL service and vice versa. Thus, it is possible to export one business process diagram to a heterogeneous system, mapping one pool to, e.g., a JADL service and another to an agent bean.

Table 1. Comparison of different implementations

Property	JADL	Agent Beans	Interpreter
Plan language	JADL++	Java	n/a
Rule language	Drools	Java	n/a
Process structure	block	block	any graph
Expressiveness	low	very high	high
Extensibility of code	good	very good	n/a
Deployable at runtime	yes	no	yes

The mapping from BPMN to agents has been developed and – to varying degrees – applied in different research projects. First, in the *SerCHo* project, the mapping to JADL was used to describe and deploy agent service orchestrations, and similar in the *Smart Senior* and *ILIas* projects. Currently, the mapping to Agent Beans and the interpreter, and particularly the mapping of semantics and planning, are being advanced in the *EMD* project for the dynamic orchestration of e-mobility services.

Business process modelling can best be applied either at an early system design stage, to visually model the interaction protocols in the core system [14], or at a later stage, for modelling individual high-level services. Both is supported by the mapping and its implementations.

5   Related Work

In part, BPMN was developed as a graphical notation for the web service orchestration language BPEL, and the resulting mapping from BPMN to BPEL [18] can be considered a point of reference for all other mappings. Here, each pool is mapped to a BPEL process, consisting mostly of assignments, calls to other services, and some event handling. Messages are always service calls or their respective results; other kinds of communication are not supported, and there is no direct mapping from start events to service starting behaviour. Thus, the mapping to BPEL does not use the full potential of BPMN.

The similarities between business processes and agents have already led to different approaches for combining process modelling and agents.

One of those approaches is *WADE (Workflows and Agents Development Environment)*, allowing to model the behaviours of JADE agents as process graphs [6] and generating working Java code from those diagrams. However, the workflow is not mapped to Java control flow statements, but encoded in a special data structure, making the generated code more difficult to follow. Also, the initially used process notation is much simpler than BPMN, limiting the expressiveness of the approach. Later, WADE has been extended to provide better support for long-running business processes, event handling, user-interaction, and Web-service integration [2] and as of today appears to be a very mature product used in many projects.

Table 2. Comparison of mappings: BPMN to X. -/o/x means no/partial/full support

Element		BPEL	JADL	Ag.Beans	Interpr.
Workflow	XOR, AND, OR Gtw.	x	x	x	x
	Event-bsd. XOR Gtw.	x	x	x	x
	Complex Gateway	-	-	-	-
	Event Handler, Error	x	x	x	x
	Event Handler, Other	x	-	x	x
Activities	Send, Receive Task	o	x	x	x
	Service Task	x	x	x	x
	User Task	o	-	o	o
	Manual Task	-	-	-	-
	Script Task	-	x	x	o
	Subprocess	o	o	x	x
	Transaction	-	-	-	-
	Call Activity	o	o	o	o
	Ad-Hoc-Subprocess	-	-	o	o
Events	Message	o	x	x	x
	Timer	x	x	x	x
	Rule	-	o	x	o
	Signal	-	-	-	o
	Escalate	-	-	-	-
	Error	x	-	x	x
	Compensate	x	-	-	-
	Cancel	-	-	-	-
	Terminate	x	-	x	x
Misc.	Properties, Assignmt.	x	x	x	x
	Multiple Lanes	-	-	-	-
	Data Objects	-	-	-	-
	Roles	-	x	x	x
	Service Starter	o	x	x	x

Another approach is *GO-BPMN (Goal-oriented BPMN)*, using BPMN processes to model the plans that are the leafs in a goal hierarchy [5]. However, only a subset of the BPMN notation is used, describing individual plans and thus only a single agent. Interactions between agents – for which BPMN would be very well suited – are not modelled at all. While the combination of BPMN with agent goals is promising, we believe that BPMN is used at the wrong level of abstraction, abandoning many of its benefits. Similarly, *Go4Flex* [4] combines BPMN with goal hierarchies for Jadex Agents.

In another work, the authors also present a mapping from AUML interaction diagrams to BPMN [19]. *AUML* interaction diagrams themselves [1] are well suited for describing the interactions between agents, but following the principle of UML, they show only this one aspect, while leaving the behaviour *in between* the interactions to be modelled with other means. In contrast, BPMN can be seen as a combination of AUML interaction- and activity -diagrams, conveying the bigger picture of the agents' actions and interactions.

Finally, there are numerous agent development methods, many of which also use business processes and similar graphical notations. One of those is i^*, which is used, among others, in the TROPOS methodology [23]. Here, the focus lies particularly on the social relationships between the agents, their goals, intentions and resulting 'strategic dependencies'. While i^* itself is not used for modelling processes, it could well be used complementary to, e.g., BPMN to model the rationale behind the agents' behaviours and interactions.

6   Conclusion

In this paper, we described a mapping from BPMN processes to multi-agent systems and exemplarily showed how this mapping has been implemented in three different fashions for the JIAC V multi-agent framework: By generating high-level JADL scripts, creating versatile agent beans, or having an agent directly interpret the processes.

Each approach has its strengths and weaknesses: Agent beans are fast and versatile, making them the best choice for the core processes of the multi-agent application, while scripts and interpreted processes are more flexible and thus best suited for dynamic and adaptable behaviours. At the same time, using the same mapping, all implementations are semantically equivalent and interoperable, such that, e.g., one part of a process system can be mapped to agent beans, while another part is interpreted.

The mapping covers most important aspects of processes and agents, such as roles and rules, activities and events, messages and services. It also supports many different process control flow structures, translating them to equivalent block-structures.

While already included in the meta-models and the mapping, the implementation does not yet support goals and semantics. For future work, we are planning to extend the mapping in this direction. The BPMN *ad-hoc* subprocess is a good candidate for this, providing a *completion condition* that closely resembles an achieve goal in agent systems, but more work is needed for the mapping to handle *ad-hoc* subprocesses with more diverse content. Also, this will require the extension of BPMN with service semantics. Both are goals of our ongoing research projects.

References

1. Bauer, B., Müller, J.P., Odell, J.J.: Agent UML: a formalism for specifying multiagent software systems. In: Ciancarini, P., Wooldridge, M.J. (eds.) AOSE 2000. LNCS, vol. 1957, pp. 91–103. Springer, Heidelberg (2001)
2. Bergenti, F., Caire, G., Gotta, D.: Interactive workflows with WADE. In: 2012 IEEE 21st International Workshop on Enabling Technologies: Infrastructure for Collaborative Enterprises, pp. 10–15 (2012)
3. Bernon, C., Cossentino, M., Gleizes, M.-P., Turci, P., Zambonelli, F.: A study of some multi-agent meta-models. In: Odell, J.J., Giorgini, P., Müller, J.P. (eds.) AOSE 2004. LNCS, vol. 3382, pp. 62–77. Springer, Heidelberg (2005)
4. Braubach, L., Pokahr, A., Jander, K., Lamersdorf, W., Burmeister, B.: Go4Flex: goal-oriented process modelling. In: Essaaidi, M., Malgeri, M., Badica, C. (eds.) Intelligent Distributed Computing IV. Studies in Computational Intelligence, vol. 315, pp. 77–87. Springer, Heidelberg (2010)
5. Burmeister, B., Arnold, M., Copaciu, F., Rimassa, G.: BDI-agents for agile goal-oriented business processes. In: Proceedings of 7th International Conference on Autonomous Agents and Multiagent Systems (AAMAS 2008), pp. 37–44. International Foundation for Autonomous Agents and Multiagent Systems, Richland, SC (2008)
6. Caire, G., Gotta, D., Banzi, M.: WADE: A software platform to develop mission critical applications exploiting agents and workflows. In: Berger, M., Burg, B., Nishiyama, S. (eds.) Proceedings of 7th International Conference on Autonomous Agents and Multiagent Systems (AAMAS 2008). Industry and Applications Track, pp. 29–36, May 2008
7. Dijkman, R.M., Dumas, M., Ouyang, C.: Semantics and analysis of business process models in BPMN. Inf. Softw. Technol. 50(12), 1281–1294 (2008)
8. Franklin, S., Graesser, A.: Is It an agent, or just a program?: a taxonomy for autonomous agents. In: Jennings, N.R., Wooldridge, M.J., Müller, J.P. (eds.) ECAI-WS 1996 and ATAL 1996. LNCS, vol. 1193, pp. 21–35. Springer, Heidelberg (1997)
9. Hirsch, B., Konnerth, T., Burkhardt, M., Albayrak, S.: Programming service oriented agents. In: Calisti, M., Dignum, F.P., Kowalczyk, R., Leymann, F., Unland, R. (eds.) Service-Oriented Architecture and (Multi-)Agent Systems Technology, vol. 10021 in Dagstuhl Seminar Proceedings, Schloss Dagstuhl - Leibniz-Zentrum für Informatik, Germany, Dagstuhl, Germany (2010)
10. Kiepuszewski, B., ter Hofstede, A.H.M., Bussler, C.J.: On structured workflow modelling. In: Wangler, B., Bergman, L.D. (eds.) CAiSE 2000. LNCS, vol. 1789, p. 431. Springer, Heidelberg (2000)
11. Küster, T., Heßler, A.: Towards transformations from BPMN to heterogeneous systems. In: Ardagna, D., Mecella, M., Yang, J. (eds.) Business Process Management Workshops. LNBIP, vol. 17, pp. 200–211. Springer, Heidelberg (2009)
12. Küster, T., Heßler, A., Albayrak, S.: Towards process-oriented modelling and creation of multi-agent systems. In: Dalpiaz, F., Dix, J., van Riemsdijk, M.B. (eds.) EMAS 2014. LNCS, vol. 8758, pp. 163–180. Springer, Heidelberg (2014)
13. Küster, T., Lützenberger, M.: An overview of a mapping from BPMN to agents (extended abstract). In: Bordini, E., Weiss, Y. (eds.) Proceedings of 14th International Conference on Autonomous Agents and Multiagent Systems (AAMAS 2015). Istanbul, Turkey, 4–8 May 2015

14. Küster, T., Lützenberger, M., Heßler, A., Hirsch, B.: Integrating process modelling into multi-agent system engineering. Multiagent Grid Syst. **8**(1), 105–124 (2012)
15. Liu, R., Kumar, A.: An analysis and taxonomy of unstructured workflows. In: van der Aalst, W.M.P., Benatallah, B., Casati, F., Curbera, F. (eds.) BPM 2005. LNCS, vol. 3649, pp. 268–284. Springer, Heidelberg (2005)
16. Lützenberger, M., et al.: A multi-agent approach to professional software engineering. In: Cossentino, M., El Fallah Seghrouchni, A., Winikoff, M. (eds.) EMAS 2013. LNCS, vol. 8245, pp. 156–175. Springer, Heidelberg (2013)
17. Mendling, J., Lassen, K.B., Zdun, U.: Transformation strategies between blockoriented and graph-oriented process modelling languages (2005)
18. OMG: Business process model and notation (BPMN) version 2.0. Specification formal/2011-01-03, Object Management Group, August 2011
19. Pokahr, A., Braubach, L.: Reusable interaction protocols for workflows. In: Workshop on Protocol Based Modelling of Business Interactions (2010)
20. Recker, J.C.: BPMN modeling - who, where, how and why. BPTrends **5**(3), 1–8 (2008)
21. van Riemsdijk, M.B., Dastani, M., Winikoff, M.: Goals in agent systems: a unifying framework. In: Proceedings of 7th International Conference on Autonomous Agents and Multiagent Systems (AAMAS 2008), pp. 713–720. International Foundation for Autonomous Agents and Multiagent Systems, Estoril, Portugal, May 2008
22. Voß, M.: Orchestrating Multi-Agent Systems with BPMN by Implementing a Process Executing JIAC Agent Using the Visual Service Design Tool. Master thesis, Humboldt Universität Berlin, May 2014
23. Yu, E.S.: Social modeling and i*. In: Borgida, A.T., Chaudhri, V.K., Giorgini, P., Yu, E.S. (eds.) Conceptual Modeling: Foundations and Applications. LNCS, vol. 5600, pp. 99–121. Springer, Heidelberg (2009)

Validating Requirements
Using Gaia Roles Models

Nektarios Mitakidis[1], Pavlos Delias[2], and Nikolaos Spanoudakis[3(✉)]

[1] School of Electronic and Computer Engineering (ECE),
Technical University of Crete (TUC), Chania, Greece
nmitakidis@isc.tuc.gr
[2] Business School, Eastern Macedonia and Thrace Institute of Technology,
Kavala, Greece
pdelias@teiemt.gr
[3] School of Production Engineering and Management (PEM),
Applied Mathematics and Computers Laboratory (AMCL),
Technical University of Crete (TUC), Chania, Greece
nispanoudakis@isc.tuc.gr

Abstract. This paper presents a method that aims at assisting an engineer in transforming agent roles models to a process model. Thus, the software engineer can employ available tools to validate specific properties of the modeled system before its final implementation. The method includes a tool for aiding the engineer in the transformation process. This tool uses a recursive algorithm for automating the transformation process and guides the user to dynamically integrate two or more agent roles in a process model with multiple pools. The tool usage is demonstrated through a running example, based on a real world project. Simulations of the defined agent roles can be used to (a) validate the system requirements and (b) determine how it could scale. This way, engineers, analysts and managers can configure the processes' parameters and identify and resolve risks early in their project.

Keywords: Model checking agents and multi-agent systems · Business process models · Agent simulation · Gaia methodology

1 Introduction

This paper aims to show how a Gaia Multi-Agent System (MAS) analysis (or architectural design) role model can be represented as a business process model. This allows employing available tools to validate specific properties of the modeled system before its final implementation. Moreover, a business partner has a greater potential to comprehend the system being modeled through intuitive process visualization.

Rana and Stout [1] highlighted the importance of combining performance engineering with agent oriented design methodologies in order to develop large agent based applications. To derive process performance measures, we need a quantitative process analysis technique. Process simulation appears to be a prominent technique that allows us to derive such measures (e.g., cycle time) given data about the activities (e.g., processing times) and data about the resources involved in the process. Through

© Springer International Publishing Switzerland 2015
M. Baldoni et al. (Eds.): EMAS 2015, LNAI 9318, pp. 171–190, 2015.
DOI: 10.1007/978-3-319-26184-3_10

process simulation an engineer can forecast the process execution time, identify possible bottlenecks and perform tests regarding the response of the process to increasing demand. Process simulation is a versatile technique supported by a range of process modeling and analysis tools [2]. However, to run a process simulation, the engineer needs a process model.

In this paper we will see how liveness formulas, an important property of agent role models, introduced by the Gaia methodology [3], and later employed by ROADMAP [4], the Gaia2JADE process [5], Gaia4E [6] and ASEME [7], can be transformed to process models. Moreover, we will present a tool that allows these models to be integrated to produce a process model of a multi-agent system using the XML Process Definition Language (XPDL) [8] portable standard. Having transformed the MAS role model to a process model, we can use simulation to validate several properties of the modeled system, and also determine its ability to scale, as early as the analysis [3] or architectural design (introduced in the second version of Gaia [9]) phases. This is demonstrated through a case study based on real world system's requirements for smart-phone services.

Therefore, this work is expected to have a high impact on (a) Agent Oriented Software Engineering (AOSE) practitioners using the Gaia methodology and its successors, who can immediately take advantage of this work to evaluate their models, (b) AOSE researchers, and practitioners of other methodologies who can use this transformation combined with method engineering to compile new methodologies, and, (c) those who use business process models for agent-based simulations [10, 11] or for communicating them to business people [12], who can now use an AOSE methodology to aid them in their modeling tasks.

In the following section we will briefly discuss the background of this work. Then, in section three, we will present the algorithm for the automatic transformation process and, in section four, the tool that allows integrating many individual agent processes to build a common process that will resemble how the different agents collaborate. In section five we will present the results of a number of simulations. In Sect. 6 we present the software process fragment that an engineer can use to integrate this method to an existing software engineering process. Section seven discusses our findings and the tool's limitations, and, finally, section eight concludes and provides an insight to future work.

2 Background

2.1 The Gaia Liveness Formulas and AOSE

The liveness property of an agent role was introduced by the Gaia methodology [3, 9]. Gaia is an attempt to define a general methodology for the analysis and design of MAS. MAS, according to Gaia, are viewed as being composed of a number of autonomous interactive agents forming an organized society in which each agent plays one or more specific roles. The latest version of Gaia defines a three phase process and at each phase the modeling of the MAS is further refined. These phases are the analysis phase, the architectural design phase, and, finally, the detailed design phase. In the analysis phase, Gaia defines the structure of the MAS using the *role model*. This model identifies the roles that agents have to play within the MAS and the interaction protocols between the different roles. The role model is further refined in the architectural design phase [9].

The objective of the Gaia analysis phase is the identification of the roles and the modeling of interactions between the roles found. Roles consist of four attributes: *responsibilities, permissions, activities* and *protocols*. Responsibilities are the key attribute related to a role since they determine the functionality. Responsibilities are of two types: *liveness properties* – the role has to add something good to the system, and *safety properties* – the role must prevent something bad from happening to the system. Liveness describes the tasks that an agent must fulfill given certain environmental conditions and safety ensures that an acceptable state of affairs is maintained during the execution cycle. In order to realize responsibilities, a role has a set of permissions. Permissions represent what the role is allowed to do and, in particular, which information resources it is allowed to access. The activities are tasks that an agent performs without interacting with other agents. Finally, protocols are specific patterns of interaction with other roles.

Gaia originally proposed some schemas that could be used for the representation of interactions between the various roles in a system. However, this approach was too abstract to support complex protocols [5]. ROADMAP [4] proposed that protocols and activities are social actions or tasks and ASEME [13] moved one step further by allowing protocols to define the involved roles processes as liveness formulas that would later be included in the liveness of the system role model (a model inspired by the Gaia roles model). This is one assumption of this work, i.e. that the protocols are a send message action, a receive message action or a combination of message send and receive actions and, possibly, other activities for each participating role.

Although the Gaia methodology does not explicitly deal with the requirements capture phase, it supposes that they exist in some kind of form before the analysis phase. ASEME supports the systematic gathering of requirements in free text form and associating them with the goals of specific actors in the System Actor-Goals Model [7]. Since ASEME has adopted a model-driven engineering approach these requirements influence the role model definition, which emerges at the end of the analysis phase.

In both cases, it makes sense to seek to validate or forecast specific properties of the system to be, based on its requirements. Until now, an analyst can only reach this goal by manually transforming the model. In this paper, we propose a systematic method for achieving the same goal. The advantages of such an approach are that it can be automated, is less error prone and faster. This is the actual research question of this work.

The liveness model has a formula at the first line (*root formula*) where activities can be connected with Gaia operators. Abstract activities must be decomposed to *activities* again connected with Gaia operators in a following formula. The operators used in the liveness formulas are:

A+ (activity A is executed one or more times)
A* (activity A is executed zero or more times)
[A] (activity A is optionally executed)
A.B (activity B executes after activity A)
A|B (activity A or B exclusively is executed)
A||B (activities A and B are executed in parallel)
A~ (activity A is executed forever, the original Gaia operator was the greek character omega "ω", however for keyboard compatibility we chose to use the tilde)

Figure 1 shows a Gaia roles model for an indicative role named *ComplexProvider*. This role employs two protocols, one for servicing a complex service request and one for requesting a simple routing service (activities are underlined in the *Protocols and Activities* field). In its liveness formula it describes the order that these protocols and activities will be executed by this role using three liveness formulas.

The liveness property is defined as a string, adhering to a grammar. The latter is defined using the Extended Backus–Naur Form (EBNF), which is a metasyntax notation used to express context-free grammars [14]. In Listing 1 we define the liveness property grammar (*char* is any lower or upper case alphabetic character).

Role: ComplexProvider

Description: This role provides an added value service in routing requests. It receives a routing request containing needed information but also the user's preferences. Firstly it decides the route type to request (public transport, car and/or pedestrian), then it composes a simple routing request and after it gets the results it sorts them according to the user's preferences.

Protocols and Activities: ComplexService, ReceiveComplexServiceRequest, DecideRouteType, SimpleService, SortRoutes, SendComplexServiceResponse, SendSimpleServiceRequest, ReceiveSimpleServiceResponse.

Responsibilities - Liveness:

CP = ComplexService+

ComplexService = ReceiveComplexServiceRequest. DecideRouteType. SimpleService.
      SortRoutes. SendComplexServiceResponse

SimpleService = SendSimpleServiceRequest. ReceiveSimpleServiceResponse.

Fig. 1. Part of the gaia role model for a role.

2.2 Metamodels and Model Transformations

Model transformation is an essential process in Model Driven Engineering (MDE). It is the process of transforming a model to another model [15]. To define a transformation an engineer needs the metamodels of the source and target models. A model is defined as an abstraction of a software system (or a part of it) and a metamodel is an abstraction defining the properties of the model. A metamodel is itself a model. For example, the metamodel of a text model can be the EBNF grammar.

A model's metamodel defines the elements that can be used by the engineer to create the (terminal) model, usually in a format defined by a metametamodel which is the language for defining metamodels. The Eclipse Modeling Framework (EMF, [16]) defines such a language, namely *ecore*, that is much like a UML Class definition. Ecore defines that a model is composed of instances of the *EClass* type, which can have attributes (instances of the *EAttribute* type) or reference other EClass instances (using the *EReference* type). *EAttributes* can be instances of terminal data types such as *string*, *integer*, *real*, etc.). EMF allows to extend existing models via inheritance, using the *ESuperType* relationship for extending an existing *EClass*.

Thus, using EMF technology, in order to define the text to model transformation that is the liveness to XPDL transformation we need the XPDL metamodel.

```
Liveness        → {Formula}
Formula         → LeftHandSide, "=", Expression
LeftHandSide    → string
Expression      → Term | ParallelExpr | OrExpr | SequentialExpr
ParallelExpr    → Term, "||", Term { "||", Term }
OrExpr          → Term, "|", Term { "|", Term }
SequentialExpr→ Term, ".", Term { ".", Term}
Term            → BasicTerm | "(", Expression, ")" |
                  "[", Expression, "]" | Term, "*" | Term, "+" |
                  Term, "~"
BasicTerm       → string
String          → char, {char | digit | "_"}
```

Listing 1. The liveness property grammar

2.3   Business Process Modeling

Software Engineering (SE) and Business Process Management (BPM) are two disciplines with clear associations. A visible influence of SE to BPM concerns quality assessment, while SE aims its attention to BPM mainly to take advantage of its advanced monitoring and controlling functions [17] and its experiment design principles. For example, following the BPM paradigm, one can find solutions about how business people and software engineers are facilitated in communicating system requirements. Stakeholders are able to get involved in the system's design, and hence to assure the alignment of the produced software with the business objectives.

Simulation is employed to quantify the impact that a process design is likely to have on its performance, and to numerically indicate the best design alternatives. Regarding business process simulation, various tools exist [18], which facilitate the adoption of BPM as a practical way for designing systems. However, a critical factor in selecting which tool is more appropriate is the modeling language used.

Popular modeling languages in designing software systems, such as the object-oriented ones (e.g., UML), lack process views, an issue that has been early identified by [17]. On the other hand, process models do not usually map clearly to a programming environment. Both approaches have their relative advantages, so it is a hard decision to spare one. This is why there have been efforts to bridge object-oriented models and process models through model transformations [17, 19].

In this work we chose the XML Process Definition Language (XPDL version 2.1) as the target language. XPDL, a standard supported by the Workflow Management Coalition (WfMC, http://www.wfmc.org), has a good potential for process interchange and heterogeneous system integration since it is used today by more than 80 different products to exchange process definitions and keeps up to date with BPMN 2.0.

The XPDL metamodel that we used for our project is shown in Fig. 2. The *Package* concept represents a set of processes and contains:

- *pools*, which represent major participant roles in a process, typically separating different organizations. A pool can contain:
  - *lanes*, which are used to organize and categorize activities within a pool according to function or role.
- *workflowProcesses*, which aggregate sets of activities and transitions
  - *activities* are represented by rounded rectangles and correspond to the execution of a task or to the functionality of a gateway, which can be:
    - *XOR* gateway (exclusively one of the outgoing transitions will be followed), which is represented by a diamond shape with the "X" character in the middle
    - *parallel* gateway (all the outgoing transitions lead to activities that will be executed in parallel), which is represented by a diamond shape with the "+" character in the middle
  - *events* are represented by circles and are specific kinds of activities that correspond to something that happens. Common events are the start of a process lane and its ending
  - *transitions*, are represented with a solid line and arrowhead and have source and target (at the arrowhead) activities and define the control flow in the workflow process
- *associations*, are represented with a dotted line and arrowhead and have source and target (at the arrowhead) activities and define the message flow between different pools. Therefore, they also have source and target pools.

3   The Transformation Algorithm

The transformation algorithm uses elements from the liveness formulas grammar (Listing 1) and the XPDL metamodel (Fig. 2). It is a recursive algorithm that takes the liveness formula expression elements from left to right and applies the templates shown in Fig. 3, gradually building the XPDL process. For all templates, the control flows from left to right, i.e. if a template follows another, then it is connected to its rightmost element. The algorithm is provided in pseudocode at the appendix.

Regarding the theoretical properties of the algorithm we believe that it can be easily proved that it is correct using induction and the assumption that if we have a correct XPDL model and replace an XPDL activity with a correct XPDL fragment (or a *well-structured fragment*, as in [20]) the resulting model is correct. The templates are all correct XPDL diagrams (well structured fragments) if they have a *start* event on their left and a transition to an *end* event on their right, as every task is on a path from the start event to the end event. Then, for each of these valid models we can easily assert that if we take a random template and replace an activity of the model with it then, again, the model is correct. Then, we hypothesize that after *n* insertions the model is correct and we insert a new random template. Then we show again that the resulting model is correct.

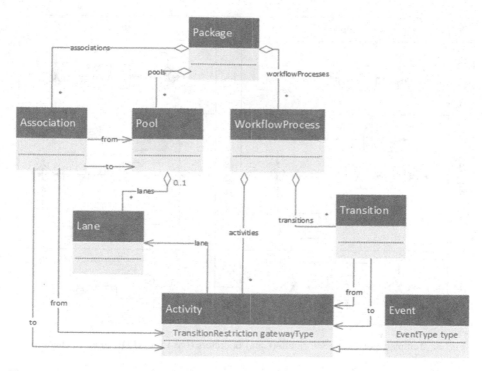

Fig. 2. The XPDL metamodel (we used the *org.enhydra* Java package defining the metamodel for XPDL 2.1, which is distributed under the GNU Free License by Together Teamsolutions Co., Ltd., http://tinyurl.com/org-enhydra)

The reader should note the common templates for the $\sim$ and + operators. Considering the semantics of the $\sim$ operator the exclusive gateway should not be used (the activity should just loop back to itself). In this way, the resulting process model would not be easily ported to existing analysis techniques as it would not pass the Proper Completion test (each workflow ends with an end event) [21]. Given the fact that in a later stage the situation could be remedied by adjusting the gateway to always return the flow to the activity, and that in the second version of Gaia there is a case where the authors allow the indefinite operator to be followed by a sequential activity [9], we believe that our approach is the best compromise for this case.

As far as the algorithm's complexity is concerned, since we have a recursive function call inside a for loop, the complexity of our algorithm is $O(n^2)$, where n is the number of activities and protocols present in the liveness formulas. The algorithm would run forever should there be circular references to *LeftHandSide* from a formula's *Expression* (or from subsequent formulas), however, we have a pre-processing step guarding against this possibility and preventing the algorithm from executing.

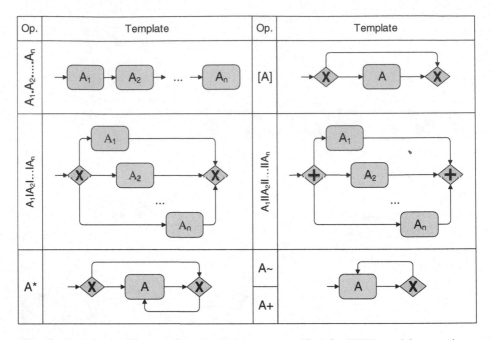

Fig. 3. Templates of liveness formula (Gaia) operators (Op.) for XPDL model generation.

4 The Liveness2XPDL Tool

The tool allows defining one or more agent roles. For each role, the user can edit a liveness formula or import a role model. We researched for the Gaia methodology and its derivatives' metamodels to create the relevant import functionality. We found documented metamodels for the Gaia [22], ROADMAP [23] and the ASEME [7] methodologies. However, Gaia's metamodel abstractly defines the LivenessProperty class and ROADMAP's metamodel file is not available on-line. Thus, we created an importer for the ASEME System Roles Model (SRM) metamodel to demonstrate the capability of our approach in importing meta-models. Since our tool is open source, interested developers can create an importer for the metamodel they prefer or they can type their formulas in the text editor.

The tool allows integrating multiple roles in the same XPDL model. We create one *Pool* instance for each role in a common *Package* (the transformation algorithm executes as many times as the participating roles with the same Package instance) and then the user defines the associations for message sending and receiving activities. Then, the tool creates the needed references of the associations to the pools and outputs the Package in XPDL format.

In this section we demonstrate the usage of the developed tool. We consider a real world system developed in the context of the ASK-IT Integrated Project[1] where a

[1] ASK-IT has been co-funded by the European Union under the 6th Framework Programme (no IST-2003-511298).

personal assistant agent on a lightweight device (e.g., a smart phone) requests services from a mediator agent (or broker). This broker has the capability to service simple requests but can also access a complex service provider agent who can offer high level services. The complex provider also needs simple services from the broker in order to compose a high level service. In our case, we consider a route calculation service that can be simple (I want to get from point A to B with a car using the quickest route) or complex (I want to get from point A to B with the best transport means according to my user's impairment needs and habits). In the second case the complex provider will

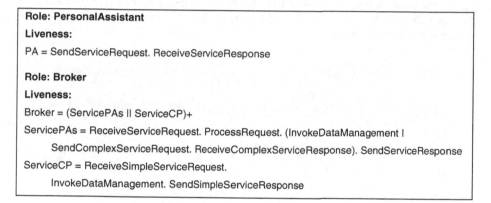

Fig. 4. The personal assistant and broker role models.

reason on the type of simple request based on the user's profile, make a simple route calculation service request to the broker and then sort the results according to the user's habits before replying to the user through the broker.

The agent roles models for the personal assistant and the broker are presented in Fig. 4 (just the role name and liveness property). The complex provider is the same with the one presented in Fig. 1.

The user starts the Liveness2XPDL tool and imports through the *File* menu the three role models, as presented in Fig. 5. Then, the user can select one role and the *Single role transformation* option from the *Transform* menu, or more than one (holding

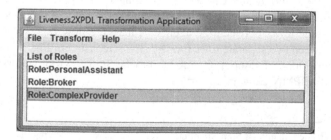

Fig. 5. The main screen of the Liveness2XPDL tool.

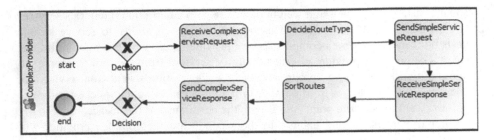

Fig. 6. The complex provider displayed in Together Workflow Editor (a graphical workflow editor implementing XPDL specification V2.1 using the BPMN graphical notation, http://www. together.at/prod/workflow/twe).

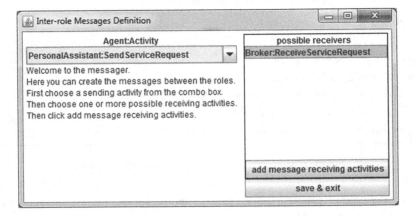

Fig. 7. The inter-role messages definition screen.

down the control key) and the *Multiple role transformation* option from the *Transform* menu. In Fig. 6 the reader can see the single role file for the Complex Provider role.

In the case of multiple roles transformation, the tool then prompts the user to select where to save and how to name the output XPDL file. If there are activities that send or receive messages the graphical interface presented in Fig. 7 helps the user to create message flows.

Finally, in Fig. 8 the reader can see the combined roles process model for all the roles used in our project. The modeler has used the graphical tool depicted in Fig. 7 to define the message flows between the agents. A message flow represents the flow of information between two separate roles (pools). The screenshot in Fig. 8 has been taken from the Signavio tool[2]. To import the model into the Signavio tool we first used a free online XPDL to BPMN conversion service[3].

---

[2] The BPM Academic Initiative of Signavio offers a web-based process modeling platform to students, lecturers and researchers, http://www.signavio.com/bpm-academic-initiative.

[3] E.g. the "Convert XPDL to BPMN" service provided freely on-line by Trisotech, http://www. businessprocessincubator.com.

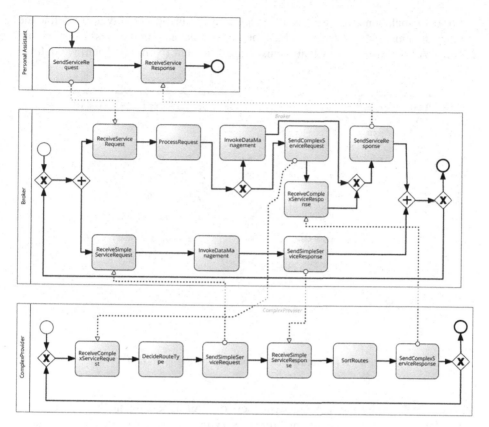

Fig. 8. The three agent roles displayed together in Signavio BPM academic initiative.

5 Simulating the Roles Interactions

In this section, we demonstrate how simulation can aid the system modeler as well as the project manager to make important decisions, mainly concerning non-functional requirements.

Initially, there were two reasons for simulating the ASK-IT system. The first was that the ASK-IT service providers needed to know if the system can satisfy non-functional user requirements, one of which was the delivery of the service within ten seconds. The frequency of service requests was calculated to be one request per 30 s. The second was to find out how the system would scale when service demand increased. The latter would be used for preparing the project's exploitation plan.

The Signavio tool allows simulating a process model involving several roles. For each simulation scenario, it allows to define:

- available resources for each role (how many instances of this role are available)
- the frequency in which a role can appear and start executing
- the percentage of times that a XOR gateway selects one or the other execution path
- activity duration (distribution type, mean and standard deviation values)
- number of simulations for each scenario

For our simulations we used several executions of function prototypes to define the activities durations. Moreover, we added the network latency in the message receiving activities. All the distributions that we used are Gaussian (Normal). Then, we defined

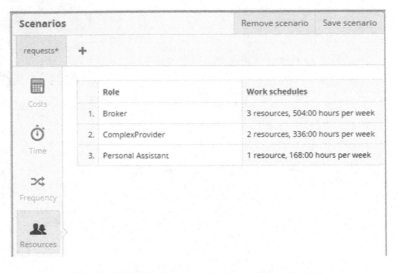

Fig. 9. Defining the scenario in the Signavio tool.

different scenarios by varying the frequency of PAs appearing in the network and asking for services, the number of brokers serving the requests and the number of complex providers (in Fig. 9 you can see a screenshot from the Signavio tool for defining a scenario).

Our experiments are presented in Fig. 10. We have validated the system to respond within 10 s in the worst case when we have an incoming request every 30 s with one broker and one complex provider. Moreover, we can see what the expected quality of service will be, while the requests' frequency rises. As far as system scaling is concerned we see that by adding more broker instances, the system performance has a better gain than by adding complex providers. Finally, we can claim that with three broker instances the system can offer the required quality of service (respond within ten seconds) even if we have a request every two seconds.

6   The Method Fragment for Validating the Analysis Model

Method fragments [24] are reusable methodological parts that can be used by engineers in order to produce a new design process for a specific situation. This allows a development team to come up with a hybrid methodology that will support the needs of specific programming and modeling competencies.

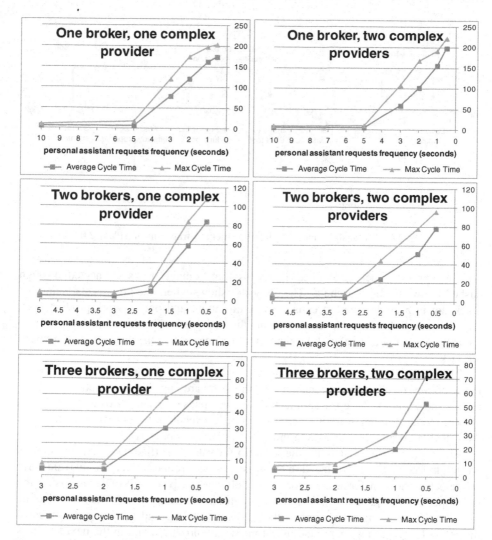

Fig. 10. Average and maximum response times in seconds (vertical axis). The horizontal axis represents the time interval between two requests (in a normal distribution).

The method fragment that corresponds to the process of validating an analysis model is presented in this section. It is defined as a software development process using the extended SPEM 2.0 language for representing agent oriented methodologies [25]. A *Software Process* is defined as a series of *Phases* that produce *Work Products*. In each phase simple or complex *tasks* take place. Tasks are achieved by *Human Roles*. Work products can be either graphical or textual models. Graphical models can be *Structural* (focusing in showing the static aspects of the system – such as class diagrams) or *Behavioral* (focusing in describing the dynamic aspects of the system – what happens as time passes). Textual models can be completely *Free* text or follow some specifications or grammar (a *Structured* work product).

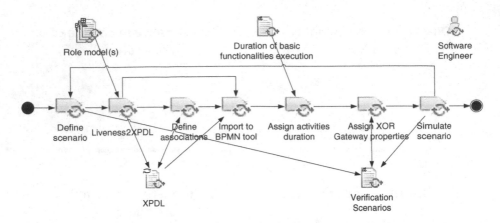

Fig. 11. The analysis model validation method fragment in SPEM 2.0.

Each process package defines a process that contains tasks connected through dashed arrows like in flowcharts. The black dot shows where the process starts and the black dot in a circle where it ends. A task has input and output work products. An arrow from a task to a work product means that the product is created (or updated) by the task. An arrow from a work product to a task means that the product is an input to the task.

This method fragment (shown in Fig. 11) can be integrated with the Gaia methodology or one of its descendants by the software engineer. It is activated at the end of the analysis phase (or architectural design phase for Gaia 2.0) to validate the system model. Its inputs are the various activities execution times (average and standard deviation) and the (Gaia) role models (the liveness property).

The engineer must first define the scenario for validation (first task). The scenario is written in free text (the "Verification Scenarios" work product). Then the relevant roles are selected and transformed to process models in the Liveness2XPDL task using the developed tool. Optionally, using the same tool, in the next task, namely "Define associations", the engineer connects the message sending and receiving activities of the roles. The XPDL work product is automatically produced and in the next task it is imported to the desired tool that will be used for simulation (in our case study Signavio). Then, the engineer assigns the activities duration and XOR gateway properties using the same tool. Finally, the engineer simulates the scenario. The process package finishes by updating the "Verification Scenarios" with the results of the simulation or is restarted to simulate a new scenario.

7   Discussion

It is not the first time that the AOSE community studies and uses business process models. There are a number of works, e.g., one for improving a process model representing the behavior of agents [11], another for proposing a method for transforming BPMN models to agent-oriented models in the Prometheus methodology [26], and another that provides a mapping of BPMN diagrams to a normalized form checking for certain structural properties, which normalized form can itself be transformed to a petri-net that allows for further semantic analysis [27].

All these works can be aligned with ours using method engineering and provide a number of new paths or possibilities for a system modeler that has come up with the Gaia analysis models. Thus, an AOSE practitioner can transform the process model outputted from our work to a system specification using the Prometheus methodology notation [26] and continue using that methodology. Another might be interested in checking certain structural properties of the process model [27].

Some preliminary results of this work have appeared in EUMAS 2010 (with informal proceedings) [28]. In that work, we provided transformation templates targeting the BPMN 1.0 metamodel. This work extends that one by targeting the XPDL metamodel, which offers a wide range of possibilities when available tools are concerned. Moreover, this work caters for integrating multiple roles in a single process model.

Although we have achieved our goals, the Liveness2XPDL tool has specific limitations. Firstly, when the user decides to create multiple associations that define message flows from an activity that will be received by different activities in other pools the method cannot automatically tell whether one of the possible paths will be followed, or all of them. The inter-agent messages definition interface allows defining such associations; however, it is not clear how these can be exploited with simulation.

An important note to the transformation approach concerns the templates' definitions. Undoubtedly, there is not a single way to express a concept with XPDL (or the BPMN notation). For example, the $A \sim$ formula can be represented either with the template illustrated in Fig. 3, or by adding the loop symbol in the rectangle. Although some good styles and practices are in use today, in practice there are no rules that guarantee an optimal design. The appropriateness of the model must every time get validated by the end user. In our case, the templates were defined considering the BPMN simulation tools features. For example, for the $A \sim$ formula, we chose that particular definition because the loop symbol would introduce sub-processes to the model, and available simulation tools have limited support for such a feature.

Moreover, in XPDL it is acceptable to create more than one transition from an activity to other activities. This option reduces the complexity of the model as it is not mandatory to use XOR gateways. However, a large number of process management tools do not accept this option and most of the times they suggest that a gateway should be placed to avoid errors. This is why we used the XOR gateway in our templates.

Finally, after the process model is produced, the user still has to provide some additional elements concerning the send/receive activities' configuration. We are currently working towards automating this step based on the following guidelines (which are now manually configured):

- All activities that stand for sending or receiving messages are labeled as message type activities.
- When a receive activity immediately follows a start event, then the start event and the activity are merged into a start event triggered by a message.

- When a receive activity immediately precedes an end event, then the two are merged into an end event triggered by a message.
- When a message is intended to be sent to one or more out of many recipients and this decision has to be evaluated during runtime, then before the "send message" activity a data-based exclusive gateway is added.

8 Conclusion

In this paper we showed how a development team that employs the Gaia methodology, or its derivatives, i.e. ROADMAP [4], the Gaia2JADE process [5], Gaia4E [6] and ASEME [7] can transform the output of the analysis phase model (Role Model) to a process model. Actually, the role's liveness property is used for the transformation.

Process models are useful paradigms as they, on one hand, allow the usage of a wide range of tools (free or proprietary) for simulation, thus providing the means to explore non-functional properties of the system under construction, even before its implementation. Therefore, project managers and engineers can evaluate the use of methods and technologies in their project, but also information about the deployment and scaling of their application. On the other hand, process models are commonly used by business stakeholders, who can now understand and appreciate a MAS analysis model. Finally, such models can be used to define agent and humans interactions based on the associations of the process model.

Herein, we presented the transformation algorithm, demonstrated the developed tool and showed how it can be used to validate a system analysis for a real world application, which was created in the context of ASK-IT project. The open Java sources and executable java jar file for the Liveness2XPDL tool can be browsed by the interested reader at github[4].

The approach that we followed has some limitations, but also opens interesting paths for future work. A very promising path lies in developing a code generation tool based on the process model and targeting the WADE[5] toolkit of the popular JADE platform. Another path is that of accommodating the definition of human-agent interactions in the modern field of Human-Agent Collectives [29], based on process models.

Appendix: The Recursive Transformation Algorithm

The pseudocode of the tranformation algorithm is presented below. The different model elements are represented as classes and their properties as class properties, accessible using the dot operator, i.e. $< classname > .<property >$. For representing a list we use a

---

[4] https://github.com/ASEMEtransformation/Liveness2XPDL.
[5] WADE is a software platform based on JADE providing support for the execution of tasks defined using the workflow metaphor, http://jade.tilab.com/wadeproject.

List class that supports the operations *add* (to add an element to the list) and *size* (to return the number of its elements). The program takes as input an XPDL Package instance and the String liveness property of an SRM Role instance.

```
Program transform(Liveness liveness, Package package)
 WorkflowProcess workflowProcess = new WorkflowProcess
 package.workflowProcesses.add(workflowProcess)
 Event startEvent = new Event
 startEvent.type = start
 workflowProcess.add(startEvent)
 Activity lastActivity = createProcess(liveness.formula₁.expression,
 workflowProcess, startEvent)
 Event endEvent = new Event
 endEvent.type = end
 workflowProcess.add(endEvent)
 Transition transition = new Transition
 transition.from = lastActivity
 transition.to = endEvent
 workflowProcess.add(transition)
End Program


Function Activity createProcess(Expression expression, WorkflowProcess
 workflowProcess, Activity activity)
 List terms = new List
 For Each termᵢ In expression
  terms.add(termᵢ)
 End For
 If terms.size() > 1 Then
  If expression Is SequentialExpr Then
 For Each termᵢ In expression
  Activity newActivity = createProcess(termᵢ, workflowprocess,
activity)
   activity = newActivity
  End for
 Else If expression Is OrExpr
  Activity xorEntryGateway = new Activity
  xorEntryGateway.gatewayType = XOR
  workflowProcess.add(xorEntryGateway)
  Transition transition = new Transition
  transition.from = activity
  transition.to = xorEntryGateway
  workflowProcess.add(transition)
  Activity xorExitGateway = new Activity
  xorExitGateway.gatewayType = XOR
  workflowProcess.add(xorExitGateway)
```

```
For Each termᵢ In expression
  Activity newActivity = createProcess(termᵢ, workflowprocess,
xorEntryGateway)
    transition = new Transition
    transition.from = newActivity
    transition.to = xorExitGateway
    workflowProcess.add(transition)
  End for
  activity = xorExitGateway
Else If expression is ParallelExpr
  //similar with orExpr, parallel gateway type instead of XOR
End If
For Each termᵢ In expression
 If termᵢ Is BasicTerm
  boolean foundLeftHandSideEqualsBasicTerm = false
  For Each formulaᵢ In liveness
  If formulaᵢ.leftHandside = termᵢ Then
    Activity newActivity = createProcess(formulaᵢ.expression,
workflowprocess, activity)
    activity = newActivity
    foundLeftHandSideEqualsBasicTerm = true
  End If
  If foundLeftHandSideEqualsBasicTerm = false
   Activity newActivity = new Activity
   workflowProcess.add(newActivity)
     Transition transition = new Transition
     transition.from = activity
     transition.to = newActivity
     workflowProcess.add(transition)
     activity = newActivity
  End If
 Else If (termᵢ is of type '(' term ')' ) Then
   Activity newActivity = createProcess(term, workflowprocess,
activity)
   activity = newActivity
 Else If (termᵢ is of type '[' term ']')Then
   //definition of the [A] template
 Else If (termᵢ is of type '*') Then
   //definition of the A* template
 Else If (termᵢ is of type '~') Then
   //definition of the A~ template
 Else If (termᵢ is of type '+') Then
   //definition of the A+ template
 End If
 End If
End For
return activity
End Function
```

References

1. Rana, O.F., Stout, K.: What is scalability in multi-agent systems? In: International Conference on Autonomous Agents. pp. 56–63. ACM, Barcelona, Spain (2000)
2. Dumas, M., La Rosa, M., Mendling, J., Reijers, H.A.: Fundamentals of Business Process Management. Springer, Berlin (2013)
3. Wooldridge, M., Jennings, N.R., Kinny, D.: The Gaia Methodology for Agent-Oriented Analysis and Design. Auton. Agent. Multi. Agent. Syst. 3, 285–312 (2000)
4. Juan, T., Pearce, A., Sterling, L.: ROADMAP: extending the gaia methodology for complex open systems. In: Proceedings of the First International Joint Conference on Autonomous Agents and Multiagent Systems part 1 – AAMAS 2002, pp. 3–10. ACM Press, New York, USA (2002)
5. Moraitis, P., Spanoudakis, N.: The GAIA2JADE process for multi-agent systems development. Appl. Artif. Intell. 20, 251–273 (2006)
6. Cernuzzi, L., Zambonelli, F.: Gaia4E: A tool supporting the design of MAS using gaia. In: Proceedings of the 11th International Conference on Enterprise Information Systems (ICEIS 2009), 6–10 May, Milan, Italy, vol. SAIC, pp. 82–88 (2009)
7. Spanoudakis, N., Moraitis, P.: Using ASEME methodology for model-driven agent systems development. In: Weyns, D., Gleizes, M.-P. (eds.) AOSE 2010. LNCS, vol. 6788, pp. 106–127. Springer, Heidelberg (2011)
8. Workflow Management Coalition: Workflow Standard Process Definition Interface - XML Process Definition Language, WFMC-TC-1025. (2008)
9. Zambonelli, F., Jennings, N.R., Wooldridge, M.: Developing multiagent systems: the Gaia methodology. ACM Trans. Softw. Eng. Methodol. 12, 317–370 (2003)
10. Pascalau, E., Giurca, A., Wagner, G.: Validating auction business processes using agent-based simulations. In: Proceedings of 2nd International Conference on Business Process and Services Computing (BPSC 2009), Leipzig, Germany, 23–24 March 2009)
11. Szimanski, F., Ralha, C.G., Wagner, G., Ferreira, D.R.: Improving business process models with agent-based simulation and process mining. In: Nurcan, S., Proper, H.A., Soffer, P., Krogstie, J., Schmidt, R., Halpin, T., Bider, I. (eds.) BPMDS 2013 and EMMSAD 2013. LNBIP, vol. 147, pp. 124–138. Springer, Heidelberg (2013)
12. Onggo, B.S.S.: BPMN pattern for agent-based simulation model representation. In: Proceedings of the 2012 Winter Simulation Conference (WSC), pp. 1–10. IEEE (2012)
13. Spanoudakis, N., Moraitis, P.: An agent modeling language implementing protocols through capabilities. In: 2008 IEEE/WIC/ACM International Conference on Web Intelligence and Intelligent Agent Technology, pp. 578–582. IEEE (2008)
14. Wirth, N.: Extended Backus-Naur Form (EBNF), ISO/IEC 14977:1996(E) (1996)
15. Sendall, S., Kozaczynski, W.: Model transformation: the heart and soul of model-driven software development. IEEE Softw. 20, 42–45 (2003)
16. Steinberg, D., Budinsky, F., Paternostro, M., Merks, E.: Eclipse Modeling Framework, 2nd edn. Addison-Wesley Professional, Boston (2008)
17. Redding, G., Dumas, M., ter Hofstede, A.H.M., Iordachescu, A.: Generating business process models from object behavior models. Inf. Syst. Manag. 25, 319–331 (2008)
18. Jahangirian, M., Eldabi, T., Naseer, A., Stergioulas, L.K., Young, T.: Simulation in manufacturing and business: a review. Eur. J. Oper. Res. 203, 1–13 (2010)
19. Cibrán, M.A.: Translating BPMN models into UML activities. In: Ardagna, D., Mecella, M., Yang, J. (eds.) BPM 2008 International Workshops, Milano, Italy, September 1–4, 2008. Revised Papers, pp. 236–247. Springer, Heidelberg (2009)

20. González-Ferrer, A., Fernández-Olivares, J., Castillo, L.: From business process models to hierarchical task network planning domains. Knowl. Eng. Rev. **28**, 175–193 (2013)
21. Van der Aalst, W.M.P.: The application of petri nets to workflow management. J. Circuits Syst. Comput. **8**, 21–66 (1998)
22. Bernon, C., Cossentino, M., Gleizes, M.-P., Turci, P., Zambonelli, F.: A study of some multi-agent meta-models. In: Odell, J.J., Giorgini, P., Müller, J.P. (eds.) AOSE 2004. LNCS, vol. 3382, pp. 62–77. Springer, Heidelberg (2005)
23. Juan, T., Sterling, L.: The ROADMAP meta-model for intelligent adaptive multi-agent systems in open environments. In: Giorgini, P., Müller, J.P., Odell, J.J. (eds.) AOSE 2003. LNCS, vol. 2935, pp. 53–68. Springer, Heidelberg (2004)
24. Cossentino, M., Gaglio, S., Garro, A., Seidita, V.: Method fragments for agent design methodologies: from standardisation to research. Int. J. Agent-Oriented Softw. Eng. **1**, 91 (2007)
25. Seidita, V., Cossentino, M., Gaglio, S.: Using and extending the SPEM specifications to represent agent oriented methodologies. In: Luck, M., Gomez-Sanz, J.J. (eds.) AOSE 2008. LNCS, vol. 5386, pp. 46–59. Springer, Heidelberg (2009)
26. Dam, H.K., Ghose, A.: Agent-based development for business processes. In: Desai, N., Liu, A., Winikoff, M. (eds.) Principles and Practice of Multi-Agent Systems, pp. 387–393. Springer, Berlin Heidelberg, Berlin, Heidelberg (2012)
27. Endert, H., Hirsch, B., Küster, T., Albayrak, Ş.: Towards a mapping from BPMN to agents. In: Huang, J., Kowalczyk, R., Maamar, Z., Martin, D., Müller, I., Stoutenburg, S., Sycara, K. (eds.) SOCASE 2007. LNCS, vol. 4504, pp. 92–106. Springer, Heidelberg (2007)
28. Delias, P., Spanoudakis, N.: Simulating multi-agent system designs using business process modeling. In: 8th European Workshop on Multi-Agent Systems (EUMAS 2010), Paris, France (2010)
29. Jennings, N.R., Moreau, L., Nicholson, D., Ramchurn, S.D., Roberts, S., Rodden, T., Rogers, A.: Human-Agent Collectives. Commun. ACM **57**, 80–88 (2014)

Programming Mirror Worlds: An Agent-Oriented Programming Perspective

Alessandro Ricci$^{(\boxtimes)}$, Angelo Croatti, Pietro Brunetti, and Mirko Viroli

DISI, University of Bologna, Via Sacchi 3, Cesena, Italy
{a.ricci,a.croatti,p.brunetti,mirko.viroli}@unibo.it

Abstract. The impressive development of technologies is reducing the gulf between the physical and the digital matter, reality and virtuality. *Mirror worlds* (MW) are agent-based systems that live on this edge. They are meant to be a conceptual blueprint for designing future smart environment systems, providing an innovative conceptual framework for investigating inter-disciplinary aspects – from cognition to interaction, cooperation, governance – concerning human-agent mixed-reality and augmented systems. In this paper we focus on the problem of how to concretely design and program mirror worlds, in particular adopting high-level programming abstractions that are provided by state-of-the-art agent-oriented programming models and technologies.

1 Introduction

Mixed reality refers to the merging of real and virtual worlds to produce new environments and visualisations where physical and digital objects co-exist and interact in real time [6]. As defined by P. Milgram and F. Kishino, it is "anywhere between the extrema of the virtuality continuum" [12], that extends from the completely real through to the completely virtual environment with augmented reality (AR) and augmented virtuality ranging between.

The fruitful integration of augmented/mixed-reality technologies and agents and multi-agent systems has been remarked along different perspectives in literature [11]. The most recent works have emphasized the value of (serious) mixed-reality games as a platform to explore scenarios in the real world that are typically hard to study in realistic settings, such as disaster response, to study the joint activities of human-agent collectives [9]. Similarly, mixed-reality testbeds have been deployed for the incremental development of human-agent robot applications [4].

A deeper integration of the research on agents and mixed reality is envisioned in [5,19,22] with the concept of *mirror world* (MW)[1], fostering a new generation of multi-agent applications based on a bidirectional *augmentation* of the physical and digital matter, the physical and the virtual reality. MWs bring together research contributions from different fields apart agents and MAS,

---

[1] The name *mirror world* has been used in honour of Gelernter's book [10] that originally inspired the first glimpses of this idea.

© Springer International Publishing Switzerland 2015
M. Baldoni et al. (Eds.): EMAS 2015, LNAI 9318, pp. 191–211, 2015.
DOI: 10.1007/978-3-319-26184-3_11

from Ambient Intelligence and smart environments, Internet-of-Things down to mixed/augmented reality. A MW can be abstractly conceived as a digital world shaped in terms of a multi-agent system, situated into some virtual environment which is *coupled* to some physical environment, *augmenting* its functionalities and the capabilities of the people that live or work inside it. Besides smart environment applications, they aim at being *laboratories* where to explore together inter-disciplinary aspects: how human/agent action, perception, cognition are enhanced and supported by MWs; how to think about the co-design of physical objects and environments and related digital counterparts; what models for interaction, coordination, organization, and governance are promoted by and can be adopted in these agent-based mixed-reality systems.

In this paper we focus on the problem of how to concretely design and program mirror worlds, in particular adopting high-level programming abstractions that are provided by state-of-the-art agent-oriented programming models and technologies. The contribution is the definition of a first programming model based on the A&A (Agents and Artifacts) meta-model [15], which provides first-class abstractions to model the environment where agents are situated. We develop a first implementation of the model upon the JaCaMo platform [1], where the A&A meta-model is integrated with BDI agents, implemented using the Jason programming language [2]. The result is a first platform that allows for prototyping simple mirror worlds, and investigate the value (and current limits) of the idea in different application domains.

Besides mirror worlds, the motivation and contribution of the paper concern – more generally – the definition and development of proper methods and techniques for modeling, designing and programming *augmented worlds*, in which Artificial Intelligence is combined with other domains such as ubiquitous computing, sensor network technologies as well as augmented reality, to shape future smart environments beyond the current vision of ambient intelligence [19, 22]. To this purpose, we believe that the availability of concrete platforms that would allow to prototype and play with these kinds of systems – starting from the simplest cases – would be important, in particular to realize if/how current agent-based models/architectures/technologies are fully effective for this job or need to be extended with new concepts and mechanisms.

The remainder of the paper is organized as follows: In Sect. 2 we provide a background about the main concepts concerning MWs. Then, in Sect. 3 we describe an agent-oriented programming model, based on A&A, and in Sect. 4 we describe a first implementation based on the JaCaMo platform. In Sect. 5 we discuss real-world applications as well as the challenges to be tackled in the mirror-world development research agenda.

2   Background: The Mirror World Idea

On the background of MWs there is the broad idea of using agent-oriented abstractions to shape the continuous real-time distributed flows of situated information generated by the physical and social layers (as devised by Smart environments, Internet of Things, Big Data contexts), as well as of the distributed

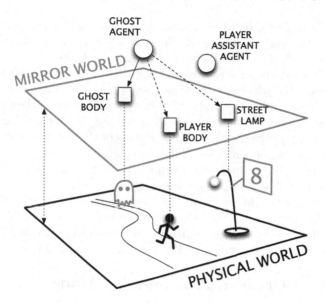

Fig. 1. An abstract representation of a mirror world, using the ghost in the city game example.

intelligent software processes that work on that information in order to provide some smart service or functionality. A mirror world can be conceived as an open society of software agents situated into a virtual environment *augmenting* some physical reality (e.g., a room, a building, a city), to which the environment is coupled. Mirroring is given by the fact that – to some extent – physical things, which can be perceived and acted upon by humans in the physical world, have a digital counterpart (or augmentation, extension) in the mirror, so that they can be observed and acted upon by agents. Viceversa, an entity in the MW that can be perceived and acted upon by software agents may have a physical appearance (or extension) in the physical world – e.g., augmenting it, in terms of augmented or mixed-reality – so that it can be observed and acted upon by humans—for instance, by means of wearable devices like smart glasses.

This implies a form of *coupling*, such that an action on an object in the physical world causes some kind of changes in one or more entities in the mirror, perceivable then by software agents. Viceversa an action by agents on an entity in the MW can have an effect on things in the physical world, perceivable by people. As MW citizens, agents are responsible of autonomously fulfilling tasks inside a MW, by properly observing/using MW things which are part of their environment and (directly/indirectly) observing and interacting with human inhabitants that act in that environment.

A simple but effective example of MW described in [19] is an extension of the mobile AR game *Ghosts in the city* (see Fig. 1). The MW is composed by a collection of treasures and ghosts distributed in some part of a city. There are two teams of human players. Their objective is to collect as much treasures as possible – walking around – without being caught by the ghosts. Players have smart glasses and a smart-phone, used as a magic wand. Ghosts are agents autonomously moving in the MW – and in the city. Players perceive ghosts by means of their smart glasses – as soon as they are in the same location. Ghosts as well can perceive the players, as soon as they are within some distance. Ghosts aim to catch human players; so they follow them as soon as they can perceive them. A ghost catches a human player by grabbing her body in the MW—this can be physically perceived by humans by means of the magic wand (trembling). Different kinds of ghosts may prefer different (physical) spots, according to some physical parameter of the spot—e.g., humidity, light, temperature. Besides perceiving the world, ghosts with enough energy could also act on it, for instance turning off a physical light (by acting on the counter-part in the MW).

In spite of being a game, the example sumarizes the basic kinds of coupling that are possible between the digital layer and the physical one. A deeper discussion about the usefulness of the MW idea can be found in [19].

3   An Agent-Oriented Programming Model

As mentioned in the introduction, the conceptual meta-model adopted for modelling and designing MWs, underlying the programming framework, is A&A (Agents and Artifacts) [15]. A&A introduces *artifacts* as first-class abstractions to model and design the application environments where agents are logically situated. An artifact can be used to model and design any kind of (non-autonomous) resources and tools used and possibly shared by agents to do their job [20]. Artifacts are collected in *workspaces*, which represent logical containers possibly distributed over the network.

In A&A artifacts are then the basic blocks to modularize in a uniform way the agent environment, which can be distributed across multiple network nodes and that eventually function also as the interface to the physical environment. As described in the literature about environments for MAS [24], such environments can be useful at different levels in engineering MAS, not only for interfacing with the external environment but also as an abstraction layer for shaping mediated interaction and coordination among agents.

From the agent viewpoint, an artifact is characterised by two main aspects: an observable state, represented by a set of *observable properties*, whose changes can be perceived by agents as observable events; a set of *operations*, which represent the actions that an agent can do upon that piece of environment. When used by BDI agents, like in the case of the JaCaMo framework (discussed in Sect. 4), artifacts observable properties are mapped into beliefs that agents have about the environment that they are perceiving, while operations become the external actions that agents can perform.

The artifact idea has been conceived by taking inspiration from Activity Theory [18] and human environments, mimicking the artifacts that are designed, shared and used by humans (as cognitive agents) to work, to live. So it is not surprising that we found such an abstraction quite natural to model mirror words, where the coupling with human physical artifacts is an essential aspect.

3.1   Modelling MWs with A&A: Mirror Artifacts and Workspaces

A MW is modelled in term of a set of *mirror workspaces*. A mirror workspace extends the concept of workspace defined in A&A with an explicit coupling with the physical world. In particular, for each mirror workspace a *map* is defined, specifying which part of the physical world is coupled by the MW. It could be a part a city, a building, a room. Each point belonging to the map has a geolocation, which can defined in terms of latitude and longitude, or using local reference systems.

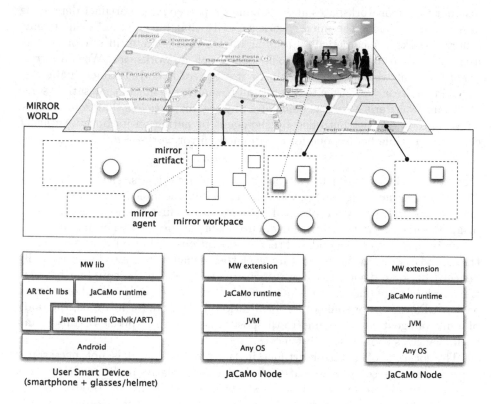

Fig. 2. Abstract view of organization of a mirror word and of the layers that characterise the MW infrastructure.

Figure 2 shows an abstract representation of the elements composing a MW, including the infrastructure levels based on JaCaMo platform, which will be discussed in Sect. 4. A mirror workspace contains a dynamic set of *mirror artifacts* — besides the normal artifacts. Mirror artifacts are artifacts anchored to some specific location inside the physical world, as defined by the map. Such location could be either a geo-location, or some trackable physical marker/object. Such a physical location/position is reified into an observable property. The position can change dynamically and can be perceived then by agents observing the artifact.

As depicted in Fig. 2, a MW can include multiple mirror workspaces spread over different computational nodes, used to run the infrastructure. Each workspace is located on some specific network node; then, when mapping a piece of a mirror world onto a mirror workspace, that part of the environment will be executed and managed on the node hosting the workspace.

Mirror Agents. An agent can perceive/continuously observe a mirror artifact in two basic ways. One is exactly the same as for normal artifacts, that is explicitly *focusing* on the artifact, given its identifier [20]. The second one instead is peculiar to mirror workspaces and accounts for perceiving an artifact depending on its position inside the mirror workspace. To that purpose, an agent joining a mirror workspace can create a *body* artifact, which is a builtin mirror artifact useful to situate the agent in a specific location of the workspace. We call *mirror agent* an agent with a body in a mirror workspace. A body artifact enables an agent in a mirror workspace to observe all the mirror artifacts that satisfy some observability criteria – such as being at a physical distance less than some radius. These criteria can be controlled by the agent by acting on its body. An agent can have multiple bodies, one for each joined mirror workspace.

Coupling. Mirror artifacts can be of two different kinds: either completely virtual, i.e., situated in some physical location but uncoupled from any physical device, or coupled to some physical artifact. In the first case, the geo-position inside the mirror (and the physical environment) is specified when instantiating the artifact, and it can be updated then by operations provided by the artifact. In the second case, at the infrastructure level, the artifact is meant to be periodically *synched* by some device which is responsible to establish the coupling between the two levels, the mirror and the physical. It can be e.g., a smartphone device with a GPS sensor, or some other localization device. So, for instance, the body of a mirror agent can be bound to the position of the smartphone of a user, and then change as soon as the user moves.

The location of a mirror artifact in the physical world is not necessarily expressed as an absolute geo-location, but could be a relative position with respect to some physical object, such as a *marker* or an existing physical object. In that case AR technologies – hardware (cameras and other sensors mounted on the smartglasses) and software (computer vision algorithms, pattern recognition) – are essential to realize the coupling between the two layers.

Coupling is not limited to the physical location: it could concern any property of the physical world, of some physical entity, that we want to make it observable to the agents living in the MW. An example could be the temperature of a room or the luminosity of a lamp or the force on some object.

Humans in the Loop. A main ingredient of mirror worlds is the capability of human situated in such environments to perceive the augment layer, by adopting devices such as smart glasses or AR helmets. This can be modelled by adopting user assistant mirror agents with a body coupled to the physical location of the human user, by means of a smart device—glass, phone, whatever. Such agents can exploit the device to communicate with the user, in terms of messages, cues, etc. In more sophisticated scenarios, the user assistant agent can superimpose to the image of the physical reality information or objects that represent some kind of extension of the reality, given the set of mirror artifacts perceived. Existing (mobile) AR frameworks – e.g., Wikitude[2] – can be exploited inside the mirror world middleware to implement these functionalities.

4   Programming Mirror Worlds in JaCaMo: A First API

A main objective and contribution of this paper is the definition of a first agent-oriented API and platform to explore the development of mirror worlds, based on the meta-model described before. To that purpose, we devised such a framework on JaCaMo [1], which natively supports the development of multi-agent systems based on BDI agents living in artifact-based environments. In particular, JaCaMo is based on the synergistic integration of three different dimensions (and technologies):

- the *agent* dimension — agents are programmed using the Jason agent programming language [2], which is a practical extension and implementation of AgentSpeak(L) [17];
- the *environment* dimension – artifact-based environments are programmed using the CArtAgO framework [21], which provides a Java API for that purpose;
- the organization dimension – organizations can be specified using the MOISE organization model and language.

JaCaMo – and in particular CArtAgO – has been recently extended so as to support *situated* workspaces and *situated* artifacts as an extension of normal workspaces and artifacts, as described in previous section. Mirror words are realized by situated workspaces equipped by specific maps, establishing a coupling with physical environments such as city zones, buildings, rooms. Mirror workspaces/artifacts are then a specialisation of situated workspaces/artifacts, based on the physical/geographical world as context defining the situated-ness.

It is worth remarking that no extension has been necessary on the agent side, that is: mirror agents are pure JaCaMo agents – i.e., Jason agents situated in artifact-based environments, organized according to the MOISE model – with a single important difference, about observation and percepts—described in the previous section.

Mirror Workspaces. Mirror workspaces are based on a workspace map that defines a geographical region of the physical environment; for instance, a rectangular region defined by vertices expressed in terms of latitude/longitude. Inside that region, a simple three dimensional euclidean system of reference is

---

[2] https://www.wikitude.com.

used to define positions and distances. Given a point expressed with respect to this system of reference, it is possible to compute (when needed) its absolute geographical position in terms of longitude/latitude/altitude by using the workspace map.

Mirror Artifacts. Mirror artifacts are characterized by:

- a *position*, defined as a point in the system of reference of the workspace map—in this case a three-dimensional vector, with coordinates expressed in meters;
- an *observability radius*, which is a distance in meters useful to specify who can perceive the artifact.

The agent body is a predefined mirror artifact with a further information:

- an *observing radius*, which is a distance useful to define which artifacts an agent can observe.

The observability radius and observing radius are meant to be properly chosen when designing the mirror artifacts and mirror agents of the systems, possibly modified at runtime. Given this information, a mirror artifact X located at the position X_{pos}, with an observability radius X_r is observable by a mirror agent with a body B, located in B_{pos}, with an observing radius B_R, iff $d <= X_r$ and $d <= B_R$, being d the distance between X_{pos} and B_{pos}.

This rule extends the basic agent-artifact observation model used in CArtAgO [20] and then in JaCaMo. In the case of pure JaCaMo agents, an agent can perceive the observable state of an artifact and the stream of the observable events related to its changes only after intentionally focusing the artifact, by means of the `focus` action. This action is analogous to the *subscribe* action in publish/subscribe systems. Thus, in order to perceive some artifact X, the agent has to know X before and intentionally issue a *focus(X)* action. In the case of mirror agents instead, a JaCaMo mirror agent can perceive mirror artifacts even without knowing them a priori and without intentionally doing a focus action, depending on *where* the artifacts are inside the workspace map with respect to the agent body, and depending on the radii.

In the remainder of the section we first provide a global picture of the API used to develop mirror worlds in JaCaMo, then we show their main features using simple examples.

4.1   API Overview

The API has been conceived with a main objective in mind, that is: to make the development of such mixed-reality worlds as "natural" as possible for MAS developers. The full code of the examples is available in [8], along with the experimental JaCaMo distribution supporting mirror worlds. The Mirror World API currently include:

- a new set of actions for creating mirror workspaces and mirror artifacts inside, including agent bodies. Among the others, used in the examples in next sections:
  - `createMirrorWorkspace(name, latitude, longitude)` – this action creates a new mirror workspace named `name`, centered at the specified latitude/longitude coordinates – without boundaries.
  - `createMirrorArtifactAtPos(name, template, initParameters, pos, observabilityRadius,?id)` – creates a new mirror artifact named `name`, specifying its template (a Java class name), location `pos` and the observability radius. Like the CArtAgO basic action `makeArtifact`, this action too allows for getting the identifier of the new artifact created as an action feedback (output parameter `id`).
  - `createMirrorArtifact(name, template, initParameters, observabilityRadius, ?id)` – A further way to create a mirror artifact, without specifying the location because the artifact is meant to be bound to some mirror world coupling device, defining and constraining its position.
  - `createAgentBodyAtPos(pos, observableRadius, observingRadius)` – creates a new agent body (attached to the agent that requested this action) in the workspace, specifying the initial position and the observation-related radii.
  - `createAgentBody(observableRadius, observingRadius)` – A further way to create agent body artifacts, analogously to mirror artifacts creation.
  These actions are implemented by a new artifact called `mw`, available by default in each mirror workspace.

- `MirrorArtifact` artifact template, extending the `Artifact` CArtAgO base class and representing the basic template to be further extended and specialized to implement specific kinds of mirror artifacts. The usage interface of this artifact includes:
  - a `pos` observable property, containing the current location in the mirror workspace of the artifact;
  - `observabilityRadius` observable property, storing the current observability radius of the artifact;
  - specific operations (`setPos`, `setObservabilityRadius`) for updating the position and the observability radius.

- `AgentBody` – a predefined artifact used to represent agent bodies. The usage interface of this artifact includes a further `observingRadius` observable property, storing the current observing radius of the agent, and the related operation `setObservingRadius` for updating such radius.

Besides, some *utility* artifacts are available providing functionalities useful for agents working in the mirror. An example is given by the `GeoTool`, which provides functionalities for converting the coordinates and compute distances. For instance, the operation `toCityPoint(Lat,Long,?Loc)` used in the examples makes it possible to compute the location ?Loc in the local system of reference of the mirror workspace of a geographical point given its latitude Lat and longitude Long[3].

4.2   Hello, Mirror World!

This first example mimics classic mobile augment reality applications. It is a very simple mirror world composed by a single mirror workspace (called mirror-example) mapped onto a city zone in the center of a city (Cesena, in this case). The mirror workspace is dynamically populated of mirror artifacts representing simple messages situated in some specific point of the city. Mobile human users walk around the streets along with their user assistant agents, running on their smartphone. As soon as user agents perceive a situated message, they display it on the smart glasses worn by the users (see Fig. 3).

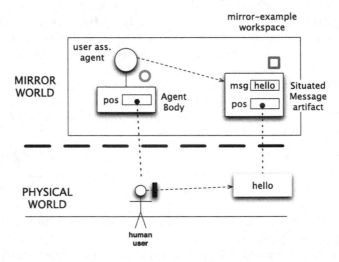

Fig. 3. In the *hello mirror world* example, each mobile user walking along the streets has a user assistant agent, with a body located at the position detected by the GPS. As soon as the user is near to a situated message, this becomes observable by the user assistant agent. The red circle and the blue rectangle are the symbols used to represent respectively agent bodies and situated messages in the map in Fig. 4.

The MAS program implementing the mirror includes:

– a majordomo agent, who is responsible of creating and setting up the MW, composed in this case by a single mirror workspace called mirror-example. The agent creates also some SituatedMessage mirror artifacts, located at some specific geo-coordinates;

---

[3] The altitude is not considered in the examples.

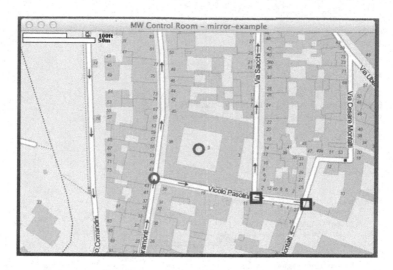

Fig. 4. The map visualised by the control room, showing the position of mirror agents (red circles) – that is, the body of mirror agents – and the position of mirror artifacts, i.e. situated messages in the example (Color figure online).

- user-assistant agents, running on the smartphone of each mobile user, whose task is to promptly react to situated messages perceived in the nearby of the user and display the corresponding message on the smart glasses;
- a control-room agent, which is responsible of showing the real-time state of the MW, represented by a map with the current location of the situated message artifacts and of the user-assistant agents (see Fig. 4). Besides, this agent is responsible also of dynamically creating new situated messages, in the positions specified by human users observing the map, by means of the GUI.

The example is useful to give a taste of the API to create mirror artifacts and agents. Figure 5 shows the source code of the majordomo agent. The goal of the agent is to initialize the mirror world. First, it creates the mirror workspace (line 19), then it joins it with the subgoal of creating some SituatedMessage mirror artifacts inside (line 24). The corresponding plan (lines 28–34) creates a couple of situated messages, storing hello #1 and hello #2, with an observability radius of 2.5 m. Besides the mirror artifacts, in the workspace the agent creates also a "normal" artifact called geotool, instance of the GeoTool auxiliary artifact, which will be used by the other agents joining the workspace. The source code of a SituatedMessage artifact is shown in Fig. 6: the artifact has a single observable property called msg (defined in line 6), storing a message specified when the artifact is created. No specific operations are provided.

Figure 7 shows the source code of the user_assistant mirror agent. The agent first creates (in its default/local workspace) a SmartGlassDevice artifact (line 8), to be used as output device to display messages, by means of the displayMsg operation. Then, the agent joins the mirror workspace and cre-

```
1    /* Majordomo agent */
2
3    /* initial beliefs */
4
5    /* the center of the mirror -- latitude/longitude */
6    poi("isi_cortile", 44.13983, 12.24289).
7
8    /* the point of interests, where to put the messages */
9    poi("pasolini_montalti",44.13948, 12.24384).
10   poi("sacchi_pasolini",44.13952, 12.24340).
11
12   /* initial goal*/
13   !setupMW.
14
15   /* the plans */
16
17   +!setupMW
18     <- ?poi("isi_cortile",Lat,Long);
19        createMirrorWorkspace("mirror-example",Lat,Long);
20        joinWorkspace("mirror-example");
21        /* create an aux artifact to help coordinate conversion */
22        makeArtifact("geotool","GeoTool",[Lat,Long]);
23        /* create the situated messages */
24        !create_messages;
25        println("MW ready.").
26
27   /* to create the situated message mirror artifacts */
28   +!create_messages
29     <- ?poi("pasolini_montalti",Lat,Lon);
30        toCityPoint(Lat,Lon,Loc);
31        createMirrorArtifactAtPos("a1","SituatedMessage",["hello #1"],Loc,2.5);
32        ?poi("sacchi_pasolini",Lat2,Lon2);
33        toCityPoint(Lat2,Lon2,Loc2);
34        createMirrorArtifactAtPos("a2","SituatedMessage",["hello #2"],Loc2,2.5).
```

Fig. 5. Hello world example: the majordomo agent.

```
1    /* Mirror artifact representing a situated message */
2
3    public class SituatedMessage extends MirrorArtifact {
4
5        public void init(String msg){
6            defineObsProperty("msg",msg);
7        }
8    }
```

Fig. 6. Code of the SituatedMessage mirror artifact.

ates its body, with observing radius of 10 meters. The body is bound to a GPSDeviceDriver device driver artifact (line 19), previously created at line 17. The device driver implements the coupling between the position detected by the GPS sensor, available on the smartphone of the user. When the human user approaches a point in the physical world where a situated message is located, the user assistant agent perceives the message and reacts by simply displaying it on the glasses (lines 24–26). When (if) the human user moves away from the mirror artifact, the belief about the message is removed and the use assistant agent reacts by displaying a further message (lines 28–30).

```
1    /* User assistant agent */
2
3    /* goal of the agent */
4    !monitor_and_display_messages.
5
6    +!monitor_and_display_messages
7      <- /* setup the smart glass device */
8          makeArtifact("viewer","SmartGlassDevice",[],Viewer);
9          +viewer(Viewer);
10
11         /* join the mirror workspace */
12         joinWorkspace("mirror-example");
13
14         /* create the agent body */
15         createAgentBody(1000,10,Body);
16         /* create the artifact used as MW coupling device */
17         makeArtifact("driver","GPSDeviceDriver",Dev);
18         /* bind the body to the device */
19         bindTo(Body)[artifact_id(Dev)];
20         println("ready.").
21
22   /* plans reacting to situated messages perceived in the mirror worlds */
23
24   +msg(M) : viewer(Dev)
25     <- .concat("new message perceived: ",M,Msg);
26         displayMsg(100,50,Msg)[artifact_id(Dev)].
27
28   -msg(M) : viewer(Dev)
29     <- .concat("message ",M," no more perceived. ",Msg);
30         displayMsg(100,50,Msg)[artifact_id(Dev)].
```

Fig. 7. Code of the user-assistant agents.

4.3 Ghosts and Traces

The second example is an extension of the previous one, where some ghost mirror agents are moving around autonomously along some streets of the city, perceiving and interacting with the situated messages as well.

The mirror artifact representing a situated message is extended (SituatedMessageExt, Fig. 8), implementing a new touch operation which increments a new n_touches observable property. The action touch is performed by user assistant agents and ghost agents each time they start perceiving the situated message.

The source code of ghost agents is shown in Fig. 9. They have a walk_around goal (line 8), and the plan for that goal (line 12) consists in repeatedly doing the same path, whose nodes (a list of point-of-interests) are stored in the path belief (line 5). They move by changing the position of their body, by executing a moveTowards action available in each mirror artifact—specifying the target point (to define the direction) and the distance to be covered (in meters). The plan for reaching an individual destination of the path (lines 23–29) simply computes the distance from the target (exploiting the computeDistanceFrom, provided by the GeoTool artifact) and then, if the distance is greater than one meter, it moves the body of 0.5 m and then goes on reaching, by requesting recursively the sub-goal !reach_dest; otherwise it completes the plan (the destination has been reached).

Ghosts too react to messages perceived while walking (plan at lines 38–41), eventually executing a `touch` action on each message encountered and printing to the console the current number of touches observed on the message. Instead, when a ghost perceives a human (lines 43–46) – by perceiving the body of the user assistant agent – it reacts by making a trembling on the smartphone owned by the human user. `body` is an observable property provided by each agent body artifact, containing the identifier of the user assistant agent which created the body. Trembling happens by executing a `tremble` action on the artifact which the user assistant agent created to enable the physical interaction with the corresponding human user. By convention, in the example, these artifacts are created with the name `user-dev-X`, where X is name of the user assistant agent. This convention allows the ghost agent to retrieve the identifier of the artifact dynamically given its logic name, by doing a lookup (line 45).

```
1   public class SituatedMessageExt extends SituatedMessage {
2
3       public void init(String msg){
4           super.init(msg);
5           defineObsProperty("n_touches",0);
6       }
7
8       @OPERATION void touch(){
9           updateObsProperty("n_touches",
10          getObsProperty("n_touches").intValue()+1);
11      }
12  }
```

Fig. 8. Code of `SituatedMessageExt` artifacts.

This example is useful to show a couple of things. The first one is the development of mirror artifacts that are not simply information augmenting the physical world, but computational entities with a behaviour and a state, which can change dynamically. The second one is the development of autonomous agents living in the mirror, able to perceive and being perceived by humans, and act on the mirror world so as to have effect in the physical reality.

4.4   Coupling with the Physical World

In this last example, some `StreetLight` mirror artifacts are placed along the streets, representing (and coupled to) physical street lights. Their state (on, off) as well as their luminosity level is made observable by means of a couple of observable properties, `light_status` and `light_level`; instead, a couple of operations are provided to switch on and off the light (`switchOn`, `switchOff`). When approaching a light, ghosts perceive the level of luminosity and, if it is higher than a certain threshold, they invert their direction. Other mirror agents could instead act upon `StreetLight` artifacts so as to have an effect on the physical world, by switching on or off the lights.

This case is useful to show mirror artifacts that have both a physical and a mirror part *in sync*, so that by observing these artifacts, mirror agents (ghosts

```
1    /* ghost agent initial beliefs */
2
3    start_pos("pasolini_chiaramonti").
4    /* path of the walk - 2 steps*/
5    path(["sacchi_pasolini","pasolini_montalti"]).
6
7    /* initial goal */
8    !walk_around.
9
10   /* plans */
11
12   +!walk_around <- !setup; !moving.
13
14   +!moving <- ?path(P); !make_a_trip(P); !moving.
15
16   +!make_a_trip([POI|Rest])
17      <- ?poi(POI,Lat,Lon);
18         !reach_dest(Lat,Lon);
19         !make_a_trip(Rest).
20   +!make_a_trip([])
21      <- ?start_pos(Start); ?poi(Start,Lat,Lon); !reach_dest(Lat,Lon).
22
23   +!reach_dest(Lat,Lon) : myBody(B)
24      <- toCityPoint(Lat,Lon,Target);
25         computeDistanceFrom(Target,Dist)[artifact_id(B)];
26         if (Dist > 1){
27            moveTowards(Target,0.5)[artifact_id(B)];
28            .wait(50);
29            !reach_dest(Lat,Lon)}.
30
31   +!setup
32      <- joinWorkspace("mirror-example",Mirror);
33         lookupArtifact("geotool",Tool); focus(Tool);
34         ?start_pos(Point); ?poi(Point,Lat,Lon); toCityPoint(Lat,Lon,P);
35         createAgentBodyAtPos(P,1000,10,Body);
36         +myBody(Body); .my_name(Me); +me(Me).
37
38   +msg(M) [artifact_id(Id)]
39      <- touch [artifact_id(Id)];
40         ?n_touches(C)[artifact_id(Id)];
41         println("new message perceived: ",M," - touch count: ",C).
42
43   +body(Who) : me(Me) & Who \== Me
44      <- .concat("user-dev-",Who,Dev);
45         lookupArtifact(Dev,DevId);
46         tremble [artifact_id(DevId)].
```

Fig. 9. Code of ghost agents.

in the example) can perceive the physical reality and by acting on them they can have an effect on it. This coupling is implemented by means of embedded devices, connected to the infrastructure.

An important point for artifacts coupled to the physical reality is that the MW infrastructure is responsible to keep track of the *synchronization* state between the digital and physical part, making it observable (to agents) if the mirror artifact is either synchronized or not, depending on the amount of time elapsed since the last synchronization done by devices. This is important in particular for agents that aim at reasoning on the state of the physical world by considering the actual value of artifact observable state.

5   Discussion

In this section we discuss some main aspects of the approach, first providing an overview of the real-world application domains where – we believe – mirror worlds can be effectively exploited, and then discussing the challenges and opportunities to be explored in MW research agenda.

5.1   Real-World Applications

As mentioned in the introduction and in [22], mirror worlds have been conceived in general as a conceptual blueprint to explore the integration of different kinds of models and technologies (multi-agent systems, augmented reality, Internet-of-Things,...) for the design and development of forth-coming open smart environments, scaling from rooms to cities.

Besides such a broad and general target, we aim at exploring their application in specific case studies that concern real-time distributed collaborative environments for teams of human agents engaged in some kind of missions across some physical environment. Mirror worlds promote the design of these applications as augmented worlds enacting forms of indirect/implicit communication and *stigmergic* mechanisms as a mean to support human collaboration [5]. This support is realized by shaping the augmented reality perceived by humans in terms of augmented entities that are dynamically arranged and manipulated by intelligent agents, populating the mirror.

A main example of collaborative application that we are investigating is given by *rescue* scenarios. The objective is to devise novel information technology supports to improve the action and coordination of rescuers engaged in civil or military missions. In that case, a mirror world is deployed on top of the geographical environment where the rescue mission takes place, where there are the wounded to be assisted. Rescuers participate to missions by means of smart glasses/helmets and a smartphone, connected through a network (local or global, depending on the context). One objective is to support as much as possible their action in a *free-hands* mode, minimizing the need of hands for using devices. Besides the rescuers situated in the field, the team includes also remote operators – both human agents (such as doctors) and software agents – following the mission and eventually producing effects on the mirror themselves. The overall objective here is to make both the action of the individual rescuer and the coordination of the team more effective, by augmenting their perception, cognitive and social capabilities through the mirror.

5.2   Challenges and Opportunities for Future Work

The concrete realization of full-fledged mirror words puts forth many important challenges, to be explored in the MW research agenda. Some main ones are sketched in the following.

Coupling – The coupling between the physical and digital layer is a challenging and critical point. Such a coupling includes, among the other, issues concerned to *localization*—every MW application implies the capability to deal with the static/dynamic physical location of people and physical/digital artifact, both outdoor and indoor. This is a well-known challenging problem in literature, and different kinds of technics have been proposed for that purpose. More generally, depending on the applications, the coupling could require also forms of physical-world *recognition and modeling*, and, more general, the real-time recognition and modelling of the *context* where human users are immersed. The research literature on *context-aware* computing and applications is a main reference in that case [7].

Distribution and Scale – MW are inherently distributed systems—even the simplest one includes some part running on the mobile user devices and some infrastructure part running on some other node on the network. So typical issues/problems of distributed systems such as intermittent connectivity, failures, latencies, lack of global clocks cannot be abstracted. Also the scale of a MW can vary depending on the specific applications. In the simple examples shown in this paper only one mirror workspace is used. Of course, complex MW may call for modelling them in terms of multiple workspaces, each one mapping some portion of the physical environment coupled by the MW. Large-scale MW will require the adoption of *cloud* services in the design of some levels of the MW infrastructure.

Organizations and Institutions – The adoption of proper agent-based organizational models and related technologies appears an important direction to be explored in order to tackle the design and programming of large-scale and open, highly dynamic MWs. Thus, we believe that the definition of proper organization and institution models is an important point in the MW research agenda, eventually integrating the contributions about *embodied organizations* that have been developed in literature [16].

To this purpose, JaCaMo already provides a first-class support for organization-oriented programming, based on the MOISE model, currently not exploited for programming MW. Thus, future work can quite easily explore the benefits and limits of this model in the context of MW.

Time in MW – *Time*, like *space*, is a main ingredient and aspect of MWs. Time in MW is necessarily distributed, in fact there is not a single global clock at the MW level. A clock exists at the individual mirror artifact level, so observable events produced by actions on mirror artifacts can be ordered in chains. So, in spite of the distribution, some level of causal consistency must be guaranteed, related to chains of events that span from the physical to the digital layers and viceversa. That is, if a mirror artifact produces a *sequence* of two events concerning the change of its observable state, the same sequence must be observed by any mirror agent observing the artifact (of the same workspace) and then indirectly every human user assisted by such agents.

As a further must-have feature, MW must support agent/human observations and actions changing the physical/digital level with some degree of *real-time* (not necessarily hard real-time). Latencies introduced by network communications and failures can make this aspect quite hard to deal with.

Degrees of Mixed/Augmented-Realities – The support in MWs for augmented/mixed reality does not necessarily require the capability of creating views on smart-glasses/helmets that merge the appearance of the physical reality with the rendering of 3D virtual objects or holograms. For many applications, the *augmented reality* perceived by a user could be limited to either messages that appear on the eyewear devices (Google-glass like), or simple symbols appearing on the FOV (Field-of-View) of the user, possibly associated to some specific element of physical reality part of the view. These functionalities are nowadays supported with a more and more level of sophistication by modern AR technologies, which witnessed an impressive progress in recent years, both at the consumer/business level – e.g., Epson Moverio BT-200, Sony SmartEyeglass, Microsoft Hololens – and at the military level – e.g., DARPA ULTRA-Vis program and prototype [23].

5.3   Related Work

In literature, the integration of agents and multi-agent systems and augmented/mixed-reality has been already explored in different ways. A survey of existing approaches is provided in [3,11].

In [11], agents embodied in a Mixed Reality Environment (referred as MiRAs, Mixed Reality Agents) are classified as along three axes: *agency*, weak or strong; *corporeal presence*, which describes the degree of virtual or physical presence and *interactive capacity*, which is about the ability of MiRAs to sense and act on the virtual and physical environment. Given that taxonomy, [3] discusses the features in particular of AuRAs (Augmented Reality Agents), which can be categorised as MiRA that can both sense and act in the virtual component of the reality but can only sense in the physical. Among the platforms available for developing AuRAs, the AFAR toolkit makes it possible to develop BDI agents for AR applications on the NeXuS mixed reality framework [14], using AgentFactory as agent programming language [13]. Conceptually, the MW toolkit based on JaCaMo presented in this paper is strongly related to AFAR, since it aims at providing a general-purpose framework and API for developing agent-based applications exploiting various degrees of augmented/mixed reality, and adopting a BDI agent programming language for implementing agents. A main difference is that in MW, the virtual layer is not based only on agents, but also on artifacts, which play a key role also for creating the coupling with the physical world, besides *representing* the augmented world itself.

The main objective of AuRAs as described in [3] is to function as *embodied interfaces* and *design paradigm*. The former mainly concerns the development of anthropomorphic interfaces, while the latter concerns software agents tasked with delivering relevant content to the user in a AR scenario. The MW idea conceptually extends these objectives by conceiving AR as one of the ingredients to develop – more generally – smart environment applications, integrating AR with pervasive/ubiquitous computing, context-aware computing, Internet of Things.

Finally, recent works have emphasized the value of (serious) mixed-reality games as a platform to explore scenarios in the real world that are typically hard to study in realistic settings, such as disaster response, to study the joint activities of human-agent collectives [9]. Similarly, mixed-reality testbeds have been deployed for the incremental development of human-agent robot applications [4].

6   Conclusion

In this paper we presented a first programming model for developing mirror worlds, and its implementation on top of the JaCaMo platform. Actually, the model is not specifically bound to JaCaMo, but refers in general to the A&A meta-model and agents based on a BDI-like model. Given such orthogonality between the agent/environment/organization dimensions, in principle it is possible to exploit the same API with agents written in different agent programming languages, not only Jason.

As remarked in Sect. 5, these are just the first steps of the overall MW research agenda [19], which include different kinds of challenges and investigations to be done in future work. However, the availability of a first platform that allows for designing and developing simple MWs could be important both for investigating the applicability of the idea to real-world applications, and for exploring further features that concern the future work, by extending and enriching the platform itself.

References

1. Boissier, O., Bordini, R.H., Hübner, J.F., Ricci, A., Santi, A.: Multi-agent oriented programming with jacamo. Sci. Comput. Program. **78**(6), 747–761 (2013)
2. Bordini, R.H., Hübner, J.F., Wooldrige, M.: Programming Multi-Agent Systems in AgentSpeak using Jason. Wiley Series in Agent Technology, Wiley (2007). http://jason.sf.net/jBook
3. Campbell, A.G., Stafford, J.W., Holz, T., OHare, G.M.: Why, when and how to use augmented reality agents (auras). Virtual Reality **18**(2), 139–159 (2014)
4. Cap, M., Pechoucek, M., Jakob, M., Novak, P., Vanek, O.: Mixed-reality testbeds for incremental development of hart applications. IEEE Intell. Syst. **27**(2), 19–25 (2012)
5. Castelfranchi, C., Piunti, M., Ricci, A., Tummolini, L.: AmI systems as agent-based mirror worlds: bridging humans and agents through stigmergy. In: Bosse, T. (ed.) Agents and Ambient Intelligence, Ambient Intelligence and Smart Environments, vol. 12, pp. 17–31. IOS Press, Amsterdam (2012)

6. Costanza, E., Kunz, A., Fjeld, M.: Mixed reality: a survey. In: Lalanne, D., Kohlas, J. (eds.) Human Machine Interaction. LNCS, vol. 5440, pp. 47–68. Springer, Heidelberg (2009)
7. Dey, A.K.: Understanding and using context. Pers. Ubiquit. Comput. 5(1), 4–7 (2001)
8. PSLAB team at DISI, C.: JacaMo-MW– mirror worlds in JaCaMo – open source distribution (2015). https://bitbucket.org/pslabteam/mirrorworlds
9. Fischer, J., Jiang, W., Kerne, A., Greenhalgh, C., Ramchurn, S.D., Reece, S., Pantidi, N., Rodden, T.: Supporting team coordination on the ground: Requirements from a mixed reality game. In: 11th International Conference on the Design of Cooperative Systems (COOP 2014) (2014)
10. Gelernter, D.H.: Mirror Worlds: or the Day Software Puts the Universe in a Shoebox...How It Will Happen and What It Will Mean. Oxford (1992)
11. Holz, T., Campbell, A.G., O'Hare, G.M., Stafford, J.W., Martin, A., Dragone, M.: MiRA - mixed reality agents. Int. J. Hum. Comput. Stud. **69**(4), 251–268 (2011)
12. Milgram, P., Kishino, F.: A taxonomy of mixed reality visual displays. IEICE Trans. Inf. Syst. **E77–D**(12), 1321–1329 (1994)
13. Muldoon, C., O'Hare, G.P., Collier, R.W., O'Grady, M.: Towards pervasive intelligence: Reflections on the evolution of the agent factory framework. In: Seghrouchni, A.E.F., Dix, J., Dastani, M., Bordini, R.H. (eds.) Multi-Agent Programming: pp. 187–212. Springer, New York (2009)
14. O'Hare, G.M., Campbell, A.G., Stafford, J.W.: Nexus: delivering behavioural realism through intentional agents. In: Proceedings of the 2005 International Conference on Active Media Technology, (AMT 2005). IEEE (2005)
15. Omicini, A., Ricci, A., Viroli, M.: Artifacts in the A&A meta-model for multi-agent systems. Auton. Agent. Multi-agent Syst. **17**(3), 432–456 (2008)
16. Piunti, M., Boissier, O., Hbner, J.F., Ricci, A.: Embodied organizations: a unifying perspective in programming agents, organizations and environments. In: Boissier, O., Fallah-Seghrouchni, A.E., Hassas, S., Maudet, N. (eds.) MALLOW. CEUR Workshop Proceedings, vol. 627. CEUR-WS.org (2010)
17. Rao, A.S.: AgentSpeak (L): BDI agents speak out in a logical computable language. In: Perram, J., Van de Velde, W. (eds.) MAAMAW 1996. LNCS, vol. 1038, pp. 42–55. Springer, Heidelberg (1996)
18. Ricci, A., Omicini, A., Denti, E.: Activity theory as a framework for MAS coordination. In: Petta, P., Tolksdorf, R., Zambonelli, F. (eds.) ESAW 2002. LNCS (LNAI), vol. 2577, pp. 96–110. Springer, Heidelberg (2003)
19. Ricci, A., Piunti, M., Tummolini, L., Castelfranchi, C.: The mirror world: Preparing for mixed-reality living. IEEE Pervasive Comput. **14**(2), 60–63 (2015). doi:10.1109/MPRV.2015.44
20. Ricci, A., Piunti, M., Viroli, M.: Environment programming in multi-agent systems: an artifact-based perspective. Auton. Agent. Multi-agent Syst. **23**(2), 158–192 (2011)
21. Ricci, A., Piunti, M., Viroli, M., Omicini, A.: Environment programming in CArtAgO. In: Seghrouchni, A.E.F., Dix, J., Dastani, M., Bordini, R.H. (eds.) Multi-Agent Programming: Languages, Platforms and Applications, vol. 2, pp. 259–288. Springer, New York (2009)
22. Ricci, A., Tummolini, L., Piunti, M., Boissier, O., Castelfranchi, C.: Mirror Worlds as agent societies situated in mixed reality environments. In: 13th International Conference on Autonomous Agents and Multiagent Systems (AAMAS 2014): The 17th International Workshop on Coordination, Organisations, Institutions and Norms, pp. AAMAS2014–W22 (2014)

23. Roberts, D.C., Snarski, S., Sherrill, T., Menozzi, A., Clipp, B., Russler, P.: Soldier-worn augmented reality system for tactical icon visualization. In: SPIE Defense, Security, and Sensing, pp. 828–305. International Society for Optics and Photonics (2012)
24. Weyns, D., Omicini, A., Odell, J.: Environment as a first class abstraction in multiagent systems. Auton. Agent. Multi-agent Syst. **14**(1), 5–30 (2007)

Evaluating Different Concurrency Configurations for Executing Multi-Agent Systems

Maicon R. Zatelli[1]([✉]), Alessandro Ricci[2], and Jomi F. Hübner[1]

[1] Federal University of Santa Catarina (UFSC), Florianópolis, Brazil
xsplyter@gmail.com, jomi.hubner@ufsc.br
[2] University of Bologna, Bologna, Italy
a.ricci@unibo.it

Abstract. Reactiveness and performance are important features of Multi-Agent Systems (MAS) and the underlying concurrency model can have a direct impact on them. In multicore programming it is interesting to exploit all the computer cores in order to improve these desirable features. In this paper we perform an experiment to evaluate different concurrency configurations that can be adopted to run an MAS and analyse the effect caused by each configuration on variables like deliberation time and response time. As a result, we identify the advantages and disadvantages for each configuration allowing thus an MAS developer to choose a suitable configuration depending upon the priorities of the application.

1 Introduction

In MAS applications it is desired that agents react promptly to changes in the environment, reply to messages fast, process other high-cost activities, and all that at the same time [23]. The model of concurrency adopted in the MAS can have a direct impact on these issues. However, most researches in MAS focus on high level issues, while the low level issues still need a deeper investigation and advances. Multicore processors, multi-threaded operating systems, thread mapping, context switch overheads are examples of issues that are not comprehensively addressed by MAS platforms [17,18,27].

Current agent languages adopt different choices of concurrency features for the MAS developer. Some allow the use of a certain number of threads to exploit the cores of a computer by means of thread pools [4,30], and such threads are shared among all agents in the MAS in order to maximize the parallelism. Other approaches create separated executions lines (physical threads or processes) for each intention [10,23,29,37,43]. Yet, others prefer to avoid the internal concurrency[1] [8,9,33]. In addition, some proposals break the agent reasoning cycle in

---

The authors are grateful for the support given by CNPq, grants 140261/2013-3, 448462/2014-1, and 306301/2012-1.

[1] Internal concurrency means that agents can perform several activities concurrently (e.g. execute more than one intention at the same time).

© Springer International Publishing Switzerland 2015
M. Baldoni et al. (Eds.): EMAS 2015, LNAI 9318, pp. 212–230, 2015.
DOI: 10.1007/978-3-319-26184-3_12

different components (such as the sense, deliberate, and act) and execute them concurrently [11,22,41].

When programming an MAS, different *concurrency configurations* can lead to different results in terms of performance and reactivity. For concurrency configuration we mean here the set of concurrency features, including their parameters, that are used to run the MAS. The analysis and comparison between these configurations — in spite of the specific agent language adopted — is interesting in order to decide which one is the most suitable for the specific application to be developed. While the overall MAS execution time is the main concern for some applications, for others a fast response time of an individual agent is desirable (i.e. the time necessary for the agent to handle some percept or message). However, a configuration that provides a suitable overall MAS execution time could not be good regarding the response time, and vice-versa.

In this paper we develop such analysis and comparison by adopting an abstract MAS architecture (Sect. 2) which allows us to experiment and tune different concurrent configurations. We are interested in evaluating MAS composed of several agents by testing different forms to launch intentions, to perform the reasoning cycle, and to distribute threads among the agents. For this paper, we focus on BDI agents because it is a highly adopted model in current agent languages.

We identify some main concurrency configurations (Sect. 3), which reflect the choices adopted by some agent programming platforms available in literature. We evaluate their performance using a test case, which has been specifically designed in order to stress the impact of concurrency configurations on some variables of interest such as the response time, overall execution time, and deliberation time. The obtained results (Sect. 4) are useful to understand the importance of developing MAS platforms that allow to choose or tune the concurrency configuration to be adopted when running an MAS application. Finally, we present conclusions and further work in Sect. 5.

2   Conceptual Model

In this section, we describe a conceptual model including the main elements that concern BDI agents and MAS that are relevant for a concurrency point of view. While Sect. 2.1 presents a conceptual model for MAS, Sect. 2.2 presents a conceptual model for BDI agents, and Sect. 2.3 presents an agent architecture and a simplified version of the agent reasoning cycle.

2.1   MAS Conceptual Model

An MAS is composed of agents, environment, and thread pools (Fig. 1). Agents are executed by thread pools composed of one or more threads. Multiple agents can be executed by the same threads of a pool and multiple threads of a pool can be used to execute a single agent. The environment can be executed by as many threads as necessary and the form that it uses threads is out of the scope

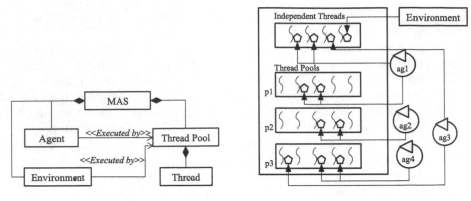

Fig. 1. MAS conceptual model.   **Fig. 2.** MAS snapshot.

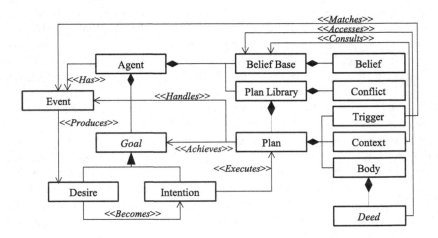

Fig. 3. Agent conceptual model.

of our work, remaining as a future work. Figure 2 illustrates the threads, agents, environment, and how they can be related to one another at run-time. Several threads can be used by the MAS in order to better exploit the computer cores. The number of threads can be greater than the number of computer cores, which means that while some threads "own the CPU", others are "sleeping". The pentagons represent threads that are being used, while threads without pentagons represent threads that are not currently being used.

Threads can be grouped in thread pools or be independent (e.g. dedicated threads to run some intentions). p1, p2, and p3 represent thread pools, each one composed of five threads, while the system also has four independent threads. Three different relations among agents and threads can be defined. The first relation is the use of dedicated thread pools, which allows each agent to have its own thread pool. This configuration is especially important if the system is composed of few agents that must perform few activities in multi-core computers. In the figure, ag1 and ag2 have their own thread pools, p1 and p2 respectively.

The second relation allows the use of shared thread pools (i.e. different agents share the same threads). It is important when the number of agents increases compared to the number of available cores in the computer. Thus, the overhead caused due context switches can be reduced. In the figure, ag3 and ag4 share p3.

Besides the use of thread pools, agents can also use other threads for more specific works (e.g. to run some intention). This configuration can be especially useful in cases where activities do not depend on the same resources and the number of activities still do not cause a high context-switch overhead. In the figure, while ag1 uses one independent thread, ag3 uses two, besides their thread pools. By default, intentions run concurrently even if they do not have one dedicated thread for each one.

2.2   Agent Conceptual Model

The agent model (Fig. 3) considers several BDI elements already adopted in BDI agent languages, such as 2APL [13] and Jason [4]. Thus, we consider concepts like beliefs, goals, intentions, desires, events, and plans. In our model, an agent is basically composed of a *belief base*, *goals*, and a *plan library*. *Beliefs* are information that the agent has at some moment. They can be about the agent itself, the environment, or other agents. *Goals* are state of affairs that the agent wants to pursue (e.g. an environmental state). While *intentions* represent the goals that the agent has already deliberated to commit to, *desires* represent the goals still not being pursued by the agent.

The plan library is composed of *plans*, which are a means to handle some event or achieve some goal, and their conflicts. A plan is composed of a unique *identifier*, a *trigger*, a *context*, and a *body*. The *trigger* is an event that the plan can handle (e.g. the adoption of some goal). The *context* is used to specify the conditions for the application of the plan and is a logical formula that must be evaluated according to the agent beliefs. The *body* is a sequence of deeds[2]. Plans can conflict with other plans, which means that some plans may not be executed concurrently. The aim of defining conflicts is to avoid an undesirable behavior of the system [24,34,35]. As plans can be added and removed at run-time, conflicts among plans can also be added and removed at run-time. The policy for adding and removing conflicts are defined by the MAS developer and it is out of the scope of this paper.

At run-time, when an agent intends something, it should start acting in order to achieve that *intention*. The proper actions for an intention come from plans that the agent has in its plan library. An intention is thus achieved by means of the execution of plans. Intentions can be created, suspended, or resumed at any time, and it is considered terminated when either the plan was executed successfully, the execution of the plan failed (e.g. the agent failed to perform an action), or the intention was dropped by the agent (e.g. the agent does not intend something anymore).

---

[2] The term *deed* is used in the same form as in [15] and it refers to several kinds of formulae that can appear in a plan body.

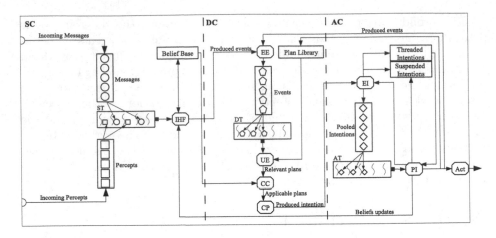

Fig. 4. Agent architecture.

Several *events* can happen at run-time. Events can produce desires for the agent (e.g. a message received by the agent can contain a request for the agent to do something, which produces a desire to be pursued). In our model we consider five kinds of events: (1) addition and deletion of beliefs; (2) messages that are sent and received by the agent; (3) percepts that are produced by the environment and perceived by the agent; (4) goals that are adopted, dropped, achieved, failed, suspended, or resumed; and (5) detection of conflicts among intentions (i.e. a new intention becomes active but it conflicts with another already running intention).

2.3   Agent Architecture

The agent architecture (Fig. 4) is inspired on some BDI models [4,11,13,22,39]. While *Beliefs*, *Plans*, *Threaded Intentions*, and *Suspended Intentions* are placed in data sets (represented by the horizontal rectangles in Fig. 4), *Messages*, *Percepts*, *Events*, and *Pooled Intentions* are placed in queues (represented by the vertical rectangles in Fig. 4) and processed by the threads in their respective components. These queues are priority queues in order to process emergencies promptly (e.g. an event notifying low battery in a robot). The priority policy is customizable by the MAS developer and agents can perform operations to retrieve and change the priority for events at run-time. The architecture has some functions (represented by octagons in Fig. 4) that define some steps of the reasoning cycle of the agent. Such functions are used, for example, to act in the environment or manipulate the data sets.

The agent is divided in three main components that can run concurrently, depending on the configuration. The aim of the concurrent architecture is to improve reactivity by allowing the agent to concurrently handle messages and percepts from the environment; handle internal events, belief updates, goal adoptions, etc.; and continue executing its intentions. The *Sense Component* (SC) is responsible for receiving the inputs from the environment (*percepts*) and from other agents (*messages*), updating the belief base, and generating events.

The *Deliberate Component* (DC) is responsible for reasoning about the events and producing new intentions to handle them. The *Act Component* (AC) is responsible for executing the intentions. Each component can have its own thread pool, named *Sense Threads* (ST), *Deliberate Threads* (DT), and *Act Threads* (AT).

```
while TRUE do
    cPercepts ← Percepts.clone()
    cMessages ← Messages.clone()
    while cPercepts ≠ ∅ and cMessages ≠ ∅ do
        Sense(cPercepts, cMessages)

    Deliberate()
    Act()
```

Code 1: Synchronous execution.

```
parallel
    while TRUE do
        Sense(Percepts,Messages) ||
    while TRUE do Deliberate() ||
    while TRUE do Act()
```

Code 2: Asynchronous execution.

The three components can also be configured to share the same thread pool. It is especially useful to reduce the number of threads in applications with more agents. For example, the MAS developer can define one single thread for each agent by configuring the ST, DT, and AT to use the same thread pool that has only one thread. In addition, all agents in the MAS could share a common thread pool. Thus, we can run the agent reasoning cycle in two distinct forms: synchronous (Code 1) and asynchronous (Code 2). In the synchronous form, each component finishes its execution before the other component starts its execution (i.e. the sense-deliberate-act cycle is executed sequentially). In the asynchronous form, the three components run concurrently and do not wait for other components to finish their execution before doing something, whether they already have something to do. However, differently from the synchronous execution, where the reasoning cycle is explicit, in the asynchronous execution the reasoning cycle is implicit by a producer-consumer strategy, where each component produces inputs for the other components. For example, the SC produces events for the DC and the DC produces intentions for the AC. Thus, the reasoning cycle is ensured because for a component to be executed it will depend on the execution of the previous component. Furthermore, if the agent must handle a whole set of percepts before to make decisions, the asynchronous configuration cannot be used. Some concurrency control mechanism or strategy must be also adopted to avoid interferences and races, given the concurrent read/write access to e.g. the belief base, caused by the concurrent execution of the sense, deliberate, act components. A simplified version of each component is explained as follows, however implementation details are not presented in this paper due lack of space.

```
Procedure Sense(pPercepts, pMessages)
    if lastInputKind = MESSAGE and pPercepts
      ≠ ∅ then
        input ← pPercepts.dequeue()
        lastInputKind ← PERCEPT
    else if pMessages ≠ ∅ then
        input ← pMessages.dequeue()
        lastInputKind ← MESSAGE

    if input ≠ NULL then
        IHF(input)
```

Code 3: Sense.

The Sense Component. The SC is responsible for the first steps of the agent reasoning cycle (Code 3). The environment enqueues the messages and percepts for the agent. Percepts and messages are then processed by the available threads in the ST. Each thread in the ST processes one message or percept at once. Thus, each thread executes the *Input Handler Function* (IHF) for the percepts, messages, and belief updates.

The IHF adds new beliefs related to percepts that are not currently in the belief base and removes beliefs that are no longer in the percepts from the environment (i.e. outdated information). The addition and removal of beliefs always produce events that are enqueued in the *Events* queue (by means of the function *Enqueue Event* (EE)) to be processed afterwards. According to some kinds of message, the IHF adds or removes the beliefs (e.g. agents can induce other agents to believe or to disbelieve something). In addition, all received messages produce events, even if they do not change the belief base (e.g. a message asking for some information). In the synchronous execution, all the percepts and messages in the queue are processed before the DC starts its execution.

```
Procedure Deliberate
    event ← Events.dequeue()
    if event ≠ NULL then
        relevantPlans ← UE(event, PlanLibrary)
        applicablePlans ← CC(relevantPlans,
        BeliefBase)
        intention ← CP(applicablePlans)
        EI(intention)
```

Code 4: Deliberate.

The Deliberate Component. The DC is responsible for processing new events by producing new intentions to handle them (Code 4). The events in the *Events* queue are individually processed by the available threads in the DT. Each thread in the DT processes one event at once. The first step to process an event is to find the relevant plans to handle the event. It is done by retrieving all plans where the trigger can be unified with the event. The function *Unify Event* (UE) is responsible for finding these plans.

The relevant plans are verified according to the their context, by means of the function *Check Context* (CC). The context of a plan determines if the plan can be applied or not in certain moments. Thus, the CC function selects which plans, from the relevant plans, are applicable considering the current state of the agent (e.g. its beliefs).

Several applicable plans can still be used to handle the event, which means that the agent could choose any of them to handle the event successfully. The function Choose Plan (CP), by default, selects the first non-conflicting plan considering the order in which they appear in the plan library. If all applicable plans conflict with some already running intention, the first one is chosen.

An intention is then produced with the chosen plan and it is added in some of the *Intentions* data sets of the agent (by means of the function *Enqueue Intention* (EI)) for a further execution. The EI adds the produced intention in the *Threaded Intentions* if it is configured as a threaded intention, otherwise, the produced intention is enqueued in the *Pooled Intentions* queue. In the synchronous execution, only one event is processed in each reasoning cycle, and after that, the execution moves to the AC.

```
Procedure Act
    intention ← PooledIntentions.dequeue()
    if intention ≠ NULL then
        PI(intention)
```

Code 5: Act.

The Act Component. The AC is responsible for the execution of intentions. They can be executed in two different forms: intentions can be executed by the available threads in the AT (*Pooled Intentions*) or be executed by dedicated threads (*Threaded Intentions*). In addition, intentions can be suspended and be placed in the **Suspended Intentions** set, remaining there until the agent resumes or drops their execution.

Each thread in the AT (Code 5) executes one deed related to certain pooled intention at once by means of the function *Process Intention* (PI). In execution of PI, the agent can perform some action in the environment, send messages to other agents, update its beliefs, adopt or drop goals, or execute any other internal action. When a deed is executed, it can also produce events. For example, when an agent adopts a new goal, an event related to it is produced and enqueued in the **Events** queue. The intention is then updated and placed at the end of the **Pooled Intentions** queue for the execution of the remaining deeds. In the synchronous execution, only one intention is processed in each reasoning cycle. After processing such intention, the execution moves to the SC and the cycle begins again.

Threaded intentions also executes the PI and produce events. The main difference is that they do not compete with other intentions to use threads, since each threaded intention has its own thread. Even in the synchronous execution, threaded intentions run independently and do not follow the default reasoning cycle.

3   Evaluation of Different Concurrency Configurations

We have implemented a prototype following the model and architecture presented in Sect. 2.3 in order to perform an experiment to evaluate different concurrency configurations[3]. The scenario for the experiment consists on executing agents that must perform certain activities, in this case we use the computation of the first n Fibonacci numbers. The implementation of the plan to compute Fibonacci numbers follows the traditional recursive approach. Thus, while the

---

[3] The prototype, experiment, and results are provided at https://sourceforge.net/p/mrzatelli/code/HEAD/tree/trunk/2015/Experiment2/.

computation of big Fibonacci numbers demand more time to be executed, the computation of small Fibonacci numbers can be executed in a short time.

All requests to compute the first n Fibonacci numbers are given to the agents in a single shot and placed in the agents perception queue at the beginning of the execution. No new requests are given to the agents during the rest of the execution and all agents work on all requests at once. The concurrent computation of Fibonacci numbers occurs without any interference among themselves. Sect. 3.1 describes how the experiment was conducted and Sect. 3.2 presents an analysis of the results.

3.1   Configurations and Experiment Setup

The experiment was performed on a computer Intel(R) Core(TM) i5-2500 CPU @ 3.30GHz (4 CPU cores) running Linux version 3.9.10-100.fc17.x86_64. Four different concurrency configurations were chosen to run the aforementioned scenario. In *Conf. 1*, the agent components run sequentially (synchronous execution), like the traditional PRS cycle [21], and each agent has only one thread. Examples of languages that adopt such approach are 2APL [13] and Jason [4]. In *Conf. 2*, the agent components run sequentially (synchronous execution), like the traditional PRS, and all the agents share the same thread pool composed of four threads (same number of cores in the computer). The use of thread pools is the approach adopted in simpAL [30], but it is also possible in Jason [4]. In *Conf. 3*, the agent components (SC, DC, and AC) run concurrently (asynchronous execution) and each one has its own thread pool composed of *four* threads. Moreover, the thread pools are shared among all agents. The asynchronous execution is an approach adopted in works like [22,41]. In *Conf. 4*, each intention is launched in different threads, which is an approach adopted in [23,43].

The configurations are also evaluated according to the number of agents in the MAS. We varied the number of agents from 5 to 10000, using the numbers of 5, 10, 50, 100, 500, 1000, 5000, and 10000. The aim is to evaluate how each configuration behaves when the number of agents changes.

The experiment was designed to analyse three variables. (1) The overall MAS execution time for the whole number of Fibonacci numbers to be computed by all the agents, which is the difference between the arrival time of the first percept and the time when the last intention has terminated. (2) The response time for each Fibonacci number, which is the difference between the arrival time of the percept and the time when the intention related to that percept has terminated. (3) The deliberation time for each Fibonacci number, which is the difference between the arrival time of the percept and the time when an intention is created to handle it. We chose the Fibonacci test case to evaluate such variables because we can easily simulate activities that demand a different execution time, stress the agent with different work loads, and simplify the experiment by using a scenario where interferences or races do not happen.

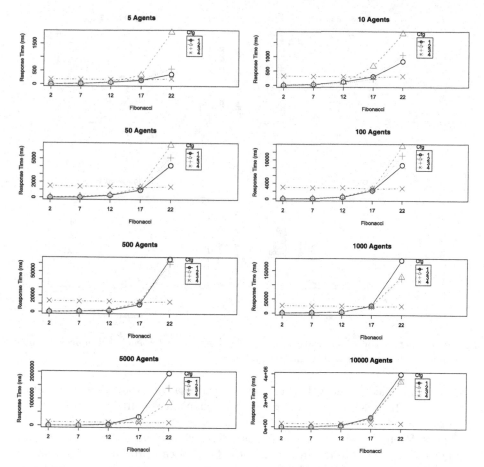

Fig. 5. Impact of the number of agents on the response time for each Fibonacci number according to each configuration (cfg).

3.2 Results

The resulting data of the experiment is presented by a series of graphs. Figures 5 and 6 present the average response time for each Fibonacci number comparing the impact caused by the number of agents in each configuration. While Conf. 1, 2, and 3 showed the expected exponential growth of the response time to compute Fibonacci numbers[4], Conf. 4 still does not show a perceptible exponential growth considering the maximum number of Fibonacci used in the experiment. Moreover, the exponential growth behavior is only possible because each agent computes the Fibonacci numbers concurrently, by interleaving among the several computations that it must perform. Even in cases where intentions are not

---

[4] This exponential growth is an expected behavior for the configurations used in this experiment because the computation of Fibonacci numbers, implemented following the traditional recursive approach, has an exponential complexity.

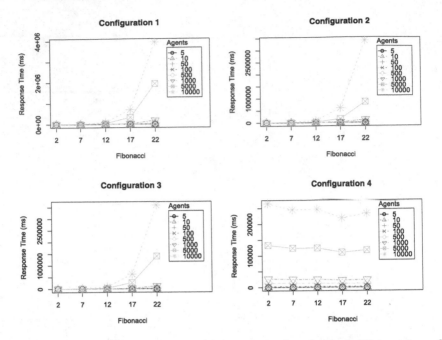

Fig. 6. Impact of the configuration on the response time for each Fibonacci number according to the number of Fibonacci numbers.

launched in dedicated threads, the agent executes a bit of a different intention in each turn. In this case, the interleaving mechanism is controlled in the agent architecture.

The different behavior for Conf. 4 is explained by the thread competition. While Conf. 1, 2, and 3 have fewer threads, Conf. 4 can produce a high number of threads that compete for the same resources (computer cores), resulting in delays to deliberate about new percepts. Thus, while the arrival order of the percepts does not seem to be an important aspect for Conf. 1, 2, and 3, it is important for Conf. 4. As another consequence, with fewer active intentions due to the delay for the thread creation, big Fibonacci numbers can be computed faster than in the other configurations, as shown in Fig. 5. The opposite behavior happens for small Fibonacci numbers. Even if the computation of small Fibonacci numbers is faster than big Fibonacci numbers, the deliberation time can harm the whole response time for small Fibonacci numbers. Therefore, as also shown in Fig. 6, Conf. 4 presents an almost constant response time independently of the Fibonacci number (considering the range of Fibonacci numbers used in this experiment) to be computed because the response time strongly depends on the deliberation time.

The reactivity of the agents could be measured by the experiment in this aspect. Small Fibonacci numbers can be thought as emergencies that the agents must react promptly. We can see that for Conf. 1, 2, and 3 the agents can respond fast to them even if they are concurrently performing other high cost activities (represented by the big Fibonacci numbers). Conf. 4, instead, takes more time to

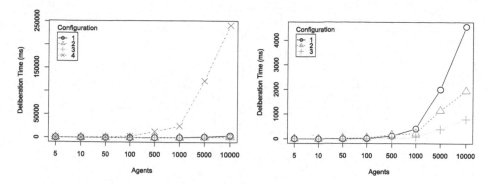

Fig. 7. Impact of the configuration on the deliberation time for each number of agents.

react to emergencies, demonstrating a worse result if reactivity is an underlying requirement for the application.

Fairness is also better in Conf. 1, 2, and 3. If an agent must perform a low cost activity it is fair to think that the agent must respond faster than the execution of a high cost activity. In addition, the computation of big Fibonacci numbers showed that Conf. 2 has the worst response time considering the number of agents lower than 500, while Conf. 1 has the worst response times considering the number of agents higher than 1000. In this point of view, Conf. 3 showed middle term behavior between Conf. 1 and Conf. 2.

Figure 7 presents the deliberation time for each configuration according to the number of agents. While Conf. 1, 2, and 3 have a fast deliberation time, Conf. 4 can take more time until the creation of some intention to compute a Fibonacci number. This result also highlights the contrast between Conf. 1, 2, and 3 (on the right). Thus, we can see that, after Conf. 4, Conf. 1 has the worst deliberation time, while Conf. 2 has some improvements, and Conf. 3 has the fastest deliberation time. This comparison helps the MAS developer to decide which configuration to adopt for an application where a fast deliberation time is necessary, for example, to handle some emergency.

Another interesting descriptor to evaluate the data produced by the experiment is the standard deviation. Figure 8 presents the standard deviation of the response time for each Fibonacci number according to the number of agents. By means of the standard deviation we can have an idea of how the response times spread out for each Fibonacci number. While Conf. 4 has a high and unstable standard deviation, Conf. 1 showed an increasing standard deviation according to the Fibonacci number to compute, and Conf. 2 and 3 showed a lower and more stable standard deviation. A lower standard deviation shows that data are more reliable and it is clustered closely around the mean, which means that we can expect that the computation of new Fibonacci numbers would be close to the mean too.

Finally, Fig. 9 presents a graphic where the overall MAS execution time for each configuration is compared according to the number of agents. While Conf. 4 presents the fastest overall MAS execution time, Conf. 1, 2, and 3 have very

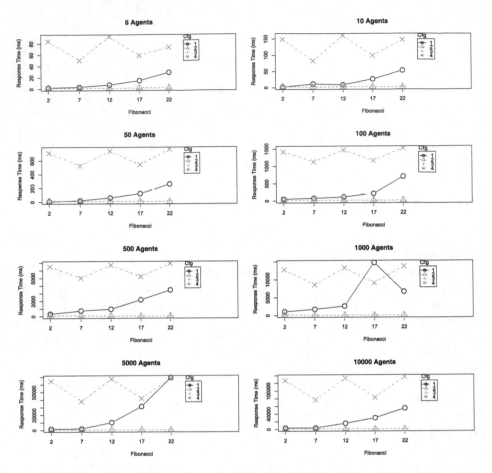

Fig. 8. Impact of the number of agents on the standard deviation of the response time for each Fibonacci number according to each configuration (cfg).

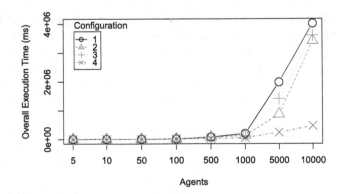

Fig. 9. Impact of the configuration on the overall MAS execution time varying the number of agents.

close times, with Conf. 1 showing the worst overall MAS execution time. The faster overall MAS execution time for Conf. 4 is explained because each intention runs in an independent thread and they are not enqueued in the Pooled intentions queue to be shared with other threads. The only overhead is caused by the context switch. In the other configurations, threads select intentions from the Pooled intentions queue. After finishing the execution of the current deed, threads need to enqueue the intention in Pooled intentions queue again. A synchronizing mechanism is necessary to control the access to the Pooled intentions queue in order to keep a consistent execution. Threads need to wait for the Pooled intentions queue be released by the thread that currently owns the access. Thus, up to 10,000 agents, the overhead caused by the Pooled intentions queue is higher than the context switch overheads.

4   Discussion

The experiment showed that each configuration has its advantages and disadvantages. On the one hand, launching intentions in dedicated threads (Conf. 4) showed better results for an overall MAS execution time and when the response time should not consider the size of the task, but the order in which the agents receive the percepts. On the other hand, configurations that do not launch intentions in dedicated threads (Conf. 1, 2, and 3) showed better results to react to emergencies. Moreover, considering an asynchronous execution for the reasoning cycle (Conf. 3), the agents showed the fastest deliberation time, while sharing thread pools among the agents (Conf. 2 and 3) is a more suitable configuration if a low standard deviation is important.

The MAS developer should be able to choose the most suitable configuration for the MAS based on the priorities for the application (e.g. fast response time). However, because most of the current agent languages have a limited set of concurrency features, the MAS developer is not able to choose the best configuration. For example, on the one hand, languages like 2APL [13], GOAL [20], JACK [16], JADE [3], Jadex [28], Jason [4], JIAC [38], simpAL [30], among others, do not provide any option to execute the reasoning cycle asynchronously. On the other hand, works that adopt an asynchronous reasoning cycle [11,12,19,22,41], do not provide any option for a synchronous execution. The number of threads are also defined differently among the different works. While some languages use a fixed number of threads for running an MAS based on the number of agents (Jadex [28], 2APL [13], GOAL [20]), computer cores (simpAL [30]), or any other policy, other works launch intentions using dedicated threads [12,23,43].

Several other features related to concurrency can be identified in the literature, however they were not included in the experiment performed for this paper. For example, some works provide operations that can be performed over intentions at run-time, such as suspend and resume their execution, and inspect their current state [3,4,28,30]. Mechanisms for join/fork are also provided by other works. Hence, it is possible to write a plan A that calls the plan B and C to run concurrently (in the same or different threads) and waits for both plans

(B and C) to get done to proceed with the execution of the current plan (plan A) [13,26]. Another feature is the use of priorities to allow the agent, based on some policy, to decide which activities to prioritize if it needs to execute several ones concurrently [14,32,42]. Finally, agents can also be composed of other agents. Sub-agents can be responsible for controlling specific parts of higher level agent, such as its beliefs or its reactive behavior [12,19,31].

The experiment presented in the paper demonstrated evidences that an agent language that provides richer options regarding to concurrency allows the MAS developer to achieve this aim and improve the MAS execution. It is important to notice that the effects caused by each configuration used in the experiment is strictly related to the scenario of the experiment. Thus, the developer will need to identify the best configuration always based on the application and its priorities. Moreover, even with the possibility to specify a wide set of concurrency configurations, some of these configurations could not be applied in all kinds of scenarios. For example, it does not make sense to run two threaded intentions that compete to use the same resources (e.g. updating the same element of the environment). At some point, one intention would need to wait for the other to release the resource. However, it is possible to use threaded intentions if they do not compete to use the same resources (e.g. working with different elements of the environment). In the case of running threaded intentions it would also be necessary to perform deeper experiments adopting other kinds of configurations to clearly see if it has some advantage or not. The same can be done when the MAS developer intend to run the agent components concurrently (asynchronously). Sometimes all the beliefs must be updated before the agent makes decisions. Otherwise, the agent could use some already outdated belief to select the applicable plans for some event that just happened. In the Fibonacci scenario, there is no need for the agents to handle all the percepts before to deliberate. Therefore, the MAS developer must consider not only the concurrency configuration, but also the characteristics of the MAS application (i.e. the result of the execution must be consistent).

In this paper, we used a very simple reasoning cycle for both synchronous and asynchronous execution, which was enough to run the experiment. Several issues still need to be addressed in order to execute more complex scenarios. Some of them are how to deal with new percepts if the agent has not finished to handle the internal events produced by the old ones; guarantee that the agent will handle emergencies promptly; and ensure a consistent context especially when the agent is selecting plans to be executed.

Other works that perform some experiments related to agents are presented in [1,2,5–7,17,25,36,40]. However, such works are mostly focused on comparing different languages, except by the work presented in [40], which makes an comparison among a parallel BDI agent architecture against sequential BDI agent architectures. As in [40], the aim of our work is to compare different configurations for agents instead of comparing different languages. The use of different languages to compare different configurations is not possible due effects caused by both variables (*language* and *configuration*). They can be mixed and the results are not reliable to evaluate the configurations.

5   Conclusions and Future Works

In this paper, we performed an experiment to evaluate different concurrency configurations for an MAS. By means of the experiment, we identified the effects caused by the use of such configurations and demonstrated the importance for an agent language to provide richer options regarding to concurrency configurations. In the future, we intend to perform further richer/more complex test cases than the Fibonacci described in the paper to enhance the evaluation and analysis. Finally, we plan to consider further configurations, with more specific and complex strategies in handling concurrency. For example, thread pools with a dynamic number of threads, which is chosen and allocated at run-time so as to optimize the MAS execution according to some objective function.

References

1. Alberola, J.M., Such, J.M., Garcia-Fornes, A., Espinosa, A., Botti, V.: A performance evaluation of three multiagent platforms. Artif. Intell. Rev. **34**(2), 145–176 (2010)
2. Behrens, T.M., Hindriks, K., Hubner, J., Dastani, M.M.: Putting apl platforms to the test: agent similarity and execution performance. Technical report, Clausthal University of Technology (2010)
3. Bellifemine, F., Bergenti, F., Caire, G., Poggi, A.: JADE - a Java agent development framework. In: Bordini, R.H., Dastani, M., Dix, J., Fallah-Seghrouchni, A.E. (eds.) Multi-Agent Programming. Multiagent Systems, Artificial Societies, and Simulated Organizations, vol. 15, pp. 125–147. Springer, New York (2005)
4. Bordini, R.H., Hübner, J.F., Wooldridge, M.: Programming multi-agent systems in AgentSpeak using Jason. Wiley, Liverpool (2007)
5. Burbeck, K., Garpe, D., Nadjm-Tehrani, S.: Scale-up and performance studies of three agent platforms. In: IPCCC 2004: IEEE International Conference on Performance, Computing, and Communications, Phoenix, AZ, USA, pp. 857–863 (2004)
6. Cardoso, R.C., Hübner, J.F., Bordini, R.H.: Benchmarking communication in actor- and agent-based languages. In: Winikoff, M. (ed.) EMAS 2013. LNCS, vol. 8245, pp. 58–77. Springer, Heidelberg (2013)
7. Cardoso, R.C., Zatelli, M.R., Hübner, J.F., Bordini, R.H.: Towards benchmarking actor- and agent-based programming languages. In: Proceedings of the 2013 Workshop on Programming Based on Actors, Agents, and Decentralized Control, AGERE! 2013, pp. 115–126. ACM, New York (2013)
8. Cicirelli, F., Furfaro, A., Giordano, A., Nigro, L.: Performance of a multi-agent system over a multi-core cluster managed by Terracotta. In Proceedings of the 2011 Symposium on Theory of Modeling & Simulation: DEVS Integrative M&S Symposium, TMS-DEVS 2011, pp. 125–133. Society for Computer Simulation International, San Diego (2011)
9. Cicirelli, F., Furfaro, A., Nigro, L.: An agent infrastructure over HLA for distributed simulation of reconfigurable systems and its application to UAV coordination*. Simulation **85**(1), 17–32 (2009)
10. Clark, K., McCabe, F.: Go! - a multi-paradigm programming language for implementing multi-threaded agents. Ann. Math. Artif. Intell. **41**(2–4), 171–206 (2004)

11. da Costa, A.L., Bittencourt, G.: From a concurrent architecture to a concurrent autonomous agents architecture. In: Veloso, M.M., Pagello, E., Kitano, H. (eds.) RoboCup 1999. LNCS (LNAI), vol. 1856, pp. 274–285. Springer, Heidelberg (2000)
12. Costa, M., Feijó, B.: An architecture for concurrent reactive agents in real-time animation. In: Brazilian Symposium on Computer Graphics and Image Processing (1996)
13. Dastani, M.: 2APL: a practical agent programming language. Auton. Agent. Multi-Agent Syst. 16(3), 214–248 (2008)
14. de Giacomo, G., Lespérance, Y., Levesque, H.J.: ConGolog, a concurrent programming language based on the situation calculus. Artif. Intell. 121(1–2), 109–169 (2000)
15. Dennis, L.A., Fisher, M., Webster, M.P., Bordini, R.H.: Model checking agent programming languages. Autom. Softw. Eng. 19(1), 5–63 (2012)
16. Evertsz, R., Fletcher, M., Frongillo, R., Jarvis, J., Brusey, J., Dance, S.: Implementing industrial multi-agent systems using JACK. In: Dastani, M., Dix, J., El Fallah-Seghrouchni, A. (eds.) PROMAS 2003. LNCS (LNAI), vol. 3067, pp. 18–48. Springer, Heidelberg (2004)
17. Fernández, V., Grimaldo, F., Lozano, M., Ordua, J.M.: Evaluating Jason for distributed crowd simulations. In: Filipe, J., Fred, A.L.N., Sharp, B. (eds.) ICAART, vol. 2, pp. 206–211. INSTICC Press (2010)
18. Fernández-Bauset, V., Grimaldo, F., Lozano, M., Orduña, J.M.: Tuning java to run interactive multiagent simulations over jason. In: Li, J. (ed.) AI 2010. LNCS, vol. 6464, pp. 354–363. Springer, Heidelberg (2010)
19. Gonzalez, A., Angel, R., Gonzalez, E.: BDI concurrent architecture oriented to goal managment. In: 2013 8th Computing Colombian Conference (8CCC), pp. 1–6, August 2013
20. Hindriks, K.V.: Programming rational agents in GOAL. In: El Fallah Seghrouchni, A., Dix, J., Dastani, M., Bordini, R.H. (eds.) Multi-Agent Programming, pp. 119–157. Springer, US (2009)
21. Ingrand, F.F., Georgeff, M.P., Rao, A.S.: An architecture for real-time reasoning and system control. IEEE Expert Intell. Syst. Appl. 7(6), 34–44 (1992)
22. Kostiadis, K., Hu, H.: A multi-threaded approach to simulated soccer agents for the robocup competition. In: Veloso, M.M., Pagello, E., Kitano, H. (eds.) RoboCup 1999. LNCS (LNAI), vol. 1856, pp. 366–377. Springer, Heidelberg (2000)
23. Lee, S.-K., Cho, M., Yoon, H.-J., Eun, S.-B., Yoon, H., Cho, J.-W., Lee, J.: Design and implementation of a multi-threaded TMN agent system. In: Proceedings of International Workshops on Parallel Processing, 1999, pp. 332–337 (1999)
24. Miller, M.S., Tribble, E.D., Shapiro, J.S.: Concurrency among strangers. In: De Nicola, R., Sangiorgi, D. (eds.) TGC 2005. LNCS, vol. 3705, pp. 195–229. Springer, Heidelberg (2005)
25. Mulet, L., Such, J.M., Alberola, J.M.: Performance evaluation of open-source multiagent platforms. In: Proceedings of the Fifth International Joint Conference on Autonomous Agents and Multiagent Systems, AAMAS 2006, pp. 1107–1109. ACM, New York (2006)
26. Muscar, A.: Exploring the design space of agent-oriented programming languages. Ph.D. thesis, University of Craiova (2013)
27. Pérez-Carro, P., Grimaldo, F., Lozano, M., Orduòa, J.M.: Characterization of the Jason multiagent platform on multicore processors. Sci. Program. 22(1), 21–35 (2014)

28. Pokahr, A., Braubach, L., Lamersdorf, W.: Jadex: a BDI reasoning engine. In: Bordini, R.H., Dastani, M., Dix, J., Fallah-Seghrouchni, A.E. (eds.) Multi-Agent Programming. Multiagent Systems, Artificial Societies, and Simulated Organizations, vol. 15, pp. 149–174. Springer, US (2005)

29. Rao, A.S.: AgentSpeak(L): BDI agents speak out in a logical computable language. In: Perram, J., Van de Velde, W. (eds.) MAAMAW 1996. LNCS, vol. 1038, pp. 2–55. Springer, Heidelberg (1996)

30. Ricci, A., Santi, A.: Programming abstractions for integrating autonomous and reactive behaviors: an agent-oriented approach. In: Proceedings of the 2nd Edition on Programming Systems, Languages and Applications Based on Actors, Agents, and Decentralized Control Abstractions, AGERE! 2012, pp. 83–94. ACM, New York (2012)

31. Rodriguez, S.A.: From analysis to design of holonic multi-agent systems: a framework, methodological guidelines and applications. Ph.D. thesis, Universit de Technologie de Belfort-Montbliard and Universit de Franche-Compt, December 2005

32. Sardina, S., De Giacomo, G., Lespérance, Y., Levesque, H.J.: On the semantics of deliberation in Indigolog&Mdash;from theory to implementation. Ann. Math. Artif. Intell. **41**(2–4), 259–299 (2004)

33. Sislák, D., Rehák, M., Pechoucek, M., Pavlícek, D.: Deployment of A-globe multi-agent platform. In: Proceedings of the Fifth International Joint Conference on Autonomous Agents and Multiagent Systems, AAMAS 2006, pp. 1447–1448. ACM, New York (2006)

34. Thangarajah, J., Padgham, L., Winikoff, M.: Detecting & avoiding interference between goals in intelligent agents. In: Gottlob, G., Walsh, T. (eds.) IJCAI, pp. 721–726. Morgan Kaufmann, San Francisco (2003)

35. Thangarajah, J., Padgham, L., Winikoff, M.: Detecting & exploiting positive goal interaction in intelligent agents. In: Proceedings of the Second International Joint Conference on Autonomous Agents and Multiagent Systems, AAMAS 2003, pp. 401–408. ACM, New York, (2003)

36. Vrba, P.: JAVA-based agent platform evaluation. In: Mařík, V., McFarlane, D.C., Valckenaers, P. (eds.) HoloMAS 2003. LNCS (LNAI), vol. 2744, pp. 47–58. Springer, Heidelberg (2003)

37. Weerasooriya, D., Rao, A., Ramamohanarao, K.: Design of a concurrent agent-oriented language. In: Wooldridge, M., Jennings, N. (eds.) Intelligent Agents. LNCS, vol. 890, pp. 386–401. Springer, Berlin, Heidelberg (1995)

38. Wieczorek, D., Albayrak, Ş.: Open scalable agent architecture for telecommunication applications. In: Albayrak, Ş., Garijo, F.J. (eds.) IATA 1998. LNCS (LNAI), vol. 1437, p. 233. Springer, Heidelberg (1998)

39. Zhang, H., Huang, S.-Y.: A parallel BDI agent architecture. In: IEEE/WIC/ACM International Conference on Intelligent Agent Technology, pp. 157–160, September 2005

40. Zhang, H., Huang, S.Y.: Are parallel BDI agents really better? In: Proceedings of the 2006 Conference on ECAI 2006: 17th European Conference on Artificial Intelligence August 29 - September 1, 2006, Riva Del Garda, Italy, pp. 305–309. IOS Press, Amsterdam (2006)

41. Zhang, H., Huang, S.-Y.: A general framework for parallel BDI agents. In: IAT, pp. 103–112. IEEE Computer Society (2006)

42. Zhang, H., Huang, S.-Y.: A general framework for parallel BDI agents in dynamic environments. Web Intell. Agent Syst. Int. J. **6**, 327–351 (2008)
43. Zheng, G.-P., Hou, Z.-Y., Yin, X.-N.: Research of the agent technology based on multi-thread in transformer substation communication. In: 2006 International Conference on Machine Learning and Cybernetics, pp. 56–60 (2006)

Author Index

Printed in the United States
By Bookmasters